"*A Course in Miracles*"
Seven Keys to Heaven

"*A Course in Miracles*"
Seven Keys to Heaven

≈ • ≈

A Simple Framework for

Understanding the Course

Donald James Giacobbe

Miracle Yoga Services

Copyright © 2013 by Miracle Yoga Services. All rights reserved.

No part of the text, cover graphics, or interior graphics of this book may be reproduced, stored in a retrieval system, or transmitted in any form or by any means: electronic, mechanical, photocopying, recording, or otherwise, without the written permission of Miracle Yoga Services.

The overall cover design, graphics, and interior layout of the text were created by Donald James Giacobbe.

Published by Miracle Yoga Services
— miracleyoga@gmail.com —
Cottonwood, Arizona

Printed in the United States of America

BISAC Subject Codes and Headings:

OCC027510 Body, Mind, and Spirit: Spirituality—*A Course in Miracles*

OCC014000 Body, Mind & Spirit—New Thought

REL012120 Religion: Christian Life—Spiritual Growth

Library of Congress Control Number: 2013911834

Giacobbe, Donald James
A Course in Miracles Seven Keys to Heaven:
A Simple Framework for Understanding the Course

ISBN 978-0-9843790-4-0

CONTENTS

~ o ~

About the Author
Preface 1
Acknowledgments 4
Introduction 5
Choosing the Ego or the Holy Spirit 13
The Tools of the Holy Spirit 21
The Door to Heaven 27
The Interrelationships of the Seven Tools 29
    The Seven Tools Lead to the Real World 35
    The Seven Tools Lead to the Face of Christ 36
Opening the Door to Heaven 37
The Holy Spirit's One Purpose 43
How to Restore Divine Love 45
Your Function for God 47
The Practice of Forgiveness 51
    "Overlooking" as a Change in Perception 52
    "Looking" as a Change in Perception 56
One Process 59
To Be Forgiving is To Be For Giving 61
Forgiveness Interrelationships 63
    Forgiveness Interrelationships Facilitate Application 63
    Christ's Vision Helps You to Forgive 64
    Miracles Help You to Forgive 67
    The Holy Instant Helps You to Forgive 69
    The Holy Relationship Helps You to Forgive 70
    Meditation Helps You to Forgive 72
    The Atonement Helps You to Forgive 78
Where is Forgiveness Leading You? 81
    Forgiveness is Leading You to the Real World 82
    Forgiveness is Leading You to the Face of Christ 85
    Seeing the Face of Christ as a Blazing Light 86
Sixty Answers to Sixty Questions 91
An Option for Study Group Leaders 175
Closing Summary 177

ABOUT THE AUTHOR

~ • ~

Donald James Giacobbe recorded his life story in his autobiography, *Memory Walk in the Light*. He was employed for sixteen years as a case manager serving developmentally disabled clients. The professional nature of his work limited his ability to express his spiritual motivations overtly, so out of necessity he served as an "undercover agent" for God.

A more direct approach to spirituality was facilitated by living with Zen Buddhist seekers and then being part of a yoga community. Later he was the director of the Aquarian Age Yoga Center in Virginia Beach, VA. He served as an instructor of meditation and yoga, teaching college courses and appearing on television. He specialized in providing yoga teacher training certification courses and leading meditation workshops and retreats. Don has attempted in his teaching of meditation to strip away the rituals of Zen Buddhism and yoga practices and transpose only the bare essence into a Christian context. Techniques of meditation inspired by Eastern sources open the mind to the influence of the Holy Spirit and enhance the use of traditional Christian practices, such as the "Jesus Prayer" and Christian contemplation. These techniques can be found in Don's book *Christian Meditation Inspired by Yoga and "A Course in Miracles": Opening to Divine Love in Contemplation*.

Don's goal is to do God's Will, be receptive to the Holy Spirit, and find Christ within the temple of his own heart. He became a monk making his vow directly to God, without the approval of a religious group. Yet he is open to the possibility of God's Will leading him to a marriage relationship. Formerly Don used the term "Christian yoga" to describe his path, which combines following Christ with yoga disciplines. In recent years he has adopted the term "Miracle Yoga" to describe his type of Christian yoga. This spiritual path is a combination of yoga and the philosophy of "A Course in Miracles" that encourages seeing with "forgiving eyes" and perceiving Christ in everyone. Don seeks to maintain a balance between opening to divine love inwardly and allowing that love to be extended outwardly to others. You can contact Don at miracleyoga@gmail.com and read his teachings on the following websites:

www.miracleyoga.org
www.christianyoga.org
www.christianmeditation.org

PREFACE

~ o ~

A Course in Miracles[1] teaches that you always have only two choices: either follow the ego or follow the Holy Spirit. The ego is teaching you that you are the body and the very limited part of your mind attached to the body. The Holy Spirit is teaching you about your true Identity, such as these Course ideas: "you *are* love,"[2] "you *are* light,"[3] and "You are the holy Son of God Himself."[4] Even if you intellectually accept what the Holy Spirit tells you about yourself, you will normally still listen primarily to the ego telling you that you are a body functioning in the world.

If you have not already learned to listen very attentively to the Holy Spirit and persistently follow His guidance, your ego will present you with many roadblocks to learning the Course. "The ego's whole continuance depends on its belief you cannot learn this course."[5] If you are a beginner, learning the spiritual principles of A Course in Miracles seems like the task that a salmon has of swimming upstream because you are going against the current of everything the ego has taught you about the world, others, and yourself. "To learn this course requires willingness to question every value that you hold."[6]

Your major handicap to learning this Course is that you do not know who you are. You function at a practical level in the world as an ego with a body. Thus you listen to the ego and allow the ego to become your teacher by default. "Let me repeat that the ego's qualifications as a guide are singularly unfortunate, and that it is a remarkably poor choice as a teacher of salvation."[7] Your ego has led the way in all your learning in the past, so it naturally volunteers to be your teacher of how to make your way to Heaven. Nevertheless, the ego is an illusion that cannot exist in the reality of Heaven. Because the ego is leading you to where it cannot go, it sets a learning goal that cannot be reached. The following Course quotation identifies the "ego's rule":

> I have said that the ego's rule is, "Seek and do not find." Translated into curricular terms this means, "Try to learn but do not succeed." The result of this curriculum goal is obvious. Every legitimate teaching aid, every real instruction, and every sensible guide to learning will be misinterpreted, since they are all for facilitating the learning this strange curriculum is against. If you

are trying to learn how not to learn, and the aim of your teaching is to defeat itself, what can you expect but confusion? Such a curriculum does not make sense. This attempt at "learning" has so weakened your mind that you cannot love, for the curriculum you have chosen is against love, and amounts to a course in how to attack yourself.[8]

The Course describes itself in this way: "This is a course in mind training." The ego thinks it represents all of your mind and thinks it is qualified to train the mind, but the goal of the ego is to justify its own existence. The Course is designed to teach that the ego is merely a false idea in your mind that you think is your identity. You—meaning who you think you are as the ego—must resign from being in the role of your teacher if you really want to learn the curriculum of the Course.

Resign now as your own teacher. This resignation will not lead to depression. It is merely the result of an honest appraisal of what you have taught yourself, and of the learning outcomes that have resulted. Under the proper learning conditions, which you can neither provide nor understand, you will become an excellent learner and an excellent teacher. But it is not so yet, and will not be so until the whole learning situation as you have set it up is reversed.[9]

After you resign as your own teacher, you must choose the Holy Spirit to be your new Teacher and persistently turn to Him every day. Even with this Guide, the Course turns your perception of the world upside down so it can be disorienting, difficult to comprehend, and even harder to apply. The book you are reading now is one way of overcoming the initial disorientation and difficulty that studying the Course presents. This book is subtitled *A Simple Framework for Understanding the Course* because it provides a foundation for navigating through the Course. The title is *"A Course in Miracles" Seven Keys to Heaven* because the Holy Spirit has given you seven ways of following the purpose of holiness and healing that lead to spiritual transformation. These seven tools of the Holy Spirit help you to simplify your learning of the multifaceted spiritual concepts in the Course. More importantly, the seven instruments show you how to put those spiritual principles into practice in your daily life.

This book can stand on its own as a preparation for studying the Course, but actually it is the third of three books that can be used in sequence to provide a thoroughly solid foundation for understanding and applying the Course principles. In case you would like to read all three of these books, here they are in their recommended sequence:

1. *An Overview of "A Course in Miracles": Introduction to the Course—What Beginners Need to Know* offers an easy-to-follow outline of your journey through the entire Course from beginning to end. In less than a hundred pages, it clarifies the spiritual principles of the Course and helps you decide if you want to deepen your understanding of this path.

2. *The Two-Month Bridge to "A Course in Miracles": A Condensed Edition of "A Course in Miracles"* gives you direct experience of the Course itself for two months. For the first month, you read a fourth of the 1249 pages of the Course. As a learning device, sixty questions are asked and concisely answered. For the second month, you do thirty of the 365 Workbook lessons. This direct experience helps you decide if you want to complete your journey through the entire Course.

3. *"A Course in Miracles" Seven Keys to Heaven* describes the impact of the seven tools of the Holy Spirit that are your means of transformation. It also identifies the interrelationships between these seven instruments showing how they all work together and eventually lead to spiritual awakening. The same sixty questions raised in *The Two-Month Bridge to "A Course in Miracles"* are presented again, and this time answered in a more complete way to review and to build on what you have previously learned.

Ideally all three books will be read in this sequence. But these are companion books that can be read in any sequence, and each book also stands on its own as a preparation for the Course. These books are not a replacement for completing all three parts of the Course. You are encouraged to study the entire *Text* and the *Manual for Teachers* and to do all of the 365 lessons in the *Workbook for Students*. If you are an experienced spiritual seeker, you may not need these three books as a preparation for the Course. If you are fully open to the guidance of the Holy Spirit, He will teach you everything you need to know about the Course. However, if you are a beginner, these three books will prepare you by opening your mind to the teachings the Holy Spirit wants you to learn and put into practice. The Course requires only that you have the "little willingness" to make the transition from an old way of thinking to a new perception of the world, others, and yourself. These three books make that transition smoother, and a full study of the Course itself will enable you to complete this transition. Then the Holy Spirit Himself will guide you: "He will direct your efforts, telling you exactly what to do, how to direct your mind, and when to come to Him in silence, asking for His sure direction and His certain Word."[10]

ACKNOWLEDGMENTS

~ o ~

I am grateful for the support, suggestions, and encouragement of my sister Lillian Blackburn. I appreciate John Francis, Julie Engsberg, Sarah Anderson, Marta MacDonald, and Shirley Bessette for serving as proofreaders. My thanks go to Amy Speach for her professional copy editing work.

1. *A Course in Miracles* quotations in this book come from the second edition that is currently in public domain. Helen Schucman is recognized as the author of the Course. However, she preferred to call herself the "scribe" of the Course. She considered Jesus Christ to be the true Author of the Course because he dictated the Course to her. The second edition of the Course was first copyrighted and published by the Foundation of Inner Peace, P. O. Box 598, Mill Valley, CA 94942-0598.

INTRODUCTION

∼ • ∼

This book highlights the seven keys to Heaven, which are the basic essential tools used by the Holy Spirit to bring about your spiritual awakening. *A Course in Miracles* explains that these seven tools are thoroughly interrelated. Also, these seven instruments for transformation cannot be understood without first explaining the larger context in which they operate, which will be described now.

You are probably familiar with the *Star Trek* science fiction stories seen on television and at the movies. Let's start with an allegory of a Star Trek Starship in a future utopia. This Starship had one Captain and a crew of one thousand members. There was no hierarchy in the crew because every Starship member was equal and had equal working functions. They lived in a utopian community of happiness in which medical advances had overcome all diseases. Nevertheless, in this utopia, one hundred crew members came to the Captain, saying that they wanted to be given a special rank higher than the other crew members. The Captain refused to grant their request because doing so would be unfair to the other nine hundred crew members. The one hundred crew members became upset at the Captain's refusal so they got together to come up with a plan to demonstrate their discontent.

On the Starship, there was a holodeck, which was a virtual reality system used for recreation to relieve the stress and isolation of shipboard life for crew personnel. The holodeck manufactured any desired kind of fantasy world depending upon whatever computer parameters were programmed into it. The dissatisfied crew members wanted to leave the Starship, but there was no place to go in outer space. Therefore, they collectively wrote a holodeck computer program that would allow them to escape into a fantasy world of their own making. They did two unique things in regard to the holodeck: First, they wrote a holodeck program that excluded any form of exit strategy that would allow them to return to the Starship if they changed their minds. Second, they each took an "amnesia pill" as soon as they entered the fantasy world of the holodeck. The pill caused them to forget everything that had happened on the Starship, including their individual identities. The amnesia pill produced a mind-altering effect that split the mind into a conscious part and subconscious part. The conscious part of the mind could only relate to the future fantasy world, and the subconscious part of the mind contained the past hidden memory of their former Starship lives. They took this amnesia pill with the intention of leaving the past behind and getting a totally fresh start with new fantasy identities in a new world.

Then the Captain got wind of what the crew was about to do. He could have stopped them by force, preventing them from going to the fantasy world of the holodeck. Yet if he held onto his hundred crew members by force, they would remain, but they would be even more discontented than before. He had to figure out a way that would allow them to choose for themselves to come back to their roles as crew members of the Starship. He had to show them that they really did not want the specialness that they sought and that they did want the equality and happiness they already had.

To address the problem, the Captain created a new Super Android and gave him the task of finding a way to entice the missing crew members to want to return and to show them how to return. The Super Android wrote modifications to the holodeck program that included an exit strategy. His program modification allowed him to have dual access to both the Starship and the holodeck fantasy world. This allowed the Super Android to be in constant communication with both the Captain and the missing crew members at the same time. The Super Android installed an Exit Door right in the holodeck fantasy world and guided any interested crew members to use this door to come back to the Starship. The door had seven locks on it, and the Super Android had seven keys that he gave to any crew member who wanted to use them to open the door and return to the Starship. The Super Android was not allowed to force anyone to listen to him and follow his advice, but he could persuade them of the truth that there was a better way available to them.

The greatest obstacle for the Super Android was the fact that the missing crew had taken the amnesia pill so had lost the memory of their Starship identities. In their fantasy world, everyone was confronted with a hostile environment. The hundred crew members had worked closely together to make this fantasy world program, but after entering the fantasy world, they separated and turned on each other. They blamed each other, and it became every man for himself. There were diseases, sickness, and physical labor that had been unknown in their former lives on the Starship.

The Super Android had to help them navigate within their fantasy world before he could help them escape. He showed them how to join with each other in cooperation, just as they had cooperated on the Starship. This joining showed them there was a better way that did not include blaming each other. It was the desire to be special that had gotten the crew into this mess, so the Super Android encouraged them to see their true equality with each other that was the essential nature of their former Starship identities. Through these lessons of the Super Android, he was showing them qualities that reflected their former life on the Starship. He was indirectly encouraging them to want to go back to the Starship, even though they could not remember ever having been there in the first place.

The Super Android built up a sense of trust in some crew members because he always told them the truth. He trained one crew member to become the Doctor. On the Starship there had been no sickness and so no need for a doctor. The Doctor guided by the Super Android showed crew members how to heal by seeing each other as equals and by joining with each other, rather than blaming each other. The Doctor used the Super Android's seven keys and showed others how to use them. When the Doctor had learned enough lessons and built up enough trust in the Super Android, he used the seven keys to open the Exit Door. When the Exit Door was opened, there was a holographic image of the Doctor, just as he had looked in his previous Starship identity. After seeing this image of himself, the effect of the amnesia pill disappeared, and the subconscious memory of his Starship identity returned to conscious awareness, which also returned the split mind to wholeness. With that memory returning, the Doctor faced two very clear choices: He could either return to the happiness of the Starship life of union and equality with others, or he could go back to the misery of the fantasy world of separateness and specialness. Finally, seeing this stark choice between happiness and misery, the Doctor made the obvious the decision to return. After the Doctor opened the Exit Door, saw the image of his Starship identity, and made his decision to return, the Captain used a transporter beam to pull the Doctor out of the holodeck's fantasy world and back to the main part of the Starship. The Captain joyfully greeted the Doctor with a wholehearted hug.

The other ninety-nine crew members saw the Doctor open the Exit Door and completely disappear into thin air. When they saw him disintegrate before their eyes, they were certain he was gone forever. They were greatly distressed about the loss of their healing Doctor. But three days later, the Doctor was transported back to the fantasy world to give them a message. He told them that he had gone to a Better World where everyone is equal and happy. He could not tell them directly about the Starship because they would not believe him. But he told them to use the seven keys and open the Exit Door themselves. He knew that if they did that, the memory of their former lives would return just as it had for him. Then the Doctor was transported, disappearing again, but he left behind a book to tell the crew how to use the seven keys to open the Exit Door.

The crew members read the book, and the Super Android helped them understand it. One by one, crew members used the seven keys to open the Exit Door. Each one saw an image of his own Starship identity, and with the return of this memory, each one was beamed back to the main part of the Starship. Then for each returning crew member, there was a Starship celebration by all the crew. Eventually they all returned to the true happiness of their Starship home. Their fantasy world that had formerly seemed so real disappeared into nothingness. A small portion of the Starship computer had been used to produce the fantasy world of the holodeck. However, once the fantasy world was abandoned, all the computer gigabytes used for the fantasy program were then used for the other Starship programs in the computer. The Super Android became a permanent member of the crew, and the holodeck was dismantled so that this same mistake would never be repeated.

That's the Star Trek allegory that can be used in order to illustrate the Course's version of how you left Heaven, represented by the Starship, and how you will return. The Captain is God the Father. The thousand crew members are the Sonship, consisting of equal parts of the one Christ. Those hundred crew members who rebelled symbolize the Sons of God who came to God and asked for "special favor." But God could only give equal love to every one of His Sons, so He could not grant any form of special love. After all, He had already given all of Himself and therefore all of His Love to every Son of God.

Just as it was impossible for the hundred crew members to leave the Starship, it was impossible for the discontented Sons of God to really leave Heaven. Since Heaven is life and reality, there is no alternative that is real. The computer program written for the holodeck stands for falling asleep in Heaven and dreaming of a fantasy world of time and space that appears real, although it is not real at all. The amnesia pill that took away the identity of crew members represents the use of the mental device called the "ego," designed to provide a separate identity tailor-made to suit the fantasy world that made separation seem real. The amnesia pill represents the loss of the awareness in Heaven of the whole mind, called "knowledge." The split of the mind into a conscious part and a subconscious part, caused by the amnesia pill in the allegory, is similar to the split mind that happened in the loss of the awareness of Heaven, which the Course calls "the separation."

The Course word *knowledge* is total awareness, so complete that there is nothing partial about it. When the all-encompassing knowledge of Heaven was thrown away, it was replaced by the partial awareness of *perception*. "The separation is merely another term for a split mind. The ego is the symbol of separation, just as the Holy Spirit is the symbol of peace."[11] The whole mind that had existed in the oneness of Heaven became split into two parts. One part of the split mind is dominated by the Holy Spirit, symbolized by the Super Android in the allegory. Just as the Super Android was made by the Captain in response to the crew separation, the Holy Spirit was created by God the Father as His Answer to the separation. Just as the Super Android had access to both the Star Trek Starship and the holodeck fantasy world, the Holy Spirit has one foot in the timelessness and formlessness of Heaven where knowledge prevails, and the other foot in the three-dimensional world of time and space where perception rules.

The part of the split mind that uses knowledge is in Heaven and is called the "Christ Mind." The other part of the split mind uses perception to function in the world, and this part is further divided into two aspects. One aspect of the perceptual mind is dominated by the Holy Spirit. It is called the "right mind" because it is devoted to only true and loving perceptions of "right-mindedness." The other aspect of the perceptual mind is dominated by the ego, which is the idea of separation. This ego aspect of the perceptual mind has a mixture of true, loving perceptions and false, unloving perceptions. The ego fosters "wrong-mindedness," which presents a false perception of God, the world, and everyone and everything in it. This false perception is based on illusions of separation and on seeking specialness.

To counteract the belief in separation and specialness, the Holy Spirit encourages you to join together with others in the common purpose of seeking what the Course identifies as a "better way" of functioning in the world, based on forgiveness and equality. In order to find this better way, the Holy Spirit teaches you to substitute wrong-mindedness with right-mindedness. Through relying on the partial but loving awareness of the right mind, you can return the split mind to the perfect wholeness of One-mindedness, which is the wholeness of knowledge in Heaven. The Holy Spirit wants to teach you that you do not really want the specialness offered by wrong-mindedness and that you do want the love and equality of right-mindedness that leads to the knowledge of Heaven, which is your true Home.

The Doctor, who was the crew member devoted to healing in the allegory, is, of course, a symbol for Jesus, the first to go to Heaven and come back to ask seekers to follow him. Just as the Doctor left behind a book to tell the crew how to open the Exit Door, Jesus has given seekers the Bible and in recent years has provided an update of his spiritual teachings, which is *A Course in Miracles*. This update on the teachings of Jesus would not have been understood two thousand years ago, but can be understood today because of the progress made in modern times in the fields of psychology and theology.

Just as the Super Android installed an Exit Door, the Holy Spirit made a "door" to Heaven, called the "real world" or the "face of Christ." There are seven keys to this door that are given by the Holy Spirit to anyone who wants to use them. The master key is *forgiveness*, and the other six keys are additional supporting instruments given by the Holy Spirit as your means of transformation. Using these keys allows you to see that there is a "better way" to navigate through the world guided by the Holy Spirit. Together the keys show you reflections of Heaven and entice you to want to return to your Home in Heaven.

Similar to the seven keys of the allegory that opened the Exit Door and revealed an image of each crew member's Starship identity, the seven keys of the Holy Spirit open the door to Heaven, which is the revealing of the "face of Christ." When a crew member saw the holographic image of his Starship identity, the amnesia pill lost its effectiveness, and he remembered his former life. Likewise, when you see the image of the face of Christ, you will see your true nature reflected there, and then you will fully remember God. "The face of Christ is looked upon before the Father is remembered."[12] Just as the Captain used a transporter beam on each crew member who opened the Exit Door and saw his Starship identity, God the Father will take the final step of your awakening. He will embrace you with His unspeakable Love and will transport you into Heaven. The whole Sonship will joyfully celebrate your awakening from your sleep in which you dreamed of a fantasy world of separation.

In the allegory, part of the Starship computer was used to run the fantasy world of the holodeck. Once the fantasy world was abandoned, all of the computer gigabytes used for the fantasy program were then returned to the Starship computer. The Starship computer symbolizes your whole mind using knowledge in Heaven. The portion of your split mind dominated by the ego is still part of your whole mind in Heaven so the part of the mind devoted to the ego cannot be destroyed. The ego cannot die because it has never truly lived. Yet when you wake up in Heaven, the ego is "undone" or reformulated. The undoing of the ego is like a computer program that is deleted. The gigabytes devoted to that deleted program are not eliminated; they are simply freed up so they become available for usage by the whole computer.

Every Son of God will come Home eventually. When that happens, the dream world of time and space will dissolve, just as when you go to bed at night and have dreams that disappear when you awaken in the morning. The part of the mind used to manufacture the dream world of earth that seems so real will simply return to your whole mind in Heaven as all forms fade into the nothingness of all illusions. With the end of illusions and the healing of the entire Sonship, the Holy Spirit's plan called the "Atonement" will be complete.

> The Holy Spirit is the Christ Mind which is aware of the knowledge that lies beyond perception. He came into being with the separation as a protection, inspiring the Atonement principle at the same time. Before that there was no need for healing, for no one was comfortless. The Voice of the Holy Spirit is the Call to Atonement, or the restoration of the integrity of the mind. When the Atonement is complete and the whole Sonship is healed there will be no Call to return. But what God creates is eternal. The Holy Spirit will remain with the Sons of God, to bless their creations and keep them in the light of joy.
>
> God honored even the miscreations of His children because they had made them. But He also blessed His children with a way of thinking that could raise their perceptions so high they could reach almost back to Him. The Holy Spirit is the Mind of the Atonement. He represents a state of mind close enough to One-mindedness that transfer to it is at last possible. Perception is not knowledge, but it can be transferred to knowledge, or cross over into it. It might even be more helpful here to use the literal meaning of transferred or "carried over," since the last step is taken by God.[13]

The Star Trek allegory is a modern-day way of explaining our journey of losing the awareness of our heavenly Home and then regaining the awareness of the tender heavenly embrace of our true Father. But the story that best expresses the deep emotions of our journey of awakening is the Biblical tale of the Prodigal Son. This familiar parable of Jesus tells the story of the youthful son who asked for his inheritance immediately so he could spend it as he saw fit. To ensure that he would no longer be under his father's influence, he went off to a "far country." From the viewpoint of the Course, the "far country" would correspond to the illusory world that the children of God made as a way of escaping the Father.

The word "prodigal" literally means *wasteful*, which describes the foolish behavior of the youthful son who squandered all of the treasure he had received. He experienced many hardships and was even starving. In his mind he compared his former life in his father's home to his current suffering, and then he made the wise choice to return to his father's home. He realized that the choice to leave his home was a mistake, and he expected that he would be reproached by his father for wasting the treasure he had been given. But the father in this story saw his returning son while he was still a long way off and was filled with compassion for him. Spontaneously the father ran to his son, threw his arms around him, and kissed him. Surprised by his father's embrace, the son confessed his error and said, "I am not worthy to be called your 'son.' Will you let me be a hired servant in your home?" But the father did not see his son as an unworthy sinner. The father, filled with joy, said, "Let's have a feast and celebrate. For this son of mine was dead and is alive again; he was lost and is found."

What normal father would not express at least a few words of resentment or reproach for his wasteful son, even if he wanted him to come back home? But this is no normal father. This father represents how our heavenly Father sees us with truly forgiving eyes and how completely He loves us. The only Biblical parable in the entire Course is this story of the Prodigal Son. Below is the Course's simplified version of this tale that explains why God the Father cares nothing about our waywardness and only wants us to have a wonderfully joyful return to our true Home.

> Listen to the story of the prodigal son, and learn what God's treasure is and yours: This son of a loving father left his home and thought he had squandered everything for nothing of any value, although he had not understood its worthlessness at the time. He was ashamed to return to his father, because he thought he had hurt him. Yet when he came home the father welcomed him with joy, because the son himself *was* his father's treasure. He wanted nothing else.
>
> God wants only His Son because His Son is His only treasure.[14]

God the Father knows that His Son is His treasure because He knows the difference between what is truly valuable and what is valueless. However, the prodigal son had to learn the difference between what is valuable and what is valueless before he could make the choice to come home. Similarly, in order to come to your heavenly Home, you must learn this same lesson and be able to correctly answer this question: *What is your treasure?* The next section elaborates upon how to make the choice to keep what is valuable as your treasure and let go of what is valueless.

CHOOSING THE EGO OR THE HOLY SPIRIT

~ o ~

The goal of the Course is to remove blocks to the awareness of the presence of love. It may appear that there are many different blocks to the awareness of the love that is already within you, but there is really only one. That block includes many masks of fear, yet all these fearful appearances are only the single block of the ego itself. The ego presents a serious stumbling block to your study of the Course. Thus as you consider the value of studying and applying the Course, you would benefit by asking yourself the question in the following quotation:

> This is the question that *must* be asked: "Where can I go for protection?" "Seek and ye shall find" does not mean that you should seek blindly and desperately for something you would not recognize. Meaningful seeking is consciously undertaken, consciously organized and consciously directed. The goal must be formulated clearly and kept in mind. Learning and wanting to learn are inseparable. You learn best when you believe what you are trying to learn is of value to you. However, not everything you may want to learn has lasting value. Indeed, many of the things you want to learn may be chosen *because* their value will not last.
>
> The ego thinks it is an advantage not to commit itself to anything that is eternal, because the eternal must come from God.[15]

The Course is attempting to teach you to seek only what is eternally valuable, but the ego does not want you to become attracted to anything that has lasting value. As you study the Course, the ego will attempt to confuse you and delay your progress by diverting your attention to considering various unimportant questions that you cannot answer.

Preoccupations with problems set up to be incapable of solution are favorite ego devices for impeding learning progress. In all these diversionary tactics, however, the one question that is never asked by those who pursue them is, "What for?" This is the question that you must learn to ask in connection with everything. What is the purpose? Whatever it is, it will direct your efforts automatically. When you make a decision of purpose, then, you have made a decision about your future effort; a decision that will remain in effect unless you change your mind.[16]

I have encountered some students who have attempted reading the Course while at the same time feeling they must protect their ego-based thought systems from the Course. One specific friend told me she does not like when the Course tells her bad things about the nature of the ego. I told her the Course does not say the ego is "bad" or "good," but does say it is *meaningless*.

> The self you made [the ego] is not the Son of God. Therefore, this self does not exist at all. And anything it seems to do and think means nothing. It is neither bad nor good. It is unreal, and nothing more than that. It does not battle with the Son of God. It does not hurt him, nor attack his peace. It has not changed creation, nor reduced eternal sinlessness to sin, and love to hate. What power can this self you made possess, when it would contradict the Will of God?
>
> Your sinlessness is guaranteed by God. Over and over this must be repeated, until it is accepted. It is true. Your sinlessness is guaranteed by God. Nothing can touch it, or change what God created as eternal. The self you made, evil and full of sin, is meaningless. Your sinlessness is guaranteed by God, and light and joy and peace abide in you.[17]

The ego has no meaning because it does not express the truth about you, and in fact it does not exist in reality. I read the following quotation to my friend because the last line seems humorous to me:

> The distractions of the ego may seem to interfere with your learning, but the ego has no power to distract you unless you give it the power to do so. The ego's voice is an hallucination. You cannot expect it to say "I am not real."[18]

This did not satisfy her, so she said that her impression was that the Course wants to destroy the ego, and she thought the ego had some good qualities too. I responded, "You made the ego so you love it, and you think it is you. But the ego does not love you in return. The Course specifically says that the ego will not be destroyed, but it will be 'undone.' The ego is part of your whole mind, and when you wake up in Heaven, you will bring your whole mind with you, including the part that was previously devoted to the ego.

"You can think of the ego as a knot in a rope, and the whole rope represents your whole mind. One way of getting rid of the knot would be to use a knife to cut the knot out of the rope, but if that happened, the rope would lose its wholeness. Destroying the ego would mean destroying part of your whole mind, which would be counterproductive, and it would be impossible since the mind God created cannot be destroyed. But the knot in the rope can be untied, which would maintain the wholeness of the rope. This symbolizes the undoing of the ego, which will return your mind to its wholeness. The ego can be undone because it is just a faulty interpretation of your reality, and the Holy Spirit can help you replace your false belief in the ego with the truth of who you are in God."

My explanation seemed to satisfy my friend, and she is still interested in learning more about the Course. Her confusion about the ego is typical of beginning Course students. The following quotation describes the ego and the conflict it engenders:

> The ego does not recognize the real source of "threat," and if you associate yourself with the ego, you do not understand the situation as it is. Only your allegiance to it gives the ego any power over you. I have spoken of the ego as if it were a separate thing, acting on its own. This was necessary to persuade you that you cannot dismiss it lightly, and must realize how much of your thinking is ego-directed. We cannot safely let it go at that, however, or you will regard yourself as necessarily conflicted as long as you are here, or as long as you believe that you are here. The ego is nothing more than a part of your belief about yourself. Your other life has continued without interruption, and has been and always will be totally unaffected by your attempts to dissociate it.[19]

"Your other life" refers to your eternal life in Heaven, where you really are right now, while dreaming of this world of separation in which you have an illusory life pretending to be an ego. Your Christ Mind is undisturbed in perfect peace in Heaven, but the dreaming portion of your whole mind has dissociated itself from your Self in Christ. Thus your mind is split into two parts:

> We have seen that there are only two parts of your mind. One is ruled by the ego, and is made up of illusions. The other is the home of the Holy Spirit, where truth abides. There are no other guides but these to choose between, and no other outcomes

possible as a result of your choice but the fear that the ego always engenders, and the love that the Holy Spirit always offers to replace it.[20]

As a result of your split mind, you have no idea what is truly valuable to you and what is not because your ego dominates your conscious awareness. Nevertheless, the Holy Spirit is in your mind, placed there by God as His Answer to the dissociation that occurred in what the Course calls the "separation." You could not really separate yourself from God, so you participated in producing the illusion of time and space and the making of the individual ego. Dissociation allows you to have two thought systems in the mind without either being aware of the other.

> The ego and the spirit do not know each other. The separated mind cannot maintain the separation except by dissociating. Having done this, it denies all truly natural impulses, not because the ego is a separate thing, but because you want to believe that *you* are. The ego is a device for maintaining this belief, but it is still only your decision to use the device that enables it to endure.[21]

In your ego condition, direct access to God the Father is lost from your conscious awareness, but the Holy Spirit keeps you connected to God and to your Christ Mind in God. Because you have free will, you must decide where you choose to place your allegiance. You have only two choices. You will always choose either the ego or the Holy Spirit. Whenever you make a choice, you may not be consciously aware of whether you have chosen the ego or the Holy Spirit. But you can determine what choice you have made by the results of your choice.

> No one who learns from experience that one choice brings peace and joy while another brings chaos and disaster needs additional convincing. Learning through rewards is more effective than learning through pain, because pain is an ego illusion, and can never induce more than a temporary effect. The rewards of God, however, are immediately recognized as eternal. Since this recognition is made by you and not the ego, the recognition itself establishes that you and your ego cannot be identical. You may believe that you have already accepted this difference, but you are by no means convinced as yet. The fact that you believe you must escape from the ego shows this; but you cannot escape from the ego by humbling it or controlling it or punishing it.[22]

The Sonship consists of equal parts of the one Christ. In Heaven before the separation, some parts of the one Christ wanted God to give them more love than He gave to other parts. But God could not give more love to some parts than others because God had already given all of Himself to every part equally, and unequal love would not be love at all. When these parts separated, they threw away their awareness of all the valuable eternal gifts God had given them and accepted a valueless illusion instead. They traded away everything for nothing. This raises the following question: How can you relearn the truth of what is truly valuable, meaning what is eternal, and let go of valuing what is valueless, meaning what is temporary and illusory?

   How can you teach someone the value of something he has deliberately thrown away? He must have thrown it away because he did not value it. You can only show him how miserable he is without it, and slowly bring it nearer so he can learn how his misery lessens as he approaches it. This teaches him to associate his misery with its absence, and the opposite of misery with its presence. It gradually becomes desirable as he changes his mind about its worth. I am teaching you to associate misery with the ego and joy with the spirit. You have taught yourself the opposite. You are still free to choose, but can you really want the rewards of the ego in the presence of the rewards of God?[23]

Workbook Lesson 133 teaches: "I will not value what is valueless." This lesson provides tests that allow you to see the difference between choosing everything and nothing so you can make the wiser choice. There are two laws that govern your decision making. The first law says that you can only choose the Holy Spirit or the ego, and you have no other alternatives. The second law is that if you choose the Holy Spirit, your choice will bring you everything, and if you choose the ego, your choice will bring you nothing. Your choice will always be a total one, bringing everything or nothing. No other outcome is possible.

   These laws apply to all your decisions of what you want, but they do not center on choosing between better or worse forms of what you want. Instead, they refer to the content of your mind that can only gain everything guided by the Holy Spirit or gain nothing guided by the ego. How is this possible? You are really choosing between Heaven and the world. When you choose the Holy Spirit, you become reconnected to Heaven where you regain everything that God gave you in your creation and that you still possess as your heavenly birthright. When you choose the ego, you identify with the illusion of the world that can give your mind nothing of any value, because it exists only in your dream of reality. Within the two laws of choosing what you want, there are four ways that you can tell whether you have chosen the Holy Spirit and everything or have chosen the ego and nothing.

> First, if you choose a thing that will not last forever, what you chose is valueless. A temporary value is without all value.[24]

The first way to perceive if you have chosen the Holy Spirit or the ego is to perceive if you have chosen what is everlasting or temporary. To choose the Holy Spirit means you are choosing eternity where value lasts forever. If you choose the ego, you are choosing the illusion of time where the ego dominates, offering nothing of lasting value.

> Next, if you choose to take a thing away from someone else, you will have nothing left. Who seeks to take away has been deceived by the illusion loss can offer gain. Yet loss must offer loss, and nothing more.[25]

Consequently, the second way to see if you have chosen the Holy Spirit or the ego is to see if you have gained or lost. To choose the Holy Spirit means both you and your brother gain everything, and there is no loss either to your brother or to you. To choose the ego means you want your brother to make a sacrifice so he will lose something and you will gain something. But what you gain is illusory and worthless so your gain is really a loss.

> Your next consideration is the one on which the others rest. Why is the choice you make of value to you? What attracts your mind to it? What purpose does it serve?[26]

Therefore, the third way to perceive if you have chosen the Holy Spirit or the ego is to perceive if you have chosen the purpose of holiness and healing or the purpose of guilt and separation. Choosing the Holy Spirit expresses the purpose of holiness and healing that corrects all errors. Choosing the ego manifests the purpose of guilt and separation that maintains that sins are real, rather than mistakes that can be corrected.

> If you feel any guilt about your choice, you have allowed the ego's goals to come between the real alternatives. And thus you do not realize there are but two, and the alternative you think you chose seems fearful, and too dangerous to be the nothingness it actually is.[27]

The fourth way to see if you have chosen the Holy Spirit or the ego is to look at the result of having chosen the purpose of holiness and healing or the result of having chosen the purpose of guilt and separation. If you have selected the Holy Spirit's purpose of holiness and healing, you will have the experience of releasing the block of guilt and bringing the awareness of love's abiding presence. If you choose the ego's purpose of guilt and separation, you will have the experience of fear and guilt that block the awareness of love's presence.

The purpose of this Workbook lesson is revealed in this quotation:

> Heaven itself is reached with empty hands and open minds, which come with nothing to find everything and claim it as their own. We will attempt to reach this state today, with self-deception laid aside, and with an honest willingness to value but the truly valuable and the real. Our two extended practice periods of fifteen minutes each begin with this: I will not value what is valueless, and only what has value do I seek, for only that do I desire to find.[28]

This Workbook lesson wants you to experience Heaven because you already have been given Heaven, and it still belongs to you. As you have the quiet times of meditation on what is valuable, you are instructed to remind yourself of what you already have by saying, "I will not value what is valueless, for what is valuable belongs to me."[29] When you choose the eternal, you are choosing what is eternally yours and is now recognized by your choosing it. When you choose what is not eternal, you are hiding what is eternally yours, and choosing what can never be yours, so you have chosen nothing.

I would like to share with you one specific way I put into practical application the idea of choosing the Holy Spirit instead of the ego, which is the same as choosing what is valuable instead of valueless. Every morning as I shake off the grogginess of sleep, I say the following words out load in order to dedicate the coming day to choosing the Holy Spirit and investing in what is valuable:

> Father, thank You for loving me. Let Your Love flow through me and bless all my brothers and sisters everywhere. They are the holy Sons of God, who deserve to wake up in Heaven. They are the Christ. They are light. They are love. I am the Holy Son of God, who deserves to wake up in Heaven. I am the Christ. I am light. I am love. I am just as holy now as when You created me. With Jesus beside me on my journey of awakening, Holy Spirit, guide my mind, choose for God for me, and be in charge of my meditation experience of the holy instant. Holy Spirit and Jesus, with your help I forgive all my brothers and sisters and forgive myself because we deserve only love and not the illusions of guilt we have fabricated to unfairly punish ourselves. I am

freed from all my past mistakes and their effects because I accept the perfect love and healing of the Atonement that corrects all errors. Amen

I am not suggesting that you repeat these same words or repeat anything as long as my example. When I started this daily morning practice of choosing what is valuable, I began by repeating out loud these two sentences: "Father, thank You for loving me." (Pause to focus on opening my mind and heart to feel God's Love and my gratitude.) "Let Your Love flow through me and bless all my brothers and sisters everywhere." (Pause to focus on God's Love blessing everyone.)

These two sentences express that my brothers and sisters and I are God's treasure. They also answer the question posed in the previous section: What is my treasure? *God and my brother and sisters joined in Christ and in love are my treasure and will always be my treasure.* The combination of giving and receiving love is a perfect example of what is eternally valuable. After all, we live in an ocean of love that we call "God." All spiritual growth is merely uncovering His unwavering divine Love that endures forever, as He waits with endless patience for the celebration of our awakening from our self-imposed dreams of separation. Only in that final awakening will we be able to recognize the full extent of our burning love for God and for all of Creation that has come forth from His Love.

Reading about all the Course ideas expressed in this book is helpful, but it is even better to put these ideas into practice. For that reason, I am suggesting that you have a daily practice of starting the day on the right track. One ideal way of starting the day is to have a quiet time of meditation in the morning as a reminder to give your day to God. Meditation will be emphasized in upcoming sections. But the simplest thing you can do right now to dedicate your day to God is to repeat a simple sentence or two in your own words. Let your words be an expression of your choice for the Holy Spirit and for what is eternally valuable. This is an easy and practical way to express your desire to accept God's plan for your life. The words you choose can be your goal for the day. With this goal, you will receive the Holy Spirit's help to arrange your day, facilitating the accomplishment of your goal.

> Once you accept His plan as the one function that you would fulfill, there will be nothing else the Holy Spirit will not arrange for you without your effort.... Nothing you need will be denied you. Not one seeming difficulty but will melt away before you reach it. You need take thought for nothing, careless of everything except the only purpose that you would fulfill.[30]

THE TOOLS OF THE HOLY SPIRIT

~ o ~

A lifetime dedicated to choosing what is valuable and rejecting what is valueless will ultimately lead to awakening in Heaven. But in everyday life is it possible for you to directly experience the state of mind called Heaven? There is one way to experience Heaven directly. The Course uses the word "revelation" to describe this profound direct experience of God. Revelation is equivalent to the deepest level of enlightenment that is the goal of Zen Buddhism and the deepest level of samadhi that is sought by the spiritual disciplines of yoga. According to the Course, revelation may occur spontaneously at any time as a glimpse of your destiny of permanent union with God in Heaven. Also, when you finally heal the split mind and return to your whole mind, God will take the final step of giving the divine embrace ushering you into Heaven. Unlike the type of revelation that can temporarily occur in your daily life, this final step is revelation as a permanent condition in which there are no more illusions of separation from God. Although everyone will eventually experience this final revelation and awaken in Heaven, the Course focuses on realistic spiritual goals that can be accomplished right now in your current ego-based condition.

Before being ready to awaken directly to God in Heaven, you must first prepare by learning how to remove the blocks to your awareness of love, such as fear, anger, guilt, and the other tools of the ego. To help you prepare for the direct experience of Heaven, the Holy Spirit offers you *indirect* experiences of Heaven that help you remove your inner blocks. Just as the ego has tools to block your awareness, the Holy Spirit has tools that open your awareness.

Lesson 133 outlined the way to evaluate if you have chosen the Holy Spirit or the ego, *after your choice is already made and acted upon to bring its results.* Now you are being encouraged to set the goal of choosing the Holy Spirit *before* you make any decisions. You will not be able to silence the voice of the ego in your mind by making the Holy Spirit your goal. The ego will speak first when you are considering any decision. Then the Holy Spirit will respond, and His answer will show you the truth and cancel out the advice offered by the ego.

The Holy Spirit does not speak first, *but He always answers*. Everyone has called upon Him for help at one time or another and in one way or another, and has been answered. Since the Holy Spirit answers truly He answers for all time, which means that everyone has the answer *now*.

The ego cannot hear the Holy Spirit, but it does believe that part of the mind that made it is against it. It interprets this as a justification for attacking its maker. It believes that the best defense is attack, and wants *you* to believe it.[31]

By choosing the goal of the Holy Spirit, you find what is valuable and let go of what is valueless. After you set this goal, the Holy Spirit provides the means of accomplishing your goal. Here is where the Holy Spirit offers you the tools that remove blocks and open your awareness. What are the attributes of these tools? They provide experiences of the four ways to determine whether you have chosen the Holy Spirit or the ego, described in Lesson 133. First, they bring what is eternal. Second, they produce a gain to your brother and to you, with no loss to either of you. Third, they represent the Holy Spirit's purpose of holiness. Fourth, they heal your split mind by removing or correcting inner blocks, such as guilt and other illusions. In summary, they would have to bring you the indirect experience of Heaven. This means having an experience of everything that is already yours, such as peace, light, and love, given to you by God in your creation,

The Holy Spirit is a Master Carpenter. He, along with Jesus, helps you to rebuild your house. You must do the carpentry work yourself, but the Master Carpenter is your instructor. He gives you His seven carpentry tools and shows you how to use them to restore your house. Your house is your split mind that needs to be restored to wholeness by replacing the ego's thought system with the Holy Spirit's thought system.

What are the specific tools recommended throughout the Course as your means of following the Holy Spirit? The Holy Spirit has numerous tools at His disposal to produce inner transformation and to heal the split mind. The Holy Spirit works at the subconscious level in this transformation process in ways that may never come to your conscious awareness. But there are seven primary keys to transformation that can be used for making and manifesting the choice for the Holy Spirit instead of the ego. These seven tools are described in the hundred-page book *An Overview of "A Course in Miracles."* This inexpensive introductory book was written as a way of preparing for *The Two-Month Bridge to "A Course in Miracles."* It is certainly recommended reading if you are guided in that direction by the Holy Spirit. The seven tools of the Holy Spirit are briefly identified in the following way:

1. FORGIVENESS

False forgiveness claims to forgive a person while still seeing him as a guilty sinner. **True forgiveness** in the Course is the practice of forgiving by recognizing that guilt and sin are unreal and that everyone deserves love. True forgiveness, which is based on right-mindedness, involves both "*overlooking and looking.*" The "overlooking" part of forgiveness looks past what is forgiven, seeing that it is entirely an illusion that never happened in reality. Thus "overlooking" consists of looking beyond error from the beginning, and thus keeps it unreal for you. Overlooking requires only that you recognize immediately at first glance that all fearful appearances of sin and guilt are illusory because they contradict the awareness that every Son of God is just as holy now as when God created him in the eternal present moment.

The "looking" part of forgiveness sees only the divine holiness and true reality of the one who is forgiven, realizing he is always worthy of only love. Because he is worthy of love, you join with him. Forgiveness removes the illusory gap between you and your brother and proves to yourself that the ego, the whole idea of separation, is an illusion.

2. CHRIST'S VISION

Christ's vision is an extension of love that replaces the ego's projection of guilt. Christ's vision enables you to see light and love in others and in the world. This is not seeing with your physical eyes, but rather perceiving the inner mental content of holiness in others. Perceiving holiness, light, and love outwardly helps you to recognize this same holiness, light, and love must be in your own mind. In this process of perceiving holiness, light, and love outwardly and inwardly, you are joining with what you see, instead of producing the sense of separation that is the result of projecting guilt. This vision of holiness, light, and love is a gift from Christ and the Holy Spirit that represents divine grace, requiring only your willingness to receive it.

3. MIRACLES

A **miracle** is an exchange in which you replace perceptions of fear with new perceptions of love and forgiveness. Light and love go to the receiver of the miracle and are returned equally to the giver of the miracle. This loving mutual exchange is a miracle, which brings healing to both the mind of the giver and receiver of forgiveness. "The ego's opposite in every way,—in origin, effect and consequence—we call a miracle."[32]

4. THE HOLY INSTANT

The holy instant is a time of joining in which normal habits of thinking and feeling are set aside. The past and future are gone in the holy instant, and you are elevated to the eternal present moment of *now* in eternity. The holy instant overcomes the ego because: "'Now' has no meaning to the ego. The present merely reminds it of past hurts, and it reacts to the present as if it *were* the past."[33] When you are letting go of the past and future in the holy instant, you are letting go of the ego. The holy instant is truly your window to Heaven though it only lasts for an instant. During this pause in normal functioning, the mind is open to receive the divine truth that reflects Heaven. The holy instant is a time of perfect communication, of giving and receiving in which God and the whole Sonship participate.

Yet in the holy instant you unite directly with God, and all your brothers join in Christ. Those who are joined in Christ are in no way separate. For Christ is the Self the Sonship shares, as God shares His Self with Christ.[34]

5. THE HOLY RELATIONSHIP

The holy relationship is a relationship in which two people join for a common purpose. Also, they must have common interests in the pursuit of that common purpose so they have the same motivation for pursuing that purpose. If both partners have the same unselfish interests, they will be united in a holy relationship. Holy relationship partners join for what they can gain together rather than for what they can gain separately with separate motivations. When the partners join in a holy relationship, the Holy Spirit enters the relationship. Although they may initially have only a mundane common purpose, the Holy Spirit will help them accept His higher purpose of holiness instead of their mundane purpose. By joining in the purpose of holiness, they overcome the ego's purpose of guilt and limit their identification with the ego itself.

Those who have joined their brothers have detached themselves from their belief that their identity lies in the ego. A holy relationship is one in which you join with what is part of you in truth.[35]

6. THE QUIET TIME (MEDITATION)

When the Course refers to setting aside periods for daily **quiet time**, it is referring to what is generally called "**meditation.**" All meditation methods involve ignoring distracting thoughts that come from the ego

A Simple Framework for Understanding the Course 25

and simultaneously focusing on a sacred goal. Thus meditation brings detachment from the ego and attraction to the divine.

It is difficult to reach out to God while at the same time feeling you are unworthy of Him. Any form of meditation that fosters the belief in your sinfulness is not effective because it is an attempt to make yourself holy while still thinking you are basically unholy. Consequently, the Course offers a variety of meditation methods and seems to be saying that any technique will be effective if it does not reinforce your sense of sinfulness.

Meditation may appear to be a solitary activity, yet you meditate to experience divine love within. Thus you are seeking union with God *and* with in the Sonship. In successful meditation you experience your oneness with God and your brothers and sisters in the Sonship, similar to the extension of love that occurs in forgiveness.

In the Manual for Teachers, the Course recommends a daily quiet time for both the morning and evening. This quiet time is referred to as very similar to, but less structured than, the practices learned in your Workbook lessons, such as the focusing methods of meditation.

> ... as soon as possible after waking take your quiet time, continuing a minute or two after you begin to find it difficult....
>
> The same procedures should be followed at night. Perhaps your quiet time should be fairly early in the evening, if it is not feasible for you to take it just before going to sleep. It is not wise to lie down for it. It is better to sit up, in whatever position you prefer. Having gone through the workbook, you must have come to some conclusions in this respect.[36]

Although meditation is important in your spiritual growth, it plays only a secondary role in the Course. Some yoga disciplines and Zen Buddhism teach that meditation is the most beneficial spiritual practice. This Eastern emphasis on inner attunement is based on the fact that extended periods of intense meditation can facilitate the most profound spiritual experiences in which the seeker completely transcends ego consciousness. What is not well understood is that when that seeker returns to his normal ego consciousness, his ego can remain essentially untouched.

Historically many Eastern gurus who came to teach in America had genuine transcendent experiences, and yet they were deeply flawed as human beings. With the exception of the most advanced gurus, such as Yogananda, Meher Baba, and Vivekananda, other less evolved gurus neglected to address the shadow side of their natures and presented a mixed bag of some virtues coexisting with ego-based shortcomings.

Consequently, these less advanced gurus uplifted many seekers, yet in numerous instances exhibited abusive behavior that caused bitter disappointment and disillusionment in some of their followers.[37]

Ingrained ego flaws need to be addressed at the form level in which they operate. Because the ego is not really transformed by leaving it behind in a temporary spiritual experience of transcendence, the hard work of spiritual growth is done at the level of perception, where the ego dwells. For this reason, the teachings of the Course are primarily focused on changing perceptions and only secondarily on focusing on one perception or one set of perceptions, as often occurs in meditation. The goal of the Course is to change your entire thought system in order to grow toward unifying your mind with all loving and true perceptions. The primary means of this gradual transformation and unification of the mind is forgiveness, rather than meditation. This process of unifying the perceptions of the mind will be explained in more detail in an upcoming section of this book.

7. ATONEMENT

The Holy Spirit has established the **Atonement** as His plan for salvation. This plan corrects all of your mistakes and all their effects so the ego and its false beliefs in sin and guilt have no power over you.

> When you feel guilty, remember that the ego has indeed violated the laws of God, but *you* have not. Leave the "sins" of the ego to me. That is what Atonement is for.[38]

When you make the choice to accept the Atonement for yourself, you temporarily experience perfect love. Your brother's mind and your mind are connected. When you accept perfect love yourself, that love extends to your brother and heals his mind along with yours. Thus accepting the Atonement is an experience of sharing and healing.

> Atonement teaches you the true condition of the Son of God. It does not teach you what you are, or what your Father is. The Holy Spirit, Who remembers this for you, merely teaches you how to remove the blocks that stand between you and what you know. His memory is yours. If you remember what you have made, you are remembering nothing. Remembrance of reality is in Him, and therefore in you.[39]

THE DOOR TO HEAVEN

~ o ~

The purpose of the seven tools of the Holy Spirit is to eventually bring your mind to a new state of consciousness as a preparation for awakening in Heaven. This new state of mind is the door to Heaven and can be called the "real world" or "the face of Christ."

The real world is a world of forgiveness. It is not a physical place, but rather a state of mind. It is a state of total right-mindedness having only true perceptions. It is unlike the earthly world that contains both wrong-mindedness and right-mindedness, meaning both false perceptions and true perceptions. The real world consists of all loving thoughts and is a reflection of Heaven. This world is found through practicing forgiveness, and it is what Christ's vision reveals. The real world is called the "happy dream" because it is an illusion, but it is an illusion that reflects the reality of Heaven. Making the shift directly from the nightmares of the earthly world to the loftiness of Heaven is too great a leap to make. First the nightmares must be set aside and replaced by the happy dreams of the real world. The loving thoughts of the real world serve as a preparation and stepping stone to Heaven.

The face of Christ at the deepest level of the real world is the *vision of the Son of God*. The face of Christ is only an image of Christ, not the real Christ. Nevertheless, when fully seen, it is an image of blazing light. Some Workbook lessons talk about this blazing light as something that you can experience in meditation.

> Yet perhaps you will succeed in going past that, and through the interval of thoughtlessness to the awareness of a blazing light in which you recognize yourself as love created you. Be confident that you will do much today to bring that awareness nearer, whether you feel you have succeeded or not.[40]

The previous quotation says that in the awareness of the blazing light "you recognize yourself as love created you." The following Workbook quotation encourages you to have a quiet time of coming into His Presence and seeing the holiest of all visions, which is the "vision of His face." This vision can be experienced in a holy instant that brings back your memory of what transcends all vision.

> Into Christ's Presence will we enter now, serenely unaware of everything except His shining face and perfect Love. The vision of His face will stay with you, but there will be an instant which transcends all vision, even this, the holiest. This you will never teach, for you attained it not through learning. Yet the vision speaks of your rememberance of what you knew that instant, and will surely know again.[41]

Seeing the blazing light in a quiet time would be unusual, but you will eventually and inevitably see it as you open the door to Heaven. The final obstacle to seeing the face of Christ is the "dark veil" of the fear of God, which must be set aside along with the fear of death.

> For this dark veil, which seems to make the face of Christ Himself like to a leper's, and the bright Rays of His Father's Love that light His face with glory appear as streams of blood, fades in the blazing light beyond it when the fear of death is gone.[42]

Practicing forgiveness with the support of the other tools of the Holy Spirit allows you to remove all the blocks to seeing the face of Christ, including removing the fear of God. Forgiveness accomplishes the goal of the Course, which is "removing the blocks to the awareness of love's presence, which is your natural inheritance."[43] The next quote describes the face of Christ as "the blazing light of truth," which returns the memory of God, "opening the door at last" to Heaven.

> Let me forgive all things, and let creation be as You would have it be and as it is. Let me remember that I am Your Son, and opening the door at last, forget illusions in the blazing light of truth, as memory of You returns to me.[44]

This image is such a perfect reflection of Heaven that seeing it in its fullness brings back the direct memory of God and facilitates your final destiny of awakening in Heaven. Yet God the Father must make the final step of your awakening so you can go from seeing the face of Christ to accepting your place in the Sonship as part of the one Christ.

INTERRELATIONSHIPS OF THE SEVEN TOOLS

~ • ~

Forgiveness, Christ's vision, miracles, the holy instant, the holy relationship, meditation as a quiet time, and the Atonement have been described as separate tools of the Holy Spirit. When I first started studying the Course, I wondered why the Text didn't have seven distinct chapters that said everything there was to say about each one of these forms of transformation. I was confused by how these ideas were scattered throughout the entire book and repeated from numerous different perspectives. There were too many descriptions to keep these ideas clearly defined as separate categories in my mind. Eventually I learned that the distinctive hallmark of these ideas is that they are not separate concepts. They are totally interrelated, and their similarities are what is most important about them rather than their differences.

In the previous section discussing Lesson 133, six similarities were already identified:

    1. They bring what is eternal.
    2. They produce an equal gain to your brother and to you.
    3. They represent the Holy Spirit's purpose of holiness.
    4. They heal your split mind by correcting errors.
    5. They offer an indirect experience of Heaven.
    6. They give you everything from God that is already yours.

Every one of the tools of the Holy Spirit is an experience of joining with your brothers and sisters. This is true even of the joining that occurs when you sit alone for a quiet time in meditation devoted to experiencing the divine within. What is this joining with your brothers and sisters? Joining is the earthly version of love, which reflects the total joining that occurs in Heaven. You "can look with love or look with hate, depending only on the simple choice of whether you would join with what you see, or keep yourself apart and separate."[45]

All seven tools of the Holy Spirit represent the choice for joining. Remember, you have only two very different choices, which are the Holy Spirit bringing everything and the ego bringing nothing. In other words, your only two alternatives are the choice to join, which brings everything, or the choice to separate, which brings nothing.

But that's not all. Yes, each tool is about joining with your brothers and sisters. Yet in addition, each tool is joined with every other tool. These tools are instruments employed by the Holy Spirit in a totally integrated way, not as separate instruments. As an analogy, you can think of these as seven musical instruments. Although each instrument has its own distinctive sound, these particular seven instruments are never used alone. They are played together, and their distinctive sounds blend seamlessly into one beautiful musical performance. The seven tools of the Holy Spirit are similarly seven instruments used together in perfect coordination to ultimately bring about spiritual awakening in Heaven. Here is how each tool is totally integrated with the other tools, with an emphasis on forgiveness:

1. INTERRELATIONSHIPS OF FORGIVENESS

In comparing the seven tools of the Holy Spirit to the performance of seven musical instruments, remember that the most important musical instrument plays the melody that is repeated throughout. In this analogy, that one central musical instrument is true forgiveness. The practice of forgiveness consists of both looking for the divine presence and overlooking the symbols of the ego, such as the body and guilt. "God is our goal; forgiveness is the means by which our minds return to Him at last."[46] Forgiveness weaves its way through all the other tools of the Holy Spirit, as shown in the interrelationships identified below:

2. INTERRELATIONSHIPS OF CHRIST'S VISION

Christ's vision is the vision coming from the Holy Spirit that can be accepted to allow you to perceive holiness in everyone and everything. "Christ's vision is the holy ground in which the lilies of forgiveness set their roots."[47] Thus Christ's vision is the power that enables you to practice forgiveness. Christ's vision lets you overlook illusions of guilt and instead perceive the holiness in your brother revealing that he is worthy of your forgiveness. Christ's vision that perceives the reflections of the divine presence in everyone is the power behind the application of the other instruments that require the perception of holiness.

3. INTERRELATIONSHIPS OF MIRACLES

A miracle is an exchange of light and love between two people. Miracles are the result of forgiveness and the divine power of Christ's vision that rely on light and love to facilitate healing. When you practice forgiveness by overlooking the ego's illusory symbols of the body and guilt, you use Christ's vision and see holiness in your brother. Christ's vision is facilitated by an inner light. "The wish to see calls down the grace of God upon your eyes, and brings the gift of light that makes sight possible."[48] This light is not physical light seen by physical eyes. "True light that makes true vision possible is not the light the body's eyes behold. It is a state of mind that has become so perfectly unified that darkness cannot be perceived at all."[49] This light brings healing. "This is the light that heals because it brings single perception, based upon one frame of reference, from which one meaning comes."[50]

The experience of forgiveness, which includes the use of Christ's vision, is an exchange unseen by the physical eyes. Light and love go from the one who forgives to the one who is forgiven. This light and love are returned in gratitude to the one who forgives so two people gain light and love with no loss to either one. This miracle of joining in light and love always happens in the holy instant and results in healing.

4. INTERRELATIONSHIPS OF THE HOLY INSTANT

The holy instant is the Holy Spirit's instrument for experiencing *now* with no past or future. Your holiness rests in eternity, not in time.

> Holiness lies not in time, but in eternity. There never was an instant in which God's Son could lose his purity. His changeless state is beyond time, for his purity remains forever beyond attack and without variability. Time stands still in his holiness, and changes not. And so it is no longer time at all. For caught in the single instant of the eternal sanctity of God's creation, it is transformed into forever. Give the eternal instant, that eternity may be remembered for you, in that shining instant of perfect release. Offer the miracle of the holy instant through the Holy Spirit, and leave His giving it to you to Him.[51]

Forgiveness lets you overlook illusions. Illusions, such as guilt, are always supported by the belief in the past and future. As you forgive by overlooking illusions of the past, you accept the reality of now, which is the holy instant in which you use Christ's vision to see the holiness of your brother in the eternal present. "For the present *is* forgiveness."[52] Thus in the practice of forgiveness, you step out of time and into the timelessness of the holy instant. "The holy instant in which you and your brother were united is but the messenger of love, sent from beyond forgiveness to remind you of all that lies beyond it. Yet it is through forgiveness that it will be remembered."[53] That same experience of an instant of eternity happens in Christ's vision, in the miracle, in the holy relationship, in the quiet time of meditation, and in the Atonement.

5. INTERRELATIONSHIPS OF THE HOLY RELATIONSHIP

The holy relationship is a relationship in which two people having common interests join for a common purpose. They may consciously join in a mundane purpose. However, in the holy instant of joining, the Holy Spirit enters and brings the new common purpose of holiness. The holy relationship is nourished by forgiveness practiced by both partners, who overlook illusions and see holiness in each other.

> Beyond the body that you interposed between you and your brother, and shining in the golden light that reaches it from the bright, endless circle that extends forever, is your holy relationship, beloved of God Himself.... Every illusion brought to its forgiveness is gently overlooked and disappears. For at its center Christ has been reborn, to light His home with vision that overlooks the world.[54]

When you join in purpose, at first glance it seems like a worldly expression. However, the ramifications of your holy relationship are astonishing if you practice forgiveness to see holiness in each other. Just as the Holy Spirit enters the holy relationship, Jesus also enters. "I am within your holy relationship..."[55] Your faithfulness to forgiveness means you hold Christ's hand that leads you to the Love of God. Your holy relationship brings you to the real world and to the face of Christ, where the memory of God returns. Then you will come Home and will joyfully take the hand of every brother in the Sonship.

> When brothers join in purpose in the world of fear, they stand already at the edge of the real world. Perhaps they still look back, and think they see an idol that they want. Yet has their path been surely set away from idols toward reality. For when they joined their hands it was Christ's hand they took and they will look on Him Whose hand they hold. The face of Christ is looked upon before the Father is remembered. For He must be unremembered till His Son has reached beyond forgiveness to the Love of God. Yet is the Love of Christ accepted first. And then will come the knowledge They are One.[56]

Partners of a holy relationship join with each other in experiencing Christ's vision, holy instants, and miracles. Either partner can accept the Atonement for himself and in so doing becomes a miracle worker, bringing healing to his partner.

6. INTERRELATIONSHIPS OF THE ATONEMENT

The holy relationship, described in the previous section, is the means through which the Atonement, God's plan of salvation, is accomplished. In the holy relationship two people join in a common purpose, and in that framework of joining, the instruments of the Holy Spirit function to bring about the Atonement. Forgiveness, Christ's vision, the holy instant, miracles, and meditation work together to produce the healing necessary for the fulfillment of the Atonement.

> This holy relationship, lovely in its innocence, mighty in strength, and blazing with a light far brighter than the sun that lights the sky you see, is chosen of your Father as a means for His Own plan. Be thankful that it serves yours not at all. Nothing entrusted to it can be misused, and nothing given it but will be used. This holy relationship has the power to heal all pain, regardless of its form. Neither you nor your brother alone can serve at all. Only in your joint will does healing lie. For here your healing is, and here will you accept Atonement. And in your healing is the Sonship healed *because* your will and your brother's are joined.[57]

The Atonement is the Holy Spirit's plan that will correct all errors of perception in the split mind and make way for awakening in Heaven. Forgiveness is the primary way the Atonement will be accomplished.

> This is not a course in philosophical speculation, nor is it concerned with precise terminology. It is concerned only with Atonement, or the correction of perception. The means of the Atonement is forgiveness.[58]

The Atonement has many definitions, but perhaps the most useful is: "Perfect love is the Atonement." If you are confused about what the Atonement is then substitute that word for the term "perfect love." The sole responsibility of the miracle worker is to accept the Atonement. That means to accept perfect love that comes from the Holy Spirit and from God Himself. This perfect love corrects every error. Indeed, this Atonement, this perfect love, is expressed in each miracle of forgiveness, and permeates all the other instruments of the Holy Spirit.

> Miracles are part of an interlocking chain of forgiveness which, when completed, is the Atonement. Atonement works all the time and in all the dimensions of time.

Miracles represent freedom from fear. "Atoning" means "undoing." The undoing of fear is an essential part of the Atonement value of miracles.

A miracle is a universal blessing from God through me to all my brothers. It is the privilege of the forgiven to forgive.[59]

7. INTERRELATIONSHIPS OF MEDITATION

At first glance, it may seem that meditation has nothing to do with forgiveness and the kind of joining that occurs in the other instruments of the Holy Spirit. But let's look deeper. During your quiet times, you can look for the divine presence within and overlook your distracting thoughts that represent the ego. Consequently, meditation is actually a form of inner forgiveness within your own mind that releases your inner grievances and guilt and recognizes the divine holiness within you.

Meditation is a quiet time of opening up to the divine presence of holiness within yourself. Similar to the way meditation is an inner form of forgiveness, so too forgiveness is a form of outer meditation in which you hold the one thought of holiness in your mind and let go of any distracting thoughts of separation presented by the ego.

But isn't meditation a solitary activity and not an act of joining as occurs in forgiveness? Meditation is considered to be a solitary activity only if its true meaning is misinterpreted or *even misquoted*. There is a Course quotation stating: "Salvation is a collaborative venture. It cannot be undertaken successfully by those who disengage themselves from the Sonship...."[60] But Jesus, as the Author of the Course, dictated the word "meditation" to Helen Schucman and not the word "salvation," which was unfortunately inserted during the editing process. Actually "the true spirit of meditation" is joining with others, as is stated in the accurate original Course quote appearing in Helen Schucman's notebooks:

> Your giant step forward was to *insist* on a collaborative venture. This *does not* go against the true spirit of meditation at all. It is inherent *in* it. Meditation is a collaborative venture with God. It *cannot* be undertaken successfully by those who disengage themselves from the Sonship, because they are disengaging themselves from me. God will come to you only as you will give Him to your brothers.[61]

When you sit down by yourself to practice meditation, you let go of your normal thinking process, and you let go of the past and future in order to bring your mind into the present instant. In other words, you experience the holy instant of now in which you join in perfect communication with God *and* with the entire Sonship.

The holy instant is a time in which you receive and give perfect communication. This means, however, that it is a time in which your mind is open, both to receive and give. It is the recognition that all minds are in communication. It therefore seeks to change nothing, but merely to accept everything."[62]

Therefore, in successful meditation in which you experience the holy instant, you join with God *and* with the Sonship so you rest in the divine presence. The recognition of the divine presence of holiness that occurs in meditation also happens in every instrument used by the Holy Spirit for the purpose of spiritual growth.

THE SEVEN TOOLS LEAD TO THE REAL WORLD

The real world is a state of mind in which all seven tools of the Holy Spirit operate. "The real world is attained simply by the complete forgiveness of the old, the world you see without forgiveness."[63] The real world of only loving perceptions is a reflection of Heaven and is not a place, although it is associated with a place in the body. That place is the crown of the head, which Eastern philosophy identifies as the "crown chakra," the most important spiritual center. It is the inner Holy of Holies. The Course refers to this place as "the holy meeting place" and "the inner altar."

All this is safe within you, where the Holy Spirit shines. He shines not in division, but in the meeting place where God, united with His Son, speaks to His Son through Him. Communication between what cannot be divided cannot cease. The holy meeting place of the unseparated Father and His Son lies in the Holy Spirit and in you. All interference in the communication that God Himself wills with His Son is quite impossible here. Unbroken and uninterrupted love flows constantly between the Father and the Son, as Both would have it be. And so it is.

Let your mind wander not through darkened corridors, away from light's center.[64]

The words "light's center" refer to this altar. This is the crown chakra, which is the holy meeting place, where God and His Son, the Christ, reside. Experiencing the holy instant, the miracle, the Atonement, and the holy relationship all rely on this world of light filled with only true and loving perceptions. Forgiveness, Christ's vision, and meditation all reveal the real world to your consciousness.

THE SEVEN TOOLS LEAD TO THE FACE OF CHRIST

In the analogy of the tools of the Holy Spirit being instruments in a musical composition, forgiveness is the instrument that plays the melody throughout. Yet the composition of all the instruments as a whole and the melody of forgiveness in particular are leading up to a final musical climax, which is represented by the face of Christ. Forgiveness does the work of dispelling all illusions, until finally there is only one last illusion, which is the face of Christ. But this final illusion is such a pure reflection of Heaven that seeing it brings back the memory of God. All false perception is replaced by true perception, and then perception itself is replaced by knowledge as God Himself takes the final step of bringing about your awakening. This transformation happens because you have seen the face of Christ, "the great symbol of forgiveness."

> *The face of Christ* has to be seen before the memory of God can return. The reason is obvious. Seeing the face of Christ involves perception. No one can look on knowledge. But the face of Christ is the great symbol of forgiveness. It is salvation. It is the symbol of the real world. Whoever looks on this no longer sees the world. He is as near to Heaven as is possible outside the gate. Yet from this gate it is no more than just a step inside. It is the final step. And this we leave to God.[65]

The face of Christ is the vision of light that represents the deepest level of the real world. Like the real world, the light of the face of Christ can be seen at first dimly at lower levels of consciousness as you gaze upon the holiness of your brothers and sisters in the world. Yet seen as it truly is with perfect clarity, it is a blazing light, which is the goal of meditation and is the power behind the holy instant, miracles, the Atonement, the holy relationship, Christ's vision, forgiveness, and the real world. This blazing light is where the Holy Spirit brings you to awaken from your dreams of separation. From here the leap to Heaven is a seamless shift from time to timelessness, from form to formlessness, from light to Light, and from love to Love.

> How lovely does the world become in just that single instant when you see the truth about yourself reflected there [in the face of Christ]. Now you are sinless and behold your sinlessness. Now you are holy and perceive it so. And now the mind returns to its Creator; the joining of the Father and the Son, the Unity of unities that stands behind all joining but beyond them all. God is not seen but only understood. His Son is not attacked but recognized.[66]

OPENING THE DOOR TO HEAVEN

~ • ~

Let's summarize the interrelationships of the seven tools of the Holy Spirit by using another analogy. Think of a child playing with wooden blocks. First he sees them as separate cubes of wood. However, as he explores what he can do with the blocks, he puts one block on top of another. Then he adds a third block. He sees that each block rests on the foundation of the block below it. He continues to stack the blocks, one on top of the other, until he has completed a tower of all seven blocks. These blocks represent the seven building blocks of the Holy Spirit used in coordination with each other.

The most important block is the bottom one. The bottom block is the cornerstone upon which the tower is built. In this analogy, forgiveness is the bottom block and cornerstone of the Course upon which all the spiritual principles depend. In their relationships with each other, the seven blocks support one another to allow the tower to rise. Similarly, every tool of the Holy Spirit supports every other tool to allow you to awake from your slumber in the world of dreams.

Instead of continuing the analogy of the seven blocks, let's switch to the analogy of a ladder with seven steps on it. In the Course, Jesus stated, "As a man I did not attempt to counteract error with knowledge, but to correct error from the bottom up."[67] The ladder represents this bottom-up correction. The ladder is put against the side of a house to reach the roof. The ground represents the lower consciousness of the world of both false and unloving perceptions combined with true and loving perceptions. The roof represents unified perception, which has only loving and true perceptions. The seven steps of the ladder are the seven tools of the Holy Spirit that correct perception by replacing false perceptions with true perceptions. This ladder symbolizing bottom-up correction elevates you to the rooftop of unified true perception. This unified perception, also called "total perception," is the consciousness of the real world and the face of Christ.

When the original separation occurred, the sense of separation from God was introduced. With this original separation, the knowledge of Heaven was replaced with the awareness of perception that perpetuates the belief in separation. Then perception itself became fragmented into various lower and higher levels of consciousness, with various needs established at each level. Correction needs to be made at each level of consciousness in which it occurs from the bottom up.

> A sense of separation from God is the only lack you really need correct. This sense of separation would never have arisen if you had not distorted your perception of truth, and had thus perceived yourself as lacking. The idea of order of needs arose because, having made this fundamental error, you had already fragmented yourself into levels with different needs. As you integrate you become one, and your needs become one accordingly. Unified needs lead to unified action, because this produces a lack of conflict.
> The idea of orders of need, which follows from the original error that one can be separated from God, requires correction at its own level before the error of perceiving levels at all can be corrected. You cannot behave effectively while you function on different levels. However, while you do, correction must be introduced vertically from the bottom up. This is because you think you live in space, where concepts such as "up" and "down" are meaningful. Ultimately, space is as meaningless as time. Both are merely beliefs.[68]

The title of this book is "*A Course in Miracles*" *Seven Keys to Heaven* because the tools of the Holy Spirit are the means for you to awaken in Heaven. These tools help you undo the sense of separation you have between you and your brother and between you and God. This sense of separation is an illusion, making you imagine you do not love God and your brothers and imagine God and your brothers do not love you. When this sense of separation is gone, the tools of the Holy Spirit have accomplished their purpose of unlocking the door to Heaven, which is an ocean of divine love. Actually the door to Heaven is more of a doorway that is forever open and waiting for you to walk through it.

> Christ is at God's altar, waiting to welcome His Son. But come wholly without condemnation, for otherwise you will believe that the door is barred and you cannot enter. The door is not barred, and it is impossible that you cannot enter the place where God would have you be. But love yourself with the Love of Christ, for so does your Father love you. You can refuse to enter, but you cannot bar the door that Christ holds open. Come unto me who hold it open for you, for while I live it cannot be shut, and I live forever. God is my life and yours, and nothing is denied by God to His Son.

At God's altar Christ waits for the restoration of Himself in you. God knows His Son as wholly blameless as Himself, and He is approached through the appreciation of His Son. Christ waits for your acceptance of Him as yourself, and of His Wholeness as yours. For Christ is the Son of God, Who lives in His Creator and shines with His glory. Christ is the extension of the Love and the loveliness of God, as perfect as His Creator and at peace with Him.[69]

Illusions make you think the door to Heaven is bolted shut. It is these illusions that must be unlocked so you will see there is nothing stopping you from regaining the awareness of your Home. Forgiveness lets you undo illusions. The face of Christ, also called the real world, is the doorway to Heaven since it is where the memory of God returns. Forgiveness and the face of Christ are the beginning and the end, the alpha and the omega. But all the other keys—Christ's vision, miracles, the holy instant, the holy relationship, the quiet time of meditation, and Atonement—are needed to bring your final awakening.

When forgiveness and the other keys of the Holy Spirit have cleared away all the illusions clouding your mind, there will still be one final illusion. The last illusion is the vision of the face of Christ. Why is this illusion an open doorway to Heaven, when all the other illusions are dark clouds covering that doorway? The face of Christ is a *positive* illusion. This final illusion is not Reality itself, but it is a perfect reflection of the Reality of Heaven. Although this book teaches you words such as the terms for the seven keys to Heaven, these words and all the other words you have ever learned become meaningless in Heaven. All words are the vocabulary of perception that depends on each word being distinctly different from every other word. Yet seeing the face of Christ represents the opportunity to abandon all perception that relies on the differences of words. You have the chance to leap from words to wordlessness, from time to timelessness, from form to formlessness, and from perception of the world to the knowledge of Heaven. The rational mind ruled by the ego has both false perceptions and true perceptions, and this combination blocks the awareness of the Christ Mind.

The face of Christ has only true perceptions and no false perceptions. Seeing this image of all true perceptions presents a perfect reflection of Heaven that shows you the reflection of your true Self, your Identity in Christ. Seeing this reflection provides the opportunity to heal the split mind, letting it return to the One-Mindedness of Heaven. The face of Christ is not the reality of Christ in Heaven; it is just an image of Christ that symbolizes Him, while also symbolizing your true Self. Since the *"face of Christ* has to be seen before the memory of God can return,"[70] can you imagine how beautiful this image must be? In order to answer that question, let's first clarify that actually seeing the face of Christ must occur in a very profound vision because it has the effect of bringing back the memory of God. What is a vision?

> True vision is the natural perception of spiritual sight, but it is still a correction rather than a fact. Spiritual sight is symbolic, and therefore not a device for knowing. It is, however, a means of right perception, which brings it into the proper domain of the miracle. A "vision of God" would be a miracle [indirect experience of the divine] rather than a revelation [direct experience of God]. The fact that perception is involved at all removes the experience from the realm of knowledge. That is why visions, however holy, do not last.[71]

Since seeing "the face of Christ involves perception,"[72] does the Course tell you what the face of Christ actually looks like when you perceive it? Below the Course describes "the vision of the Son of God." It is not a great leap of interpretation to see that this specific "vision of the Son of God" is just another name for seeing the face of Christ.

> Beyond the body, beyond the sun and stars, past everything you see and yet somehow familiar, is an arc of golden light that stretches as you look into a great and shining circle. And all the circle fills with light before your eyes. The edges of the circle disappear, and what is in it is no longer contained at all. The light expands and covers everything, extending to infinity forever shining and with no break or limit anywhere. Within it everything is joined in perfect continuity. Nor is it possible to imagine that anything could be outside, for there is nowhere that this light is not.
> This is the vision of the Son of God, whom you know well. Here is the sight of him who knows his Father. Here is the memory of what you are; a part of this, with all of it within, and joined to all as surely as all is joined in you. Accept the vision that can show you this, and not the body. You know the ancient song, and know it well. Nothing will ever be as dear to you as is this ancient hymn of love the Son of God sings to his Father still.[73]

What an awesome vision! It must be amazing to directly see since this is a vision of all-encompassing light. The face of Christ is more than an ordinary vision because it is the final vision of perception that ends perception and makes the transfer to knowledge possible. Perception always involves a perceiver and an object of perception, and these two must be separate from each other. Unlike perception, the knowledge of Heaven is the full awareness of union so there is no sense of separation. What must happen in seeing the face of Christ that allows this vision of the Son of God to be the final perception of separation? How does this final separation facilitate the transformation that brings union—that restores the knowledge of Heaven to the mind?

Here is an analogy to describe what this profound vision does: Imagine you are looking at a supernatural mirror. As you look at this mirror, you see yourself reflected there. Then you notice "little edges of light around"[74] the image of your body. You step closer to the mirror to get a better look, and as you do, you see your whole body shining in light. You step even closer, and the light gets even brighter. The whole mirror fills with light, and the image of your body fades and becomes transparent in your sight. Then your mind merges with the mirror, and your body drops out of your awareness. Now you are in the mirror, and you are merging with the light, not observing the light from a distance. In fact, you feel at home in this light. You have left the three-dimensional world of bodies. You have entered a two-dimensional world of light, and you are one with the light. Then one more strange thing happens: Without your body awareness, you feel you are actually *becoming* the light. Your center is a point of light, and your "arms" are rays of light extending outward infinitely. Finally, the two-dimensional world fades away, and you are transported to a one-dimensional world, which is a "dimensionless dimension" that is everywhere all at once. Here you are a being of eternal light in union with all the other beings of light. Here "you *are* light."[75] Here "you *are* love,"[76] forever one with the Source of Light. You realize you have been here all along and have never left this state of mind, except in your former illusions of separation. Perhaps this analogy of being transported from the three-dimensional world to the two-dimensional world and finally to the one-dimensional world is close to what will really happen when you wake up in the Light of Heaven. Notice the parallels between this analogy and the following quotation:

> We share one life because we have one Source, a Source from which perfection comes to us, remaining always in the holy minds which He created perfect. As we were, so are we now and will forever be. A sleeping mind must waken, as it sees its own perfection mirroring the Lord of life so perfectly it fades into what is reflected there. And now it is no more a mere reflection. It becomes the thing reflected, and the light which makes reflection possible. No vision now is needed. For the wakened mind is one that knows its Source, its Self, its Holiness.[77]

The previous quotation indicates that your sleeping mind, dreaming of the world, will see a vision of divine perfection, which is a reflection of your own perfection. Then your sleeping mind must awaken as it fades into its reflection and becomes more than a mere reflection. "It becomes the thing reflected, and the light which makes reflection possible."[78] Your sleeping mind becomes the light. You leave behind your last vision of light and become the awakened mind that knows your Source in God. This reflection of light that awakens your sleeping mind must be none other than the face of Christ that must be seen in order to bring back the memory of God.

This quotation referring to a reflection of light is very similar to the previously described mirror analogy. The face of Christ is like this two-dimensional mirror in the analogy that serves as a transition place between the three-dimensional world of form and the one-dimensional world, which is really the *One-dimensional* world of Heaven. Although the image of a mirror is used as an analogy, this mirror of light is a close representation of the face of Christ. Through seeing the face of Christ, your mind will literally be lifted out of the body, out of form into the final illusion in the form of a two-dimensional circle of light described in the vision of Christ. Then this final form of a circle of light expanding infinitely transports you from all form to formlessness. When you reach this final reflection of the truth, there will be no sign saying, "the face of Christ," or "the vision of the Son of God," or "God's Final Judgment." But you will have a universal experience of the ineffable "blazing light," mentioned below, that will usher you into the Arms of God:

> God has come to claim His Own. Forgiveness is complete.
> And now God's *knowledge*, changeless, certain, pure and wholly understandable, enters its kingdom. Gone is perception false and true alike. Gone is forgiveness, for its task is done. And gone are bodies in the blazing light upon the altar to the Son of God. God knows it is His Own, as it is his. And here They join, for here the face of Christ has shone away time's final instant, and now is the last perception of the world without a purpose and without a cause. For where God's memory has come at last there is no journey, no belief in sin, no walls, no bodies, and the grim appeal of guilt and death is there snuffed out forever.
> O my brothers, if you only knew the peace that will envelop you and hold you safe and pure and lovely in the Mind of God, you could but rush to meet Him where His altar is. Hallowed your Name and His, for they are joined here in this holy place. Here He leans down to lift you up to Him, out of illusions into holiness; out of the world and to eternity; out of all fear and given back to love.[79]

THE HOLY SPIRIT'S ONE PURPOSE

~ o ~

When you first start to study the Course, do not be concerned if some of the concepts seem too complex to understand right away. If you ask the Holy Spirit for help and are still confused, it is perfectly all right to simply move on to reading other parts. No one understands the Course in one reading. The Course is like an onion that reveals its layers at deeper and deeper levels with each reading. That is why it needs to be read repeatedly and studied over a period of time, rather than reading it as you would a fictional story.

The seven tools of the Holy Spirit interwoven with each other may seem complex to the rational mind, but their content is really very simple. In fact, these seven instruments have a single unified inner content. Within a world addicted to complex outer appearances, this single content is so simple that it cannot be seen as just the one thing it truly is. To explain this simplicity of content within the complexity of form, imagine that you are a jewelry appraiser of diamonds. You use a microscope to assess the quality of a large diamond with many facets. If you look through just one facet on the surface of the diamond, you can see deep into the center of the diamond and see its absolute clarity and purity. Then you look through another facet and then another, and you realize that every single facet provides that same window to the perfect beauty found at the center of the diamond.

In this analogy, each facet of the diamond represents a different tool used by the Holy Spirit for you to see what the Holy Spirit loves to see and wants you to see—the holiness of the Son of God that is your Identity—symbolized by the beauty at the center of the diamond. Each instrument of the Holy Spirit shows you the beautiful face of Christ that represents the reality of your own Self in Christ. In all the complexity of your search in your daily life, you are seeking and ideally will learn to see only one thing—your own holiness. It is your own holiness that will lead to the awakening of your true Self from your dream of separation.

> Seeing with Him will show you that all meaning, including yours, comes not from double vision, but from the gentle fusing of everything into *one* meaning, *one* emotion and *one* purpose.

God has one purpose which He shares with you. The single vision which the Holy Spirit offers you will bring this oneness to your mind with clarity and brightness so intense you could not wish, for all the world, not to accept what God would have you have. Behold your will, accepting it as His, with all His Love as yours.[80]

What is this one purpose that God shares with you? God's Will for you, as well as your own true will, is to wake up in Heaven. Your one purpose is really two overlapping purposes in perfect harmony. The Holy Spirit has a short-term purpose for you to perceive holiness in every aspect of your daily life in order to heal your split mind. The Holy Spirit has a long-term purpose of awakening you to your true Self. In order to accomplish your one long-term purpose of waking up in Heaven, you will need to accept your one function, which is healing that is accomplished by your short-term purpose of perceiving holiness.

In the future as you read the pages of the Course itself, it will be helpful to pay particular attention to all of the information related to the seven instruments of the Holy Spirit. And of these, make sure that you are especially alert to every mention of the Holy Spirit's tool of forgiveness. Of all seven interrelated instruments of the Holy Spirit, the central one is forgiveness. Your forgiveness will reveal the beauty of every Son of God whom you forgive.

Can you imagine how beautiful those you forgive will look to you? In no fantasy have you ever seen anything so lovely. Nothing you see here, sleeping or waking, comes near to such loveliness. And nothing will you value like unto this, nor hold so dear. Nothing that you remember that made your heart sing with joy has ever brought you even a little part of the happiness this sight will bring you. For you will see the Son of God. You will behold the beauty the Holy Spirit loves to look upon, and which He thanks the Father for. He was created to see this for you, until you learned to see it for yourself. And all His teaching leads to seeing it and giving thanks with Him.[81]

The practice of forgiveness is your primary function because it is your best single reminder of your purpose of perceiving holiness in the world, in others, and in yourself. With each daily step on the path of forgiveness, you bring yourself one step closer to awakening to your true nature in Heaven, which is your destiny, as it is the destiny of every child of God. The next sections focus on learning how to practice forgiveness.

HOW TO RESTORE DIVINE LOVE

Love is not one of the keys to Heaven because love is what you are. The keys to Heaven reveal the love that is you. All seven keys reveal this love, but there is one master key that incorporates all the other keys.

Imagine that you can let your love expand to include everyone and everything that exists. This is God's Love. Because it is God's Love, it is your love since you are a part of God Himself. You already possess this love as your true nature given to you in your creation. What is required for you to become aware of this love you have never lost? *Forgiveness* is the answer *A Course in Miracles* offers to this question. Forgiveness is the master key that reveals your love nature and leads to opening the door to Heaven. You have darkened your own mind, and forgiveness brings back light to your darkened mind, revealing your abiding love for all that exists. Your mind has been darkened by the poison of illusions. Forgiveness is the antidote for this poison.

> God does not forgive because He has never condemned. And there must be condemnation before forgiveness is necessary. Forgiveness is the great need of this world, but that is because it is a world of illusions. Those who forgive are thus releasing themselves from illusions, while those who withhold forgiveness are binding themselves to them. As you condemn only yourself, so do you forgive only yourself.
>
> Yet although God does not forgive, His Love is nevertheless the basis of forgiveness. Fear condemns and love forgives. Forgiveness thus undoes what fear has produced, returning the mind to the awareness of God. For this reason, forgiveness can truly be called salvation. It is the means by which illusions disappear.[82]

Forgiveness does not bring the knowledge of Heaven, but it does bring your readiness for knowledge. Similarly, forgiveness does not teach you how to love, but merely reveals the divine love that is already within you. Forgiveness is your function that brings back the eternal light and love now hidden in darkness. Nevertheless, God Himself must take the final step beyond forgiveness in which you accept your true nature of love.

Yet even forgiveness is not the end. Forgiveness does make lovely, but it does not create. It is the source of healing, but it is the messenger of love and not its Source. Here you are led, that God Himself can take the final step unhindered, for here does nothing interfere with love, letting it be itself. A step beyond this holy place of forgiveness, a step still further inward but the one *you* cannot take, transports you to something completely different. Here is the Source of light; nothing perceived, forgiven nor transformed. But merely known.

This course will lead to knowledge, but knowledge itself is still beyond the scope of our curriculum. Nor is there any need for us to try to speak of what must forever lie beyond words. We need remember only that whoever attains the real world, beyond which learning cannot go, will go beyond it, but in a different way. Where learning ends there God begins, for learning ends before Him Who is complete where He begins, and where there *is* no end. It is not for us to dwell on what cannot be attained. There is too much to learn. The readiness for knowledge still must be attained.

Love is not learned. Its meaning lies within itself. And learning ends when you have recognized all it is *not*. That is the interference; that is what needs to be undone. Love is not learned, because there never was a time in which you knew it not. Learning is useless in the Presence of your Creator, Whose acknowledgment of you and yours of Him so far transcend all learning that everything you learned is meaningless, replaced forever by the knowledge of love and its one meaning.[83]

YOUR FUNCTION
FOR GOD

~ o ~

Have you ever thought what it would be like to be in Heaven? According to the Course, God is "Divine Abstraction."[84] Heaven must be an abstract state of mind, very difficult to fully understand because the human mind is oriented toward awareness of the concrete world of time and space. The Course describes Heaven as a place, or rather a state of awareness consisting of total joyful sharing:

> God, Who encompasses all being, created beings who have everything individually, but who want to share it to increase their joy. Nothing real can be increased except by sharing. That is why God created you. Divine Abstraction takes joy in sharing. That is what creation means. "How," "what" and "to whom" are irrelevant, because real creation gives everything, since it can create only like itself. Remember that in the Kingdom there is no difference between *having* and *being*, as there is in existence [in the world]. In the state of being the mind gives everything always.[85]

In this total heavenly sharing you give all of yourself to all parts of the Sonship, and all parts of the Sonship give all of themselves to you. God giving all of Himself to the Sonship makes all this sharing possible. This is a total sharing of love in which you give all of your love away as a means of increasing love rather than losing it. You can only begin to understand this total sharing by realizing that "*you* are an idea" in the Mind of God:

> You do not find it difficult to believe that when another calls on God for love, your call remains as strong. Nor do you think that when God answers him, your hope of answer is diminished. On the contrary, you are more inclined to regard his success as witness to the possibility of yours. That is because you recognize, however dimly, that God is an idea, and so your faith in Him is strengthened by sharing. What you find difficult to accept is the fact that, like your Father, *you* are an idea. And like Him, you can give yourself completely, wholly without loss and only with gain. Herein lies peace, for here there *is* no conflict.[86]

As an idea in the mind of God, you have a function that God would have you fill. It is your function to *create* in Heaven. The ability to create is related to the type of total sharing described in the two previous quotations. But can you really understand your function of creating by sharing? The Course says: "Creation cannot even be conceived of in the world."[87] Therefore, it is totally impossible for you to fully comprehend what your true function of creation entails. Yet the Course offers clues that suggest the nature of your lofty heavenly function:

> It is your Father's holy Will that you complete Himself, and that your Self shall be His sacred Son, forever pure as He, of love created and in love preserved, extending love, creating in its name, forever one with God and with your Self. Yet what can such a function mean within a world of envy, hatred and attack?[88]

When you return to Heaven, you will perfectly understand how to create. You will no longer be limited by the body or the belief in the ego. You will accept your unlimited Identity. You will create simply by giving all of yourself to every part of the Sonship and to God. Creation will flow through you to extend God's Love. You will be one with creating so no explanation will be necessary because you will have the all-encompassing knowledge of Heaven. However, right now there is no need to figure out what creation will be like. Currently your only task is to heal your split mind in order to bring back your whole mind to the awareness of Heaven where you are sleeping now.

> Therefore, you have a function in the world in its own terms. For who can understand a language far beyond his simple grasp? Forgiveness represents your function here. It is not God's creation, for it is the means by which untruth can be undone. And who would pardon Heaven? Yet on earth, you need the means to let illusions go. Creation merely waits for your return to be acknowledged, not to be complete.[89]

Forgiveness is your function because you are in a world in which some things are true and other things are false. Forgiveness helps you to discern what is true as true and what is false as false. It allows illusions made of false perceptions, such as fear and guilt, to disappear and be replaced by true perceptions that are reflections of Heaven. Forgiveness reveals the truth about the body. It allows the body to be seen in its true function as a device for communicating and connecting rather than as an image of separation.

A Simple Framework for Understanding the Course

Forgiveness gently looks upon all things unknown in Heaven, sees them disappear, and leaves the world a clean and unmarked slate on which the Word of God can now replace the senseless symbols written there before. Forgiveness is the means by which the fear of death is overcome, because it holds no fierce attraction now and guilt is gone. Forgiveness lets the body be perceived as what it is; a simple teaching aid, to be laid by when learning is complete, but hardly changing him who learns at all.[90]

Forgiveness will eventually teach you that you are not a body. When you function without a body in Heaven, your mind will no longer make errors. Death will be no more. Anger will be impossible. There will be nothing to fear. There will be only perfect peace and happiness born of extending love forever as you perform your heavenly function of creating.

Only forgiveness can relieve the mind of thinking that the body is its home. Only forgiveness can restore the peace that God intended for His holy Son. Only forgiveness can persuade the Son to look again upon his holiness.[91]

In addition to teaching you that you are not a body, forgiveness will also teach you that you are not the ego that is attached to the belief in the body. You will see you are not an ego by not accepting your brother as an ego. In your brother you will see the mirror of yourself. If you project your own belief in sin and guilt onto your brother, you will believe you are a guilty sinner, although the forms of his sins may be very different from the forms of your sins. If you withdraw all your beliefs that your brother has sinned and that he is guilty, you will clearly recognize that you have not sinned and you are not guilty.

Forgiveness changes your perception of sins, which seem real and uncorrectable. Your changed perception sees only mistakes that can be corrected. After all, "the Son of God can make mistakes,"[92] but cannot sin. You must protect the belief in your brother's holiness to preserve the truth in your own mind of your own holiness. As you use forgiveness to awaken your brother from his dream of sin and guilt, you will see you are not bound by sin and guilt. His awakening is your awakening. The Holy Spirit has given you a special function to perform in the Atonement, the plan for awakening all the Sons of God. The Course states your special function is a form of forgiveness perfectly suited to your life and relationships.

> Such is the Holy Spirit's kind perception of specialness; His use of what you made, to heal instead of harm. To each He gives a special function in salvation he alone can fill; a part for only him. Nor is the plan complete until he finds his special function, and fulfills the part assigned to him, to make himself complete within a world where incompletion rules.
> Here, where the laws of God do not prevail in perfect form, can he yet do *one* perfect thing and make *one* perfect choice. And by this act of special faithfulness to one perceived as other than himself, he learns the gift was given to himself, and so they must be one. Forgiveness is the only function meaningful in time. It is the means the Holy Spirit uses to translate specialness from sin into salvation. Forgiveness is for all. But when it rests on all it is complete, and every function of this world completed with it. Then is time no more. Yet while in time, there is still much to do. And each must do what is allotted him, for on his part does all the plan depend. He *has* a special part in time for so he chose, and choosing it, he made it for himself. His wish was not denied but changed in form, to let it serve his brother and himself, and thus become a means to save instead of lose.[93]

Fulfilling your function of forgiveness heals your mind and enables you to see the face of Christ. The quotation below states that when you see this gift of God, "you have been forgiven." Thus you have completed your function of forgiveness in time, and in so doing, you are finally ready to accept your divine function of creating in the timelessness of Heaven.

> And what He gives is always like Himself. This is the purpose of the face of Christ. It is the gift of God to save His Son. But look on this and you have been forgiven.
> How lovely does the world become in just that single instant when you see the truth about yourself reflected there. Now you are sinless and behold your sinlessness. Now you are holy and perceive it so. And now the mind returns to its Creator; the joining of the Father and the Son, the Unity of unities that stands behind all joining but beyond them all. God is not seen but only understood. His Son is not attacked but recognized.[94]

Intellectually understanding your special function of forgiveness is the first step in healing your mind and healing the minds of your brothers. This understanding is then your motivation for actually practicing forgiveness, which will be addressed in the next section.

THE PRACTICE OF FORGIVENESS

~ o ~

The focus in this book has been on gaining a basic foundation for understanding the principles of the Course. This simple framework is provided by zeroing in on the seven tools of the Holy Spirit, the seven keys to Heaven. Forgiveness has been identified as the central message of the Course and the most useful tool for transformation leading to awakening in Heaven. Certainly you must understand how to forgive as it is described in the Course in order to practice forgiveness. But how do you learn to "understand all things created as they really are"? You might assume that understanding comes first and then forgiveness. Yet the Course maintains that real understanding of all created things can only come *after* practicing forgiveness. "And it is recognized that all things must be first forgiven, and *then* understood."[95]

The point here is that the Course itself is not really interested in just fostering a lofty philosophy. Rather, the Course says, "...it is the practical with which this course is most concerned."[96] The Course is primarily designed to teach you how to practice forgiveness. Nevertheless, often seekers who fully accept the intellectual understanding of forgiveness presented in the Course are still unsure about how to actually practice forgiveness. Therefore, this section switches the emphasis from the intellectual understanding of forgiveness to its practical application, which is addressed in the Workbook.

In the second month of *The Two-Month Bridge to "A Course in Miracles,"* six of the thirty Workbook lessons describe in detail how to forgive an individual. These are Lessons 46, 68, 78, 121, 134, and 161. These lessons were chosen because they provide examples of how to forgive a particular person. In general, the later Workbook lessons are systematically more advanced than the earlier lessons. This is also true of these six lessons on forgiveness so that Lesson 161 is the closest to the ideal of truly manifesting forgiveness.

If you still do not know how to practice true forgiveness, keep in mind you only need to do two activities—*overlooking and looking*. Both of these activities represent a change in perception. First let's discuss how to practice the overlooking aspect, which is the most misunderstood.

"OVERLOOKING" AS A CHANGE IN PERCEPTION

The first aspect of forgiveness is a change in perception from a form of overlooking guided by the ego to a form of overlooking guided by the Holy Spirit. The ego guides your normal daily consciousness to overlook the divine presence in the world and all reflections of reality. It wants you to see only temporary illusions, such as sins, guilt, and outer forms and bodies and to be convinced that these illusions are real. The ego can only convince you of the reality of the world by overlooking the divine presence and true reflections of reality. The overlooking aspect of forgiveness is a reversal of the ego's form of overlooking. Guided by the Holy Spirit, you can learn to forgive by a new kind of overlooking that looks past the illusions of the ego and does not accept them as real in any way. The ideal way of practicing the overlooking of forgiveness is described in the following Text quotations:

> Atonement is for all, because it is the way to undo the belief that anything is for you alone. To forgive is to overlook. Look, then, beyond error and do not let your perception rest upon it, for you will believe what your perception holds. Accept as true only what your brother is, if you would know yourself. Perceive what he is not and you cannot know what you are, because you see him falsely. Remember always that your Identity is shared, and that Its sharing is Its reality.[97]

> The ego, too, has a plan of forgiveness because you are asking for one, though not of the right teacher. The ego's plan, of course, makes no sense and will not work. By following its plan you will merely place yourself in an impossible situation, to which the ego always leads you. The ego's plan is to have you see error clearly first, and then overlook it. Yet how can you overlook what you have made real? By seeing it clearly, you have made it real and *cannot* overlook it.[98]

If you mentally review the errors of others in any kind of detail, you will look upon "his errors as real, and you have attacked yourself."[99] Errors are not real, but your analysis and interpretation of them will make them seem real to yourself. "To perceive errors in anyone, and to react to them as if they were real, is to make them real to you."[100] In the longer quotation above the key point is this: "To forgive is to overlook. Look, then, beyond error and do not let your perception rest upon it, for you will believe what your perception holds."

If you follow the ego's plan, you will not be able to practice the overlooking of forgiveness. The following three sentences from the prior quotation bear repeating: "The ego's plan is to have you see error clearly first, and then overlook it. Yet how can you overlook what you have made real? By seeing it clearly, you have made it real and *cannot* overlook it." To follow the Holy Spirit's plan, you must overlook error right away so that it will remain unreal for you before its *imaginary reality* takes a foothold in your mind. "Forgiveness through the Holy Spirit lies simply in looking beyond error from the beginning, and thus keeping it unreal for you."[101]

Let's imagine you are a sanitation worker, and you see a plastic bag of trash on the roadside. All you have to do is throw it into the garbage truck and then move on to the next plastic bag and do the same. But if you stop to look inside the plastic bag and examine every bit of trash, you will just be delaying your work of throwing out the trash. Similarly, overlooking consists of just identifying illusions as illusions, and then immediately looking past them without wasting your time on analyzing them any further. Yet this overlooking cannot be done by you alone. You need to rely on the help that comes from your Guide, the Holy Spirit.

> You have a part to play in the Atonement, but the plan of the Atonement is beyond you. You do not understand how to overlook errors, or you would not make them. It would merely be further error to believe either that you do not make them, or that you can correct them without a Guide to correction. And if you do not follow this Guide, your errors will not be corrected. The plan is not yours because of your limited ideas about what you are. This sense of limitation is where all errors arise. The way to undo them, therefore, is not *of* you but *for* you.[102]

Ideally you will call upon the Holy Spirit to do this overlooking. Also, ideally you will have the clear intellectual understanding that you must overlook error right in the beginning before it becomes real to you. But there is still a gap between the ideal practice of overlooking and what actually happens when you first attempt to implement overlooking. One problem is that you have been so conditioned by the ego that in the beginning you cannot immediately overlook errors. The other problem is that your mind is not currently a blank slate. Right now, stored in your mind are a whole host of past grievances that seem real to you when they come to your conscious awareness.

Let's compare your first attempts at practicing overlooking with learning to practice meditation for the first time. A beginning meditator has the goal of having a quiet mind with a focus on one thought, but he will immediately be assailed by a whole series of distracting thoughts. It takes a long time to reduce these distracting thoughts and to master meditation. Similarly, in your first forgiveness practice of overlooking, you may be overwhelmed by distracting grievances. Be gentle with yourself if you cannot immediately let go of the grievances in your mind. But understand that these grievances only have the convincing appearance of reality, yet they are not real at all. Eventually, with continued practice, you will be able to offer these grievances to the Holy Spirit, Who will replace them with miracles of forgiveness.

The Course Workbook realizes that at first you will have difficulty overlooking the grievances already in your mind, and you will want to analyze them instead of following the ideal path of disregarding them immediately. For example, one early Workbook exercise, Lesson 78, describes analyzing specific grievances you want to overlook in your practice of forgiveness.

> You will attempt to hold him in your mind, first as you now consider him. You will review his faults, the difficulties you have had with him, the pain he caused you, his neglect, and all the little and the larger hurts he gave. You will regard his body with its flaws and better points as well, and you will think of his mistakes and even of his "sins."[103]

This lesson takes into account that you are a beginner in practicing forgiveness so you are likely to still be dwelling on the nature of the specific grievances you hold against the one you want to forgive. This lesson meets you where you are now in your learning forgiveness, but the Course wants you to make progress beyond the practice described here of reviewing all the shortcomings of the one you want to forgive. Lesson 134 has a similar process of looking at the "sins" and "offenses" of another, but it is a step forward in learning forgiveness because it emphasizes doing this with the goal of letting go of your ideas of sin.

> Then choose one brother as He will direct, and catalogue his "sins," as one by one they cross your mind. Be certain not to dwell on any one of them, but realize that you are using his "offenses" but to save the world from all ideas of sin. Briefly consider all the evil things you thought of him, and each time ask yourself, "Would I condemn myself for doing this?"[104]

Instead of the process of reviewing the faults of others suggested in Lesson 78, Lesson 134 recommends that you let the "sins" of others lightly cross your mind, but cautions you not to dwell on any one of them. But both of these lessons are not exactly the best examples of the ideal application of the overlooking aspect of forgiveness.

As was previously stated, the ideal way of practicing the overlooking of forgiveness is to overlook error immediately so that it will remain unreal for you. This is the ideal form of overlooking that you need to learn how to practice, even if you cannot practice it correctly in your first attempts at forgiveness. You want to learn how to go beyond the analyzing of faults in Lesson 78 and even beyond the lighter touch of cataloguing "sins" in Lesson 134. You want to learn how to overlook faults not by making any sort of evaluation of them, but simply by seeing right in the beginning that they are totally illusory. To overlook errors literally means to look *over* them, not *at* them. In other words, to overlook is to ignore or look past them so you do not let them find a home in your consciousness.

Of the six forgiveness lessons in the book *The Two-Month Bridge to "A Course in Miracles,"* the last one, Workbook Lesson 161, comes closest to the true overlooking of forgiveness. The Course considers the body to be an illusion that hides your reality. "Who sees a brother as a body sees him as fear's symbol."[105]

In Workbook Lesson 161, you do look at the body, but you see it merely as an outer mask that "conceals from you the sight of one who can forgive you all your sins." Then you are encouraged to look past this outer mask to the reality beyond it. Unlike earlier Lessons 78 and 134, there is no analysis of illusions in Lesson 161 because "Your readiness is closer now..." so you will come nearer to the ideal way of manifesting Christ's vision.

> Today we practice in a form we have attempted earlier. Your readiness is closer now, and you will come today nearer Christ's vision. If you are intent on reaching it, you will succeed today. And once you have succeeded, you will not be willing to accept the witnesses your body's eyes call forth.
>
> Select one brother, symbol of the rest, and ask salvation of him. See him first as clearly as you can, in that same form to which you are accustomed. See his face, his hands and feet, his clothing. Watch him smile, and see familiar gestures which he makes so frequently. Then think of this: What you are seeing now conceals from you the sight of one who can forgive you all your sins; whose sacred hands can take away the nails which pierce your own, and lift the crown of thorns which you have placed upon your bleeding head.[106]

Notice that choosing a person to forgive consists of asking you to "select one brother, symbol of the rest." Unlike earlier, less advanced Workbook lessons, there is no need to focus on someone who has offended you. You are not forgiving specific offenses. Instead, you are forgiving the mask that every seeker presents to hide his holiness. Anyone can be chosen, and he can represent every other brother. After all, every brother wears the mask of the body, which is a reminder of the belief in fear. "Yet bodies are but symbols for a concrete form of fear."[107] In spite of this symbol of fear worn on the outside, every brother is equally worthy of love and therefore worthy of forgiveness. Anyone can become your savior by your willingness to overlook the mask his body presents and see the divine within him.

"LOOKING" AS A CHANGE IN PERCEPTION

The second aspect of forgiveness is a change in perception from a form of looking guided by the ego to a form of looking guided by the Holy Spirit. The ego guides your normal daily consciousness to focus on seeing temporary illusions, such as sins, guilt, and outer forms and bodies, and to be convinced that these illusions are real. The ego can only convince you of the reality of the world by keeping your attention focused on the masks of reality. The looking aspect of forgiveness is a reversal of the ego's form of looking. The ego looks for grievances and reminders of hurts, which justify its very existence. Using the ego's vision given by the body's eyes will provide a sense of separation and alienation.

Using Christ's vision, you switch from the ego's vision to the Holy Spirit's vision. This change in vision manifests the looking aspect of forgiveness, which enables you to look for holiness in your brother instead of grievances. Using the Holy Spirit's gift of vision results in joining with your brother. This joining is a miracle resulting in healing in which there is an exchange of light and love. You become a savior for your brother and your brother becomes your savior as you see holiness rather than guilt in each other. Guided by the Holy Spirit, you can learn to forgive by this new kind of looking that looks for the divine presence in the world and in all reflections of reality.

The main idea of Lesson 78, "Let miracles replace all grievances," is an example of overlooking grievances and looking for the light hidden by your false interpretation of your brother. The goal here is to make your enemy into your friend, who then becomes your savior.

A Simple Framework for Understanding the Course   57

> Through seeing him behind the grievances that you have held against him, you will learn that what lay hidden while you saw him not is there in everyone, and can be seen. He who was enemy is more than friend when he is freed to take the holy role the Holy Spirit has assigned to him. Let him be savior unto you today. Such is his role in God your Father's plan....
>
> Then let us ask of Him Who knows this Son of God in his reality and truth, that we may look on him a different way, and see our savior shining in the light of true forgiveness, given unto us.[108]

Lesson 121, "Forgiveness is the key to happiness," asks you to close your eyes and look for the light in your brothers. First you are asked to see light in someone you falsely interpreted as an "enemy" and then to see the same light in a friend. The exercise is designed to demonstrate that when you are guided by the Holy Spirit, the same divine light can be seen in every brother. Then in your holy sight, every brother becomes your savior, whom you heal and who heals you.

> Now close your eyes and see him in your mind, and look at him a while. Try to perceive some light in him somewhere; a little gleam which you had never noticed. Try to find some little spark of brightness shining through the ugly picture that you hold of him. Look at this picture till you see a light somewhere within it, and then try to let this light extend until it covers him, and makes the picture beautiful and good.
>
> Look at this changed perception for a while, and turn your mind to one you call a friend. Try to transfer the light you learned to see around your former "enemy" to him. Perceive him now as more than friend to you, for in that light his holiness shows you your savior, saved and saving, healed and whole.
>
> Then let him offer you the light you see in him, and let your "enemy" and friend unite in blessing you with what you gave. Now are you one with them, and they with you. Now have you been forgiven by yourself.[109]

Lesson 161, "Give me your blessing, holy Son of God," is a step forward from the earlier lessons on forgiveness. "Your readiness is closer now, and you will come today nearer Christ's vision."[110] Here you do not place your attention on your false interpretations of grievances or your perception of anyone as your enemy. Here you chose anyone as a symbol of everyone because you must learn to forgive everyone equally. "One brother is all brothers."[111] The fundamental change in looking that happens is a shift away from seeing other bodies with your body's eyes. Instead of the vision given by the body, the looking of forgiveness is the gift of the Holy Spirit. This is Christ's vision, which reveals the divine presence in your brother. Lesson 161 offers one of the best descriptions of what Christ's vision can reveal to you:

> This do the body's eyes behold in one whom Heaven cherishes, the angels love and God created perfect. This is his reality. And in Christ's vision is his loveliness reflected in a form so holy and so beautiful that you could scarce refrain from kneeling at his feet. Yet you will take his hand instead, for you are like him in the sight that sees him thus.[112]

Lesson 161 goes a step beyond the other lessons on forgiveness because it invites you to ask your brother for his blessing. This is another way of asking for a miracle because every miracle is an exchange of blessings in which light and love are extended back and forth between two people. Here is what this lesson encourages you to ask of your brother to whom you give and receive forgiveness:

> *Give me your blessing, holy Son of God.*
> *I would behold you with the eyes of Christ,*
> *and see my perfect sinlessness in you.*[113]

> And He will answer Whom you called upon. For He will hear the Voice for God in you, and answer in your own. Behold him now, whom you have seen as merely flesh and bone, and recognize that Christ has come to you. Today's idea is your safe escape from anger and from fear. Be sure you use it instantly, should you be tempted to attack a brother and perceive in him the symbol of your fear. And you will see him suddenly transformed from enemy to savior; from the devil into Christ.[114]

Collectively Lessons 78, 121, and 161 are showing you a very similar result produced by the new way of looking used in forgiveness. This is the common result: The change in perception in your mind results in a change in perception in your brother. Your forgiven brother becomes more than just a friend; he becomes your savior. You join with your brother and recognize you are equals. Your forgiveness of your brother enables you to forgive yourself. The holiness you see in your brother belongs to you as well. Your acceptance of Christ in your brother allows you to accept Christ in yourself.

ONE PROCESS

~ o ~

Forgiveness has been identified as a process of overlooking and looking. Below is a simple outline that summarizes how this practical process always involves overlooking what the ego offers and looking for what the Holy Spirit offers. The practice of overlooking and looking is your means of not only manifesting forgiveness, but also of manifesting the other six tools of the Holy Spirit. This is just one process, yet each tool emphasizes a slightly different aspect of overlooking what is unreal and looking for what is real.

FORGIVENESS —
  Overlooking all your projections of guilt
  Looking for the divine holiness in others

CHRIST'S VISION —
  Overlooking the body and your own judgments of your brother
  Looking for light, Christ, and the Holy Spirit's judgment of holiness

MIRACLES —
  Overlooking false perceptions of grievances
  Looking for miracles as equal exchanges of light and love

HOLY INSTANT —
  Overlooking time based on the past and future
  Looking for the timelessness of now and connection with the Sonship

HOLY RELATIONSHIP —
  Overlooking differences and separateness from others
  Looking for joining with others in the common purpose of holiness

MEDITATION —
  Overlooking multiple mental distractions and inner grievances
  Looking for one sacred thought and then for the Divine Presence

ATONEMENT —
  Overlooking sickness and errors
  Looking for healing and correction that eventually lead to awakening

The previous list shows how all seven tools of the Holy Spirit use the one process of overlooking and looking. However, forgiveness itself *is* overlooking and looking. The other six tools are different ways of describing this process of forgiveness that always overlooks the unreal and looks for the real. Forgiveness is a sorting process of discrimination in which the meaningless is discarded and the meaningful is retained.

Aspects of true forgiveness can be seen in Eastern yoga philosophy. The demanding path of Jnana Yoga uses mental discrimination to bring about the direct experience of union with God. Jnana Yoga allows you to choose between two specific forms of discrimination. One approach uses denial in a positive way, letting you deny all illusions. The seeker repeats the Sanskrit "neti, neti, neti," meaning "not this, not this, not this" as a way of encountering God by observing all distractions that are not part of God. The purpose is to negate mental rationalizations, illusions, and other blocks to the nonconceptual meditative awareness of reality. Ideally, when all things are negated, only the Self remains. To reach the goal of experiencing divine union, this negation must be taken to an extreme level, which makes this a very difficult path.

In contrast to using negation to deny and release ego identifications, the other Jnana Yoga method of discrimination employs the positive Sanskrit affirmation "Tat Tvam Asi," which lets the seeker identify with his true Self in God. The various literal translations, "Thou art that," "That thou art," or "You are that," affirm that you are the Self. The Jnana Yoga seeker can use a method that either negates ego illusions or affirms the Self but never uses both approaches at the same time.

The genius of true forgiveness in the Course is that it simultaneously uses both approaches together to deny what is not divine and to affirm what is divine. The overlooking aspect of forgiveness looks past all distracting illusions, seeing they are unreal. Overlooking sees illusions do not exist and so can be denied and disregarded. The looking aspect of forgiveness looks for the divine. Whereas the two approaches of Jnana Yoga are focused on the goal of *directly* experiencing God, true forgiveness offers you the goal of *indirectly* experiencing God by perceiving the divine presence in your brothers and sisters. This goal is more realistically attainable than the direct experience of God.

Consistently practicing forgiveness your whole life will eventually lead to your awakening in Heaven. Forgiveness takes you to the doorway of Heaven in the real world. There you will be like the Biblical prodigal son on his knees before his father, who has no thoughts of reproach and wants only to joyously celebrate the return of his lost son. As your true Father, God Himself will take the final step of bringing you to your eternal Home where you will celebrate with all of the Sonship.

TO BE FORGIVING
IS
TO BE FOR GIVING

~ o ~

Forgiveness is an enlightened form of self-interest. The main idea of Workbook Lesson 126 is "All that I give is given to myself." How is that possible? In everyday life, giving seems to result in the loss of what is given away. According to the Course, *giving and receiving are the same*. Thus giving is a way of *keeping* because you get back whatever you give away. This means that you must be careful about what you intend to give. If your mind is focused on giving negativity, you will keep that negativity in your own mind. Thus it is important to direct the mind in a positive way, such as using the mind to practice true forgiveness.

You do not understand forgiveness. As you see it, it is but a check upon overt attack, without requiring correction in your mind. It cannot give you peace as you perceive it. It is not a means for your release from what you see in someone other than yourself. It has no power to restore your unity with him to your awareness. It is not what God intended it to be for you.

Not having given Him the gift He asks of you, you cannot recognize His gifts, and think He has not given them to you. Yet would He ask you for a gift unless it was for you? Could He be satisfied with empty gestures, and evaluate such petty gifts as worthy of His Son? Salvation is a better gift than this. And true forgiveness, as the means by which it is attained, must heal the mind that gives, for giving is receiving. What remains as unreceived has not been given, but what has been given must have been received.[115]

It is a mistake to think that forgiveness is the giving of a gift you give to another who is guilty and who does not deserve that gift. True forgiveness recognizes that the one you forgive is your equal who always deserves only love. When you forgive your brother, you are giving him your perception of his true holiness, which was given to him by God in his creation. Because "giving is receiving," the perception of holiness you give away is retained in your own mind so you are indirectly affirming your own holiness.

To be forgiving is to be *for giving*. To be "for giving" means to have the purpose of sharing light, love, and holiness with your brother whom you see as your equal. But you cannot accomplish the purpose of giving light, love, and holiness unless you are first willing to participate in *giving up* your perceptions that would block your giving. Thus just as forgiving is a process of overlooking and looking, it is also an expression of "giving up and giving." Overlooking is motivated by your desire to give up what is overlooked. Looking is motivated by your purpose of giving in the form of sharing as equals, which is a reflection of the sharing as equals that occurs in Heaven. This same two-part expression of "giving up and giving" that happens in true forgiveness also happens in the activation of all the keys to Heaven. Each of the seven tools of the Holy Spirit, listed below, involves a different aspect of giving up blocks and giving in the form of sharing light, love, and holiness:

FORGIVENESS —
  Giving up illusions of guilt
  Giving and receiving the perception of holiness

CHRIST'S VISION —
  Giving up reliance on your physical sight
  Giving and receiving the vision of holiness

MIRACLES —
  Giving up grievances and other false perceptions
  Giving and receiving true perceptions of light and love

HOLY INSTANT —
  Giving up the past and future
  Giving and receiving connection with the Sonship now

HOLY RELATIONSHIP —
  Giving up the perception of separation from others
  Giving and receiving by having the common purpose of holiness

MEDITATION —
  Giving up distracting and self-condemning thoughts
  Giving and receiving inner communion with the Sonship and God

ATONEMENT —
  Giving up sickness and errors
  Giving and receiving the healing of the mind

FORGIVENESS INTERRELATIONSHIPS

~ o ~

FORGIVENESS INTERRELATIONSHIPS FACILITATE APPLICATION

Forgiveness has been described concisely as overlooking and looking, but to be more precise, it is a change in your perception of what you are overlooking and a change in your perception of what you are looking for. This change in perception is really a reversal of your normal understanding. Normally you overlook the divine and look for what the world presents. Forgiveness overlooks what the world presents and looks for the divine. This understanding is required in order to put your forgiveness into practical application. You cannot apply forgiveness if you do not understand it. And you cannot understand forgiveness if you think this concept stands alone. Forgiveness is fully integrated with every other important aspect of the Course.

The Course emphasizes forgiveness, even when the word itself is not used. For example, Lesson 133, "I will not value what is valueless," describes how to discriminate between what is valueless and what is valuable. The things that are temporary and offered by the ego are valueless. What is eternal and is offered by the Holy Spirit is valuable. You are encouraged to let go of what is valueless and accept what is valuable. This sorting out process does not address forgiveness directly. Yet this same sorting out process is what happens when you practice forgiveness in which you overlook the ego and body of your brother and look for the valuable divine presence in your brother.

Another example is Lesson 108, "To give and to receive are one in truth," which refers to the "true light" that makes Christ's vision possible. This "true light" is given and received simultaneously when practicing forgiveness, just as the perception of love and holiness is given and received simultaneously, as was described in the previous section.

> True light that makes true vision possible is not the light the body's eyes behold. It is a state of mind that has become so unified that darkness cannot be perceived at all. And thus what is the same is seen as one, while what is not the same remains unnoticed, for it is not there.

This is the light that shows no opposites, and vision, being healed, has power to heal. This is the light that brings your peace of mind to other minds, to share it and be glad that they are one with you and with themselves. This is the light that heals because it brings single perception, based upon one frame of reference, from which one meaning comes.

Here are both giving and receiving seen as different aspects of one Thought whose truth does not depend on which is seen as first, nor which appears to be in second place. Here it is understood that both occur together, that the Thought remain complete.[116]

Many spiritual principles indirectly describe forgiveness, but the best examples are the other six tools of the Holy Spirit. Understanding these tools can significantly improve your practice of forgiveness. Previously the interrelationships between forgiveness and the other six tools of the Holy Spirit were identified. Now let's discuss how these interrelationships have a direct impact on the practical application of forgiveness.

CHRIST'S VISION HELPS YOU TO FORGIVE —

Many Course students study the Text and do the Workbook lessons and still have these kinds of complaints: *I can't let go of grievances. I can't see light in anyone. I can't see the divine in anyone. I don't know how to forgive.* You can't learn to forgive if you feel the task is entirely up to you. Forgiveness is always accomplished by a combination of you *and* the Holy Spirit. Your task is to directly invite the Holy Spirit and open your mind to His gift, which is also the gift of Christ. This gift is Christ's vision. It is called Christ's vision because Christ is seeing through you in your practice of forgiveness. Christ's vision is not optional; it is required for the practice of forgiveness. Just as a light bulb needs electricity to light up, forgiveness needs Christ's vision to produce miracles of light and love that result in healing.

Lesson 15, "My thoughts are images that I have made," explains that your mind projects your thoughts outwardly so you see only images you have projected. These are dream images of your dreaming mind so the body's eyes are seeing outer forms that are illusions. The body itself is the best example of a dream image projected from the dreaming mind.

It is because the thoughts you think you think appear as images that you do not recognize them as nothing. You think you think them, and so you think you see them. This is how your "seeing" was made. This is the function you have given your body's eyes. It is not seeing. It is image making. It takes the place of seeing, replacing vision with illusions.[117]

Lesson 30, "God is in everything I see because God is in my mind," describes "a new kind of 'projection.'"[118] The word "projection" normally has a negative connotation, which is associated with projecting guilt onto others. This usual kind of projection involves projecting illusory images, such as the image making that shows the body, which is a symbol of both fear and guilt. The Course describes the body as only an image that covers your perception of the light that lies beyond it.

> The body will remain guilt's messenger, and will act as it directs as long as you believe that guilt is real. For the reality of guilt is the illusion that seems to make it heavy and opaque, impenetrable, and a real foundation for the ego's thought system. Its thinness and transparency are not apparent until you see the light behind it. And then you see it as a fragile veil before the light.[119]

Christ's vision enables you to overlook the body and look for the light that shines behind it. In addition to being a symbol of fear and guilt, the body is also a symbol of the desire to be separate, which is the foundation of the ego. You overlook fear, guilt, and separation because of the "new kind of 'projection'" described in Lesson 30. This new kind of projection is not a projection of illusory images.

> Today we are trying to use a new kind of "projection." We are not attempting to get rid of what we do not like by seeing it outside. Instead, we are trying to see in the world what is in our minds, and what we want to recognize is there. Thus, we are trying to join with what we see, rather than keeping it apart from us. That is the fundamental difference between vision and the way you see.[120]

What is this new kind of "projection" that is based on joining with what you see? It is Christ's vision in which you "project" light and love, although this kind of projection is more correctly called "extension." In Christ's vision you "extend" the light in your own mind in order to connect with that same light in others. Christ's vision is about two kinds of joining. First you invite the gift of Christ's vision into your own mind and join with it. Then you use Christ's vision to join with your brother. "Yet it [your ability to see] can look with love or look with hate, depending only on the simple choice of whether you would join with what you see, or keep yourself apart and separate."[121] If you look with love, you will be using Christ's vision for joining; if you look with hate, you will be using the body's eyes for separating.

When you look with love, you join with your brother, and you are practicing forgiveness. "Forgiveness is the healing of the perception of separation."[122] Thus if you want to put forgiveness into practical application, it will help you to open your heart to your brother and feel that you are joining with him. In your union with him, you will see Christ in Him and confirm that Christ must be in you as well.

When you are accepting the gift of Christ's vision, you are actually allowing light to come into your own mind, which in turn extends to the mind of your brother. "For light must come into the darkened world to make Christ's vision possible even here. Help Him to give His gift of light to all who think they wander in the darkness, and let Him gather them into His quiet sight that makes them one."[123] Sometimes the word "light" in the Course is interpreted figuratively, but often this word can be interpreted literally, as is the case in the following passage:

> Christ's vision has one law. It does not look upon a body, and mistake it for the Son whom God created. It beholds a light beyond the body; an idea beyond what can be touched, a purity undimmed by errors, pitiful mistakes, and fearful thoughts of guilt from dreams of sin. It sees no separation. And it looks on everyone, on every circumstance, all happenings and all events, without the slightest fading of the light it sees.[124]

Christ's vision represents the divine power that enables you to practice forgiveness. Christ's vision allows you to overlook the body and other projections of guilt, and instead see the true holiness in every Son of God.

> And this you give today: See no one as a body. Greet him as the Son of God he is, acknowledging that he is one with you in holiness.
>
> Thus are his sins forgiven him, for Christ has vision that has power to overlook them all. In His forgiveness are they gone. Unseen by One they merely disappear, because a vision of the holiness that lies beyond them comes to take their place. It matters not what form they took, nor how enormous they appeared to be, nor who seemed to be hurt by them. They are no more. And all effects they seemed to have are gone with them, undone and never to be done.
>
> Thus do you learn to give as you receive. And thus Christ's vision looks on you as well. This lesson is not difficult to learn, if you remember in your brother you but see yourself. If he be lost in sin, so must you be; if you see light in him, your sins have been forgiven by yourself. Each brother whom you meet today provides another chance to let Christ's vision shine on you, and offer you the peace of God.[125]

A Simple Framework for Understanding the Course

MIRACLES HELP YOU TO FORGIVE —

Just as forgiveness and Christ's vision are inseparable, miracles cannot be separated from either forgiveness or Christ's vision. "Miracles are natural signs of forgiveness. Through miracles you accept God's forgiveness by extending it to others."[126] A miracle is defined as a change in perception in which light and love go from one mind to another and is returned. In this exchange both parties experience an increase of light and love, with no loss to either one.

Christ's vision is the miracle in which all miracles are born. It is their source, remaining with each miracle you give, and yet remaining yours. It is the bond by which the giver and receiver are united in extension here on earth, as they are one in Heaven. Christ beholds no sin in anyone. And in His sight the sinless are as one. Their holiness was given by His Father and Himself.[127]

Forgiveness is the home of miracles. The eyes of Christ deliver them to all they look upon in mercy and in love. Perception stands corrected in His sight, and what was meant to curse has come to bless. Each lily of forgiveness offers all the world the silent miracle of love.[128]

Miracles are the results of practicing forgiveness and using Christ's vision. Miracles bring about the healing of relationships and also the healing of the mind. Miracles are the natural outcome of cooperating with the Holy Spirit in His plan of salvation. Forgiveness is the function of the Holy Spirit, but you also have a function of forgiveness assigned to you as your part in fulfilling God's plan of awakening all seekers, who are the sleeping parts of the Son of God.

Follow the Holy Spirit's teaching in forgiveness, then, because forgiveness is His function and He knows how to fulfill it perfectly. That is what I meant when I said that miracles are natural, and when they do not occur something has gone wrong. Miracles are merely the sign of your willingness to follow the Holy Spirit's plan of salvation, recognizing that you do not understand what it is.[129]

Let's say hypothetically that you hold a grievance toward someone, and you want to practice forgiveness to fulfill your part in God's plan of salvation. But you cannot seem to do it. Other than calling upon the Holy Spirit, what is the most useful thing to know about miracles that will help you to succeed in your practice? Perhaps you can overcome your block to forgiveness by reminding yourself your brother is your equal so he deserves the miracle of forgiveness as much as you do. "Unless you think that all your brothers have an equal right to miracles with you, you will not claim your right to them because you were unjust to one with equal rights."[130]

The focus of Lesson 108, "To give and to receive are one in truth," is a spiritual principle that is the basis for forgiveness. This principle is likewise the basis of the exchange of light and love that happens in all miracles. Both the forgiver and the forgiven give and receive the same light and love simultaneously. The primary significance of this sharing is that it is an equal exchange between equal Sons of God. You and your brother have already been forgiven by God for everything that has ever happened or ever will happen. But if you withhold your forgiveness from your brother—from any brother—you will not recognize you have been forgiven. If you forgive everyone, you will not exclude yourself from the forgiveness that you have given and God has given to you.

God's forgiveness of you is not an overlooking of what you deserve; His forgiveness is a fulfillment of what you deserve. God's perspective is that you deserve love and only love. In order to forgive everyone, you will have to realize that all your brothers deserve only love. You must see every brother as either expressing love in his positive expressions or calling for love in his mistakes. By practicing forgiveness you answer his call for love by supplying the love he is calling for. Your loving response to his call for love expresses your forgiveness and manifests miracles, which heal your mind and your brother's mind equally.

You might assume that there are many different miracles. Indeed you can have many experiences of miracles. However, when you experience all these miracles you are actually experiencing just one miracle—the same miracle.

> There is one miracle, as there is one in reality. And every miracle you do contains them all, as every aspect of reality you see blends quietly into the one Reality of God. The only miracle that ever was is God's most holy Son, created in the one Reality that is his Father. Christ's vision is His gift to you. His Being is His Father's gift to Him.[131]

There is only one miracle because the miracle is a holy instant of directly experiencing your Identity. Why do you exchange light and love with your brother in the miracle of forgiveness? It is not because you are in a process of joining with him as it appears to you. You are not in the act of joining because you are *already* united with your brother. You are just clearing away the illusions that prevented you from recognizing that you are eternally united to your brother. Each miracle of forgiveness simply reveals a glimpse of your shared Identity. This glimpse is not a full awakening of your true Self, but is a partial healing of your mind and a reminder of your place in the Sonship as a part of the one Christ.

The miracle is always there. Its presence is not caused by your vision; its absence is not the result of your failure to see. It is only your awareness of miracles that is affected. You will see them in the light; you will not see them in the dark.[132]

THE HOLY INSTANT HELPS YOU TO FORGIVE —

What role does time play in your practice of forgiveness? All the blocks to forgiveness are based on believing that illusions are real. For example, grievances seem like things that have happened and must be real. But the things that happened are all in the past, and the past does not exist, so you must remind yourself that your grievances are not real. Your grievances are about the past, but you must be holding them in your mind now in order for them to block your ability to forgive. Even if you intellectually see the past as unreal, how do you actually experience that the past is unreal? This direct experience of releasing the past comes to you every time you experience a holy instant, which is an encounter with *now*. For an instant you step out of time, and you join with God and with your brothers and sisters in the Sonship.

When do you experience the holy instant? You experience the holy instant every time you call upon any one of the other six tools of the Holy Spirit. Just as there is only one miracle, there is only one holy instant because there is only one eternal *now*. This one holy instant is waiting for you to open your mind to it. For example, the quotation below describes the opening of your mind that occurs in Christ's vision, which is your means for letting go of the past.

> The savior's vision is as innocent of what your brother is as it is free of any judgment made upon yourself. It sees no past in anyone at all. And thus it serves a wholly open mind, unclouded by old concepts, and prepared to look on only what the present holds. It cannot judge because it does not know. And recognizing this, it merely asks, "What is the meaning of what I behold?" Then is the answer given. And the door held open for the face of Christ to shine upon the one who asks, in innocence, to see beyond the veil of old ideas and ancient concepts held so long and dear against the vision of the Christ in you.[133]

An open mind is needed because it is not focused on all the unnecessary baggage of the past that merely blocks your acceptance of the gift of Christ's vision, which brings forgiveness with it. Likewise, when you engage in a holy relationship, experience meditation, or accept Atonement, your mind is open and experiences the holy instant. Similarly, you cannot perceive the real world or the face of Christ unless the mind is open and the holy instant enters.

What all this means for the practical application of forgiveness is that you can remind yourself that you can facilitate forgiveness by merely looking upon your brother stripped of all his past. This in turn strips your own mind of all your past grievances, which you are holding onto now. "For the present *is* forgiveness."[134] In the direct experience of now, you can clearly see that the grievances of the past are totally unreal and have no place in the holy instant. "Everyone seen without the past thus brings you nearer to the end of time by bringing healed and healing sight into the darkness, and enabling the world to see."[135]

THE HOLY RELATIONSHIP HELPS YOU TO FORGIVE —

The holy relationship provides a training ground for you to learn how to forgive. If you have a significant person in your life with whom you have a common purpose, the Holy Spirit has entered this relationship. When the Holy Spirit enters the holy relationship, the common purpose both partners have chosen is replaced by the Holy Spirit's purpose of holiness. With the new goal of holiness, both partners must learn how to practice forgiveness, which facilitates the perception of holiness.

> Beyond the body that you interposed between you and your brother, and shining in the golden light that reaches it from the bright, endless circle that extends forever, is your holy relationship, beloved of God Himself. How still it rests, in time and yet beyond, immortal yet on earth. How great the power that lies in it. Time waits upon its will, and earth will be as it would have it be. Here is no separate will, nor the desire that anything be separate. Its will has no exceptions, and what it wills is true. Every illusion brought to its forgiveness is gently overlooked and disappears. For at its center Christ has been reborn, to light His home with vision that overlooks the world.[136]

In the previous quote, the most pertinent sentence is: "Every illusion brought to its forgiveness is gently overlooked and disappears." You learn your most important lessons of how to forgive through your closest holy relationships. But the Course wants you to forgive everyone without exception. How do you do that? Your practice of forgiveness learned in your holy relationship may seem like just a small part of the massive task of being able to forgive everyone. But the Course maintains that your learning in a specific situation needs to be generalized to every situation.

A Simple Framework for Understanding the Course 71

Similarly, learning to forgive one person needs to be generalized to the forgiveness of everyone. When you forgive anyone, you use Christ's vision to manifest true perception, consisting of only loving thoughts. This true perception is transferable to perceiving everyone, once it is learned. The central idea of the generalization of your learning of true perception is clearly stated in the instructions for the Workbook:

> The purpose of the workbook is to train your mind in a systematic way to a different perception of everyone and everything in the world. The exercises are planned to help you generalize the lessons, so that you will understand that each of them is equally applicable to everyone and everything you see.
>
> Transfer of training in true perception does not proceed as does transfer of the training of the world. If true perception has been achieved in connection with any person, situation or event, total transfer to everyone and everything is certain. On the other hand, one exception held apart from true perception makes its accomplishments anywhere impossible.[137]

Unlike the holy relationship, the special relationship acts like an exclusive club of two in which each partner feels he is trading his lack of specialness for the greater specialness taken from his partner. This forms an ivory tower mentality of separation. The two partners in their specialness are pitted against the world of less special people so differences are highlighted.

In contrast to the special relationship, the holy relationship fosters a deep sense of equality between each partner and, just as importantly, equality with everyone else. "Here [in the holy relationship] is belief in differences undone. Here is the faith in differences shifted to sameness."[138] This sense of sameness and equality with your brother means you can see how everything you learn about relating to your partner also applies to how you need to relate to everyone else. You will learn in your holy relationship to place your faith in the truth and in the holiness you see in every brother in every situation.

> There is no situation that does not involve your whole relationship, in every aspect and complete in every part. You can leave nothing of yourself outside it and keep the situation holy. For it shares the purpose of your whole relationship, and derives its meaning from it.
>
> Enter each situation with the faith you give your brother, or you are faithless to your own relationship. Your faith will call the others to share your purpose, as the same purpose called forth the

faith in you. And you will see the means you once employed to lead you to illusions transformed to means for truth. Truth calls for faith, and faith makes room for truth. When the Holy Spirit changed the purpose of your relationship by exchanging yours for His, the goal He placed there was extended to every situation in which you enter, or will ever enter. And every situation was thus made free of the past, which would have made it purposeless.[139]

In the holy relationship, you forgive each other, and you become saviors for each other. But then you generalize your learning to realize that everyone to whom you extend forgiveness becomes your savior and you become his savior. Instead of the exclusiveness of the special relationship, the holy relationship "must extend, as you extended when you and he [your partner] joined."[140] The holy relationship is a means of extending holiness to other relationships. "The extension of the Holy Spirit's purpose [of holiness] from your relationship to others, to bring them gently in, is the way in which He will bring means and goal in line."[141] Your holy relationship is not only the means of your salvation; it is the means through which salvation comes to many others through the Holy Spirit.

Through your holy relationship, reborn and blessed in every holy instant you do not arrange, thousands will rise to Heaven with you. Can you plan for this? Or could you prepare yourself for such a function? Yet it is possible, because God wills it. Nor will He change His Mind about it. The means and purpose both belong to Him. You have accepted one; the other will be provided. A purpose such as this, without the means, is inconceivable. He will provide the means to anyone who shares His purpose.[142]

It is no dream to love your brother as yourself. Nor is your holy relationship a dream.... It will become the happy dream through which He [the Holy Spirit] can spread joy to thousands on thousands who believe that love is fear, not happiness. Let Him fulfill the function that He gave to your relationship by accepting it for you, and nothing will be wanting that would make of it what He would have it be.[143]

MEDITATION HELPS YOU TO FORGIVE —

Many students believe that the Course emphasis on forgiveness means that the interior life of quiet times spent in prayer and meditation is not very relevant or important. This certainly disregards the clear Course recommendation that teachers of God set aside quiet times in

A Simple Framework for Understanding the Course 73

the morning and evening for interior communion. Another tendency of many Course students is to place forgiveness and meditation into two very separate categories that have nothing to do with each other. Here is the Course passage showing the true connection between forgiveness and the inner asking of prayer.

> Prayer is a way of asking for something. It is the medium of miracles. But the only meaningful prayer is for forgiveness, because those who have been forgiven have everything. Once forgiveness has been accepted, prayer in the usual sense becomes utterly meaningless. The prayer for forgiveness is nothing more than a request that you may be able to recognize what you already have.[144]

Prayer is inner asking, which is different than meditation. To show the connection between forgiveness and meditation, it is necessary to understand the practice of meditation and then compare it to the practice of forgiveness. First the practice of meditation is a means of learning how to control the mind, which is significant because the Course describes itself as "a course in mind training."[145] Meditation can be defined as continuously holding one thought, one true perception, in the mind to the exclusion of other thoughts. The first time you practice meditation you discover that you cannot easily control the mind because of interfering thoughts that distract you from your one chosen focusing thought. But after repeated practice, you can learn to train your mind to hold its attention on one thought and ignore distracting thoughts.

Workbook Lessons 183 and 184 are the only two examples in the Course of holding one thought in the mind continuously. These two lessons are like the mantra meditation of yoga in which you focus entirely on your choice of the Name of God. But in most Workbook lessons you meditate by first holding the thought for the day in your mind and then letting it go. But if distracting thoughts interfere with your meditation, you temporarily return to repeating the thought for the day. The following is an excerpt from Workbook Lesson 41 that introduces the formal practice of meditation:

> There will be only one long practice period today. In the morning, as soon as you get up if possible, sit quietly for some three to five minutes, with your eyes closed. At the beginning of the practice period, repeat today's idea very slowly. Then make no effort to think of anything. Try, instead, to get a sense of turning inward, past all the idle thoughts of the world. Try to enter very deeply into your own mind, keeping it clear of any thoughts that might divert your attention.

From time to time, you may repeat the idea if you find it helpful. But most of all, try to sink down and inward, away from the world and all the foolish thoughts of the world. You are trying to reach past all these things. You are trying to leave appearances and approach reality.[146]

The most powerful distracting thoughts are the ones that carry an emotional charge, such as thoughts of fear or anger that have been suppressed. These hidden emotional thoughts can suddenly pop into the mind during meditation. An experienced meditator can ignore even these emotional thoughts and in so doing release the hidden negative effects they have on the subconscious mind. Frequently these emotional thoughts are thoughts of self-condemnation, temporary resentments, or long held grievances toward others. If you examine these emotional thoughts as they pass through your mind, you will not be able to overlook them, and you will not be able to look for the one holy thought you have chosen as your focus. You can notice thoughts as they pass through your mind as long as you do so "without involvement," which would distract your mind. Workbook Lesson 44 states:

Begin the practice period by repeating today's idea with your eyes open, and close them slowly, repeating the idea several times more. Then try to sink into your mind, letting go every kind of interference and intrusion by quietly sinking past them. Your mind cannot be stopped in this unless you choose to stop it. It is merely taking its natural course. Try to observe your passing thoughts without involvement, and slip quietly by them....

If resistance rises in any form, pause long enough to repeat today's idea....

If you are doing the exercises correctly, you should experience some sense of relaxation, and even a feeling that you are approaching, if not actually entering into light. Try to think of light, formless and without limit, as you pass by the thoughts of this world. And do not forget that they cannot hold you to the world unless you give them the power to do so.[147]

Noticing passing thoughts without involvement as described above corresponds to the overlooking that occurs in forgiveness. The thought of light corresponds to the looking for the divine in the practice of forgiveness. Thus the mind training of meditation follows the same exact procedure of overlooking and looking as forgiveness, which has been described previously in this book. Also, there is a releasing of grievances and replacing them with true perception, which is identical for both meditation and forgiveness. Perhaps the most important common ground is that both meditation and forgiveness emphasize the intention of holiness. The form of your meditation practice is not as significant as your awareness of this inner content of holiness.

> Think of what you are saying; what the words mean. Concentrate on the holiness that they imply about you; on the unfailing companionship that is yours; on the complete protection that surrounds you.[148]

> While no particular approach is advocated for this form of exercise, what is needful is a sense of the importance of what you are doing; its inestimable value to you, and an awareness that you are attempting something very holy.[149]

How much is meditation a part of the Workbook? Every Workbook lesson has one central thought that is to be used as the focus for the day. This daily mental focusing on the thought of the day can be considered meditation in a general sense. There are many Workbook lessons that instruct you to set aside five minutes out of every hour in the day. These may be considered "mini-meditations" in which you hold the thought for the day in your mind. Lessons 221 to 356 make up the second part of the Course, and these final lessons are introduced with these words:

> We will continue with a central thought for all the days to come, and we will use that thought to introduce our times of rest, and calm our minds at need. Yet we will not content ourselves with simple practicing in the remaining holy instants which conclude the year that we have given God. We say some simple words of welcome, and expect our Father to reveal Himself, as He has promised. We have called on Him, and He has promised that His Son will not remain unanswered when he calls His Name....
> We say the words of invitation that His Voice suggests, and then we wait for Him to come to us.[150]

Although meditation is a process of holding one thought in the mind, the primary attunement practice of the Workbook is the letting go of the one thought for the day and opening to the divine presence without words. "Words will mean little now. We use them but as guides on which we do not now depend. For now we seek direct experience of truth alone."[151] This could be called a meditation practice, yet the more correct term is *contemplation*, which is wordless attunement. Whether you practice meditation using words or practice wordless contemplation, you are still ignoring distracting thoughts and opening to the divine presence. This two-part process of inner attunement is still the same kind of overlooking and looking that happens in forgiveness.

Forgiveness is an experience of the holy instant. It manifests miracles, it results in healing, and it uses Christ's vision. Do these factors that happen in forgiveness also happen in meditation? Yes, they do happen in successful meditation. In meditation you let go of the past and future to be fully present now in the holy instant. In this holy instant of meditation, you are no longer alone; you join with the presence and holiness of all your companions in the Sonship and with God. During this unified state of mind, you extend miracles as exchanges of light and love. This extension of miracles is unlike forgiveness in which you choose a specific person for your miracles. Yet in both meditation and forgiveness, the Holy Spirit extends your miracles to others in the Sonship, whom you may never meet in person. Christ's vision is a gift of "true light" that comes into your mind to produce "a state of mind that has become so unified that darkness cannot be perceived at all."[152] When you open your mind to the Holy Spirit, this light comes in as divine grace, whether it is an expression of forgiveness or meditation. In both cases you join in holiness with your brothers in Christ.

How about the Atonement, the real world, and the face of Christ in relation to forgiveness and meditation? When you accept true light into your mind in both forgiveness and meditation, you are also accepting the perfect love of the Atonement that heals the mind. Just as the practice of forgiveness leads to one destination called the real world or the face of Christ, meditation leads to the same destination.

So how are meditation and forgiveness different? Forgiveness is a way of healing your mind that starts with focusing on one specific outer relationship. You release your grievances and see the holiness in this person. You experience a miracle of joining with him so you become saviors for each other. Meditation is likewise a way of healing your mind, but unlike forgiveness, you start by looking within first. However, your inward seeking releases inner grievances and leads to miracles of joining with your brothers in the Sonship. Although forgiveness has an outer starting point and meditation has an inner starting point, they use the same device of overlooking and looking to arrive at the same healing of the mind. *In summary, forgiveness is actually an outer form of meditation focused on seeing the divine in others, which indirectly heals your own mind. Similarly, meditation is an inner form of forgiveness in which you directly forgive your own mind.*

When you blame your brother by projecting guilt onto him, you are depriving your brother of the love he deserves as the holy Son of God.

This becomes a boomerang that only seems to relieve you of the guilt you have projected. In fact, perceiving guilt in your brother actually reinforces your belief that you are guilty. Your first attempts at a reversal of thinking in which you withdraw your projection of guilt upon your brother may initially be painful. What is the cause of this temporary pain? When your brother is no longer your scapegoat for guilt, you will be tempted to replace your outer blaming with inner blaming of yourself. "The beginning phases of this reversal are often quite painful, for as blame is withdrawn from without, there is a strong tendency to harbor it within."[153] If you focus your forgiveness only outwardly by withdrawing your projections of blame onto others, you might at least temporarily indulge in self-condemnation. "Self-blame is therefore ego identification, and as much an ego defense as blaming others."[154] Since meditation is a form of inner forgiveness, it helps you to directly overcome self-condemnation. After all, you deserve inner forgiveness of yourself as much as your brother deserves your outer forgiveness. Your dual practice of forgiving others outwardly and forgiving yourself in meditation reinforces the idea that both your brother and you are holy, and you both deserve love and forgiveness equally.

Now let's consider the topic of this section: How can meditation help you to practice forgiveness? If you do not understand the link between forgiveness and meditation, you will imagine that forgiveness is just a one-time decision that you make, without appreciating the degree of focusing the mind that is required. Perhaps you have heard someone say, "I just can't forgive this person" or "I just can't meditate." Typically I will respond to both statements identically by asking this question: "On a daily basis, how much time, effort, and mental focusing have you devoted to this activity (forgiveness or meditation)?"

What you can learn from meditation is that you need to focus your mind in order to practice forgiveness successfully. "All learning involves attention and study at some level."[155] Studying forgiveness involves learning the Course principles, but then applying those principles of forgiveness means focusing your attention just as you focus the mind in meditation. My advice for learning meditation is to set aside a period of time every morning and evening to do it, just as the Course recommends for the teacher of God. Learning to clear your mind through overlooking and looking in your daily meditation will become the foundation for practicing forgiveness. Just as meditation takes daily time and effort, developing a forgiving mind takes daily time and effort. The practices of meditation and forgiveness work together in harmony toward the common goal of eventually healing the mind. This will at last result in awakening in your true Home in Heaven.

THE ATONEMENT HELPS YOU TO FORGIVE —

The Atonement corrects the separation. "The separation is merely another term for a split mind."[156] The separation was your first mistake, the first example of your *miscreation*. You continue to make the mistake of miscreating, also called "projection," whenever you are afraid.

> You have been fearful of everyone and everything. You are afraid of God, of me and of yourself. You have misperceived or miscreated Us, and believe in what you have made. You would not have done this if you were not afraid of your own thoughts. The fearful *must* miscreate, because they misperceive creation. When you miscreate you are in pain.[157]

Fortunately everyone will eventually fully accept the Atonement. This will finally end the mistake of miscreating. You will stop projecting with the split mind in this world of perception and will return the whole mind to creating, which is the extending of love in the knowledge of Heaven.

> The acceptance of the Atonement by everyone is only a matter of time. This may appear to contradict free will because of the inevitability of the final decision, but this is not so. You can temporize and you are capable of enormous procrastination, but you cannot depart entirely from your Creator, Who set the limits on your ability to miscreate. An imprisoned will engenders a situation which, in the extreme, becomes altogether intolerable. Tolerance for pain may be high, but it is not without limit. Eventually everyone begins to recognize, however dimly, that there *must* be a better way. As this recognition becomes more firmly established, it becomes a turning point.[158]

The ultimate goal everyone is seeking is to heal the split mind. One part of the split mind is the realm of the Holy Spirit that contains only expressions of love in the real world. The other part of the split mind is dominated by the ego, and it contains both false perceptions and true perceptions. The purpose of the Holy Spirit is to correct all the false perceptions and allow the entire rational mind to be filled with only true perceptions of love. The healed mind becomes so much of a reflection of Heaven that the transfer from loving perception to the knowledge of Heaven becomes possible. The Atonement is accomplished by the manifesting of forgiveness that heals the mind. The ego as a totally separate "individual consciousness" was the original mistake that facilitated the separation. Analyzing this original mistake will not correct it. But forgiveness that overlooks the ego and looks for the divine is the way to overcome the error of separation.

This is not a course in philosophical speculation, nor is it concerned with precise terminology. It is concerned only with Atonement, or the correction of perception. The means of the Atonement is forgiveness. The structure of "individual consciousness" is essentially irrelevant because it is a concept representing the "original error" or the "original sin." To study the error itself does not lead to correction, if you are indeed to succeed in overlooking the error. And it is just this process of overlooking at which the course aims.[159]

There is a strong link between forgiveness and Atonement. If you can manifest forgiveness, it means you must have accepted the Atonement. "If what you offer is complete forgiveness you must have let guilt go, accepting the Atonement for yourself and learning you are guiltless."[160] When you accept the Atonement for yourself, you forgive your own mind and also extend miracles that forgive and heal to others.

The sole responsibility of God's teacher is to accept the Atonement for himself. Atonement means correction, or the undoing of errors. When this has been accomplished, the teacher of God becomes a miracle worker by definition. His sins have been forgiven him, and he no longer condemns himself. How can he then condemn anyone? And who is there whom his forgiveness can fail to heal?[161]

Since accepting Atonement for yourself is your means of becoming a miracle worker and extending forgiveness, it seems obvious that focusing on accepting the Atonement will help you practice forgiveness. But specifically how do you get a handle on what it really means to accept the Atonement? The most helpful definition of Atonement is: "Perfect love is the Atonement."[162] In your practice of forgiveness, you can mentally focus on inviting the Atonement into your mind. However, perhaps a better way to do this is to focus on accepting perfect love into your mind—with the understanding that you are in fact accepting the Atonement. Whether you focus on the word "Atonement" or the words "perfect love," you are still inviting the Holy Spirit and the divine presence into your awareness. Your welcoming of divine assistance facilitates your practice of forgiveness. The gift of divine grace enables you to overlook ego-based perceptions and accept loving perceptions into your mind, bringing healing to yourself and others.

There is also another way, a personal way, to accept the Atonement. Instead of using the word "Atonement" or the words "perfect love" to accept the Atonement, you can use the word "Jesus." Why? Because Jesus in the Course says of himself, "I am the Atonement."

The forgiven are the means of the Atonement. Being filled with spirit, they forgive in return. Those who are released must join in releasing their brothers, for this is the plan of the Atonement. Miracles are the way in which minds that serve the Holy Spirit unite with me for the salvation or release of all of God's creations.

I am the only one who can perform miracles indiscriminately, because I am the Atonement. You have a role in the Atonement which I will dictate to you. Ask me which miracles you should perform. This spares you needless effort, because you will be acting under direct communication.[163]

Calling on perfect love to accept the Atonement is the same as calling on Jesus because, "The name of Jesus Christ as such is but a symbol. But it stands for love that is not of this world."[164] The Course also says of Jesus, "So has his name become the Name of God, for he no longer sees himself as separate from Him."[165] Jesus plays the central role in the Holy Spirit's plan of Atonement. "Everyone has a special part to play in the Atonement, but the message given to each one is always the same; *God's Son is guiltless.*"[166] The Course provides a helpful image called the "circle of Atonement" that helps you visualize your function of forgiveness. Jesus is inside this circle of holiness, and he is welcoming everyone to come inside. "In guiltlessness we know Him, as He knows us guiltless. I [Jesus] stand within the circle, calling you to peace. Teach peace with me, and stand with me on holy ground."[167] Jesus asks you to join with him in forgiving everyone. By doing so, you invite everyone inside the circle. Everyone is holy, but your brothers who stand outside the circle imagine that they are guilty. If you see guilt in any brother outside the circle, you will believe you are guilty, and you will join your brother outside the circle of Atonement. This image of the circle of Atonement helps you to forgive because it reminds you that healing your brother of his mistaken belief in guilt will heal your mind of your own belief in guilt. Forgiveness is an enlightened form of self-interest because it enables you to claim your holiness by seeing guiltlessness in everyone.

Each one you see you place within the holy circle of Atonement or leave outside, judging him fit for crucifixion or for redemption. If you bring him into the circle of purity, you will rest there with him. If you leave him without, you join him there. Judge not except in quietness which is not of you. Refuse to accept anyone as without the blessing of Atonement, and bring him into it by blessing him. Holiness must be shared, for therein lies everything that makes it holy.[168]

WHERE IS FORGIVENESS LEADING YOU?

~ o ~

There is only one problem and one solution. "Everyone in this world seems to have his own special problems. Yet they are all the same, and must be recognized as one if the one solution that solves them all is to be accepted."[169] Your one problem is separation caused by the original mistake, described in this way:

> You do not realize the magnitude of that one error. It was so vast and so completely incredible that from it a world of total unreality *had* to emerge. What else could come of it? Its fragmented aspects are fearful enough, as you begin to look at them. But nothing you have seen begins to show you the enormity of the original error, which seemed to cast you out of Heaven, to shatter knowledge into meaningless bits of disunited perceptions, and to force you to make further substitutions.
>
> That was the first projection of error outward. The world arose to hide it, and became the screen on which it was projected and drawn between you and the truth. For truth extends inward, where the idea of loss is meaningless and only increase is conceivable. Do you really think it strange that a world in which everything is backwards and upside down arose from this projection of error? It was inevitable. For truth brought to this could only remain within in quiet, and take no part in all the mad projection by which this world was made. Call it not sin but madness, for such it was and so it still remains. Invest it not with guilt, for guilt implies it was accomplished in reality. And above all, *be not afraid of it.*[170]

The original error was a mistake, but it would be an additional error to feel either guilty or fearful about that mistake. The one error of separation, as your one problem, requires only one simple solution: forgiveness. The solution is forgiveness because forgiveness heals the perception of separation.

FORGIVENESS IS LEADING YOU TO THE REAL WORLD —

As a Course student, your short-term goal is to practice forgiveness. Your long-term goal is to bring your mind into the real world as a preparation for spiritual awakening. The real world consists of all loving thoughts, all true perceptions. It's a reflection of the Love of Heaven. Since it is not reality, but only a reflection of reality, why is it called the "real world"? Because loving thoughts are the world's only reality:

> Every loving thought that the Son of God ever had is eternal. The loving thoughts his mind perceives in this world are the world's only reality. They are still perceptions, because he still believes that he is separate. Yet they are eternal because they are loving. And being loving they are like the Father, and therefore cannot die. The real world can actually be perceived. All that is necessary is a willingness to perceive nothing else. For if you perceive both good and evil, you are accepting both the false and the true and making no distinction between them.[171]

The world you see around you represents combining true and loving perceptions with false and fearful perceptions. To find the real world, you must learn to filter out the false and fearful perceptions so only the true and loving perceptions remain. Forgiveness is your means of finding the real world because it relies on overlooking false and fearful perceptions and looking for true and loving perceptions.

> The real world is a symbol, like the rest of what perception offers. Yet it stands for what is opposite to what you made. Your world is seen through eyes of fear, and brings the witnesses of terror to your mind. The real world cannot be perceived except through eyes forgiveness blesses, so they see a world where terror is impossible, and witnesses to fear can not be found.
> The real world holds a counterpart for each unhappy thought reflected in your world; a sure correction for the sights of fear and sounds of battle which your world contains. The real world shows a world seen differently, through quiet eyes and with a mind at peace. Nothing but rest is there. There are no cries of pain and sorrow heard, for nothing there remains outside forgiveness. And the sights are gentle. Only happy sights and sounds can reach the mind that has forgiven itself.[172]

How does the real world help you practice forgiveness? It helps by serving as your goal. Keeping your goal of finding the real world helps you to be mindful of your task. Having a picture in your mind of what you want to accomplish is very helpful both for motivation and for focusing your mind toward achieving your desired outcome. The Course provides many vivid pictures of the real world for your benefit.

> The real world is attained simply by the complete forgiveness of the old, the world you see without forgiveness.
> All this beauty will rise to bless your sight as you look upon the world with forgiving eyes. For forgiveness literally transforms vision, and lets you see the real world reaching quietly and gently across chaos, removing all illusions that had twisted your perception and fixed it on the past. The smallest leaf becomes a thing of wonder, and a blade of grass a sign of God's perfection.[173]

At first glance, it may seem obvious that guilt is everywhere in the world, but that is the great illusion that forgiveness unmasks. The world you see around you is simply a projection of your guilt, caused by seeing only with the body's eyes. In order to see guilt, you must have denied the true holiness in your brother, who is the holy Son of God. But there is a positive kind of denial, which is the denial of guilt. "Your only calling here is to devote yourself, with active willingness, to the denial of guilt in all its forms."[174] If you use Christ's vision in your practice of forgiveness, you will see holiness in everyone and everything. This strips the world of the guilt you have projected and enables you to perceive the real world.

> This world of light, this circle of brightness is the real world, where guilt meets with forgiveness. Here the world outside is seen anew, without the shadow of guilt upon it. Here are you forgiven, for here you have forgiven everyone. Here is the new perception, where everything is bright and shining with innocence, washed in the waters of forgiveness, and cleansed of every evil thought you laid upon it. Here there is no attack upon the Son of God, and you are welcome. Here is your innocence, waiting to clothe you and protect you, and make you ready for the final step in the journey inward. Here are the dark and heavy garments of guilt laid by, and gently replaced by purity and love.[175]

Reminding yourself about the real world is your motivation for forgiveness because the real world is your transition point to awakening in Heaven. If you are immersed in the fearful nightmares of this world, your fearful thinking will make you too afraid to make the great leap to Heaven. Your mind must become filled with the loving perceptions of the real world before you can make the leap to knowledge, the loving nonperceptual awareness of Heaven. "In Heaven, where the meaning of love is known, love is the same as union."[176] The real world is not a physical place, but rather a state of mind focused entirely on perceptual love. This love state is so much like the love of Heaven that the transfer from loving perception to the knowledge of Heaven becomes possible.

> Every child of God is one in Christ, for his being is in Christ as Christ's is in God. Christ's Love for you is His Love for His Father, which He knows because He knows His Father's Love for Him. When the Holy Spirit has at last led you to Christ at the altar to His Father, perception fuses into knowledge because perception has become so holy that its transfer to holiness is merely its natural extension. Love transfers to love without any interference, for the two are one.... When this has been accomplished, perception and knowledge have become so similar that they share the unification of the laws of God.[177]

Forgiveness leads you to the real world, and the real world leads you to Heaven. The world of form has many separate perceptions, some true and loving perceptions and some false and unloving perceptions. The real world has only loving perceptions that are not separate. The loving perceptions of the real world bring "total perception" instead of partial perception. This "total perception" is also called "redeemed perception," and it unifies the mind. It is a union in which loving thoughts produce oneness that is so much like the knowledge of Heaven that the transfer from perception to knowledge is the natural result.

> And you who share God's Being with Him could never be content without reality. What God did not give you has no power over you, and the attraction of love for love remains irresistible. For it is the function of love to unite all things unto itself, and to hold all things together by extending its wholeness.
>
> The real world was given you by God in loving exchange for the world you made and the world you see. Only take it from the hand of Christ and look upon it. Its reality will make everything else invisible, for beholding it is total perception. And as you look upon it you will remember that it was always so. Nothingness will become invisible, for you will at last have seen truly. Redeemed perception is easily translated into knowledge, for only perception is capable of error and perception has never been. Being corrected it gives place to knowledge, which is forever the only reality. The Atonement is but the way back to what was never lost. Your Father could not cease to love His Son.[178]

FORGIVENESS IS LEADING YOU TO THE FACE OF CHRIST —

Just as the practice of forgiveness is leading you to the real world, forgiveness is likewise leading you to the face of Christ. The real world and the face of Christ are two sides of the same coin. When you look on the real world side of this coin, you perceive all the loving thoughts of this world. When you look on the face of Christ side of this coin, you see a perfect reflection of the light of Heaven. The difference between the real world and the face of Christ is simply whether you are looking for love or looking for light, yet light and love are one. The real world and the face of Christ are two names to describe one unified state of mind, which is likewise called the "holy meeting place," "God's altar," and the "borderland" between the world of form and Heaven. Although this unified state of mind is not a place, it can be associated with a place, according to Eastern philosophy. It is associated with the seventh chakra, the crown spiritual center at the top of the head, and this will be elaborated upon in the next section.

Similar to the real world being a reflection of the Love of Heaven, the face of Christ is a world of light that is a reflection of the Light of Heaven. In effect the real world and the face of Christ are two terms that describe the same unified state of mind that reflects Heaven. Thus the face of Christ serves the same purpose as the real world. Both are the same doorway to Heaven, yet there is a minor difference: The real world can be called the "doorway of love," and the face of Christ can be called the "doorway of light." Just as the physical sun always shines brightly while clouds obscure its bright rays of light, the face of Christ shines its light brightly while being clouded over by illusions of fear. The entire purpose of the Course is to remove all the illusions covering the face of Christ through the application of forgiveness. When all the clouds of illusion are removed, forgiveness has done its job of revealing the face of Christ:

> No clouds remain to hide the face of Christ. Now is the goal achieved. Forgiveness is the final goal of the curriculum. It paves the way for what goes far beyond all learning. The curriculum makes no effort to exceed its legitimate goal. Forgiveness is its single aim, at which all learning ultimately converges. It is indeed enough.[179]

Guided by the Holy Spirit as your Teacher, you will increasingly experience forgiveness as a very fulfilling spiritual practice because it is the most effective means of accomplishing the goal of leading you to the face of Christ. Notice in the following quotation that Christ "stands beside the door to which forgiveness is the only key." The door opened by forgiveness reveals the "shining face of Christ."

Forgiveness has a Teacher Who will fail in nothing. Rest a while in this; do not attempt to judge forgiveness, nor to set it in an earthly frame. Let it arise to Christ, Who welcomes it as gift to Him. He will not leave you comfortless, nor fail to send His angels down to answer you in His Own Name. He stands beside the door to which forgiveness is the only key. Give it to Him to use instead of you, and you will see the door swing silently open upon the shining face of Christ. Behold your brother there beyond the door; the Son of God as He created him.[180]

SEEING THE FACE OF CHRIST AS A BLAZING LIGHT —

Like seeing some but not all of the sun's light shining through a thin cloud, you can see some but not all of the face of Christ in the shining faces of your brothers and sisters. But similar to looking directly at the brilliant sun itself, the deepest level of seeing the face of Christ is the seeing of a blazing light. This blazing light is being hidden by your last illusory false perception—your fear of God, which in the quotation below is called the "fourth obstacle" to finding peace:

> The fourth obstacle to be surmounted hangs like a heavy veil before the face of Christ. Yet as His face rises beyond it, shining with joy because He is in His Father's Love, peace will lightly brush the veil aside and run to meet Him, and to join with Him at last. For this dark veil, which seems to make the face of Christ Himself like to a leper's, and the bright Rays of His Father's Love that light His face with glory appear as streams of blood, fades in the blazing light beyond it when the fear of death is gone.[181]

When you can finally release your fear of God, you will see the face of Christ and see the blazing light emanating from it. When will that happen to you? It could happen at any time, but in fact this seldom happens in everyday life for the vast majority of people. It is not that God is reluctant to show you this remedy that would reveal your memory of Him and of His Love. Unfortunately you are not prepared to see this blazing light and not prepared to experience awe, which is appropriate to feel in the presence of your Creator. You would confuse awe with fear and reject the blazing light that you see in this vision.

> A solid foundation is necessary because of the confusion between fear and awe to which I have already referred, and which is often made. I have said that awe is inappropriate in connection with the Sons of God, because you should not experience awe in the presence of your equals. However, it was also emphasized that awe is proper in the Presence of your Creator. I have been

careful to clarify my role in the Atonement without either over- or understating it. I am also trying to do the same with yours. I have stressed that awe is not an appropriate reaction to me because of our inherent equality. Some of the later steps in this course, however, involve a more direct approach to God Himself. It would be unwise to start on these steps without careful preparation, or awe will be confused with fear, and the experience will be more traumatic than beatific. Healing is of God in the end. The means are being carefully explained to you. Revelation may occasionally reveal the end to you, but to reach it the means are needed.[182]

Let's look at an interpretation of this blazing light that is not found in the Course, but rather is based on Eastern philosophy. Yoga philosophy maintains there are seven chakras that are spiritual centers associated with nerve plexuses in the spine. The highest center is the crown center related to the top of the head. There are blocks, or "knots," along the spine that are purified through spiritual practices. When the blocks are removed, the kundalini energy at the base of the spine at the root center can be released and can rise up to the top of the head. This can happen in a spiritual experience of ecstasy called "samadhi" or in the Buddhist tradition called "enlightenment." This is an experience of light and at the deepest level an experience of blazing light. This experience is called "revelation" in the prior quotation ending with these words: "Revelation may occasionally reveal the end to you, but to reach it the means are needed."[183] The "end" here refers to seeing the blazing light of the face of Christ, which requires the preparation of practicing forgiveness.

Many Eastern philosophies also believe that at death the kundalini energy rises up to and through the top of the head and does not return as it does in spiritual experiences. People who have had near-death experiences often describe leaving the body behind and then having a profound opening to light, although they do not typically report seeing the blazing light. Unlike near-death experiences, the actual final death experience includes the severing of what the psychic Edgar Cayce called "the silver cord," a connecting link between the spirit and the body. In my opinion, when this silver cord is finally severed, that is the time that the blazing light can be seen if there is an openness to this experience. Tibetan Buddhist death rites involve whispering to the deceased person to look for the light—especially the bright white light. The person who has died has an opportunity to accept this inner light and merge with it for total spiritual fulfillment. However, if the afterlife seeker does not accept the light, he will eventually become reincarnated and so will have another opportunity—another lifetime to accept the light.

I believe you will probably have your best chance to see the blazing light of the face of Christ when you experience death in which the spirit exits through the top of the head. But, as was quoted previously, "...to reach it [the end of the spiritual path] the means are needed." Your persistent daily practice of forgiveness offers the necessary means that prepare you to appropriately experience wonder and awe in the presence of God and embrace the blazing light. If you do not prepare yourself by living a life of forgiveness, the rightful profound wonder and awe that you would normally experience in the presence of God would be interpreted in your mind as fear. If you are not prepared for Heaven, "awe will be confused with fear, and the experience will be more traumatic than beatific."[184] This fearful misinterpretation will result in rejecting the blazing light of the face of Christ, and reincarnation will be the inevitable outcome of confusing awe with fear. Yet the Holy Spirit guides you to accept the Atonement and God has promised that eventually you will open the door to Heaven and go Home. Just as the face of Christ brings back the memory of God, the following quotation confirms that Christ's face is indeed "the blazing light of truth" that dispels illusions and returns the memory of God:

> *I thank You, Father, for Your plan to save me from the hell I made. It is not real. And You have given me the means to prove its unreality to me. The key is in my hand, and I have reached the door beyond which lies the end of dreams. I stand before the gate of Heaven, wondering if I should enter in and be at home. Let me not wait again today. Let me forgive all things, and let creation be as You would have it be and as it is. Let me remember that I am Your Son, and opening the door at last, forget illusions in the blazing light of truth, as memory of You returns to me.*[185]

In addition to forgiveness, meditation also prepares your mind to accept the blazing light of the face of Christ. For example, Workbook Lesson 67 recommends a form of meditation to let go of all thoughts. If there are distracting thoughts, it is recommended to repeat the words, "Love created me like Itself."[186] This lesson states that when the mind is guided by the ego, it is "preoccupied with false self-images"[187] and other mistaken ideas that limit our awareness. If you can get past the many fluctuating thoughts of the ego, there is the possibility that you can see the dazzling light that reveals your true nature:

> *Yet perhaps you will succeed in going past that, and through the interval of thoughtlessness to the awareness of a blazing light in which you recognize yourself as love created you. Be confident*

that you will do much today to bring that awareness nearer, whether you feel you have succeeded or not.[188]

Previously this book has acknowledged that true forgiveness is outer meditation and meditation is inner forgiveness. Thus both forgiveness and meditation used in harmony combine for the purpose of helping you perceive holiness in others and in yourself. Some meditators can actually feel light rising up the spine, coming into the crown center at the top of the head and overflowing. According to Edgar Cayce, when the Twenty-Third Psalm says: "Thy rod and thy staff, they comfort me," the "rod" refers to the endocrine glands in the front of the body and the "staff" refers to the seven spiritual centers associated with the spine. When this psalm says: "Thou anointest my head with oil; my cup runneth over," it is referring to the overflowing of inner light. When an experienced meditator focuses on a single sacred thought and then transitions to wordless contemplation, he can sometimes feel his mind is being filled with light. In the crown of his head, it feels as if his "cup runneth over" with light that is extending to the whole Sonship.

Meditation can facilitate this experience, but it can happen any time there is a true openness to receiving this inner light. Christ is literally "the anointed one." An inner experience of being anointed with this overflowing of light is the beginning of opening the mind to the blazing light of the face of Christ. This is also an example of welcoming the "True light that makes true vision possible..."[189] It is a healing light. "This is the light that heals because it brings single perception..."[190] The focusing of the mind is this single perception, which is referred to by the words of Jesus in the Bible, "If therefore thine eye be single, thy whole body shall be full of light."[191]

> The wish to see calls down the grace of God upon your eyes, and brings the gift of light that makes sight possible. Would you behold your brother? God is glad to have you look on him. He does not will your savior be unrecognized by you. Nor does He will that he remain without the function that He gave to him.[192]

Of course, you can still invite the grace of true light and Christ's vision without this conscious experience of light during meditation. You can manifest Christ's vision at any time in your everyday life. This is your training ground for learning the lessons of forgiveness and love. You can become a savior to your brother by seeing your own divine nature reflected in him and in so doing allow him to be your savior.

> And to each one has He allowed the grace to be a savior to the holy ones especially entrusted to his care. And this he learns

when first he looks upon one brother as he looks upon himself, and sees the mirror of himself in him. Thus is the concept of himself laid by, for nothing stands between his sight and what he looks upon, to judge what he beholds. And in this single vision does he see the face of Christ, and understands he looks on everyone as he beholds this one. For there is light where darkness was before, and now the veil is lifted from his sight.

The veil across the face of Christ, the fear of God and of salvation, and the love of guilt and death, they all are different names for just one error; that there is a space between you and your brother, kept apart by an illusion of yourself that holds him off from you, and you away from him. The sword of judgment is the weapon that you give to the illusion of yourself, that it may fight to keep the space that holds your brother off unoccupied by love.[193]

Your judgment of your brother is what keeps you apart from him. But forgiveness enables you to let go of your judgment of your brother so you can see the light in him. The reflections of divine Light are everywhere so the glimmerings of the face of Christ can be seen shining through every one of your brothers and sisters. Consequently, the best way to become ready to eventually see the blazing light is to open your heart to loving all your brothers and sisters and to focus on seeing the divine in them in the here and now.

Vision is freely given to those who ask to see.

Your brother's sinlessness is given you in shining light, to look on with the Holy Spirit's vision and to rejoice in along with Him. For peace will come to all who ask for it with real desire and sincerity of purpose, shared with the Holy Spirit and at one with Him on what salvation is. Be willing, then, to see your brother sinless, that Christ may rise before your vision and give you joy. And place no value on your brother's body, which holds him to illusions of what he is. It is his desire to see his sinlessness, as it is yours. And bless the Son of God in your relationship, nor see in him what you have made of him.

The Holy Spirit guarantees that what God willed and gave you shall be yours. This is your purpose now, and the vision that makes it yours is ready to be given. You have the vision that enables you to see the body not. And as you look upon your brother, you will see an altar to your Father, holy as Heaven, glowing with radiant purity and sparkling with the shining lilies you laid upon it.[194]

SIXTY ANSWERS TO SIXTY QUESTIONS

~ o ~

This section contains sixty questions and answers, although many of these are two-part questions. Quotations from the Text and the Manual for Teachers follow each question and provide information addressing each question. Also, after each set of quotations is a commentary on the quotations that provides a direct answer to each question. These are the same exact questions raised in the book *The Two-Month Bridge to "A Course in Miracles."* In that book, each two-part question is written as a single sentence. However, for the sake of greater clarity here in this book, you will see in the paragraphs below that sometimes a two-part question is divided into a part "A" sentence and part "B" sentence. In *The Two-Month Bridge to "A Course in Miracles"* the questions are answered simply and briefly in order to introduce the Course principles. Here in the information below, the answers are elaborated upon to build on your learning. However, if you are a beginner who is encountering these questions for the first time, you will still benefit from reading this information. A wide variety of topics are addressed and arranged consecutively from the beginning to the end of the Course.

The seven essential tools of the Holy Spirit are forgiveness, Christ's vision, miracles, the holy instant, the holy relationship, the quiet time of meditation, and the Atonement. To help you focus on the Holy Spirit's seven tools for awakening, they will each be displayed with bold letters in this section. The seven tools of the Holy Spirit will lead you to the "real world" and to the "face of Christ," so these terms will also be in bold letters.

QUESTION 1A. Why is the Course summarized by these two lines: "Nothing real can be threatened. Nothing unreal exists"?

(After each question there are relevant quotations. Each quotation begins with a page number and reference number, which indicates the chapter, section, paragraph, and lines where that quotation can be found in the second edition of the Course.)

Page 1. T-in.1: 6-8. *The course does not aim at teaching the meaning of love, for that is beyond what can be taught. It does aim, however, at removing the blocks to the awareness of love's presence, which is*

your natural inheritance. *The opposite of love is fear, but what is all-encompassing can have no opposite.*
Page 1. T-in.2:1-4. *This course can therefore be summed up very simply in this way:*

> *Nothing real can be threatened.*
> *Nothing unreal exists.*

Herein lies the peace of God.

ANSWER 1A. The Course is summarized by these two lines because it highlights the clear distinction between changeless reality, which can never be attacked, and changing illusions, which are unreal and do not even exist. The whole Course is a learning experience of discriminating between reality and illusions. Discrimination allows you to achieve the aim of the Course, which is *"removing the blocks to the awareness of love's presence, which is your natural inheritance."* The Course teaches that love is present within you now, as are all the other aspects of reality including Christ and all your brothers and sisters in the Sonship. Reality in you also includes Heaven and all its qualities, such as timelessness, formlessness, light, eternal joy, and perfect peace. These are the divine attributes of God the Father, Who is Reality Itself. All these aspects of reality will be revealed as your inheritance from the Father after you remove the blocks to the awareness of reality. The line "Nothing real can be threatened" means your inheritance can never be lost. The line "Nothing unreal exists" means the blocks to your awareness of reality are all only illusions of reality that do not exist. All things made by the ego and the ego itself are illusions. Although illusions are unreal and do not exist, they can temporarily block your awareness of reality by your believing in them. Therefore, the Course asks you to recognize reality as what it is within you and to place your firm belief in reality as it truly is. If you hold on to your belief in illusions, you will make these illusions seem real to you, and the true nature of reality will be hidden from you. Consequently, the Course asks you to recognize illusions as unreal and nonexistent and to withdraw your belief in them. Adding what is true and letting go of what is false involves the combination of overlooking illusions and looking for reality. This process of overlooking and looking is the fundamental practice of true **forgiveness** in the Course. When this change in perception happens as you **forgive** your brother, it is called a "**miracle**," which is facilitated by the action of the Holy Spirit.

QUESTION 1B. What is a **miracle** and who benefits from the expression of a **miracle**?

A Simple Framework for Understanding the Course

Page 3. T-1.I.3:1-3. **Miracles** occur naturally as expressions of love. The real **miracle** is the love that inspires them. In this sense everything that comes from love is a **miracle**.

Page 3. T-1.I.9:1. **Miracles** are a kind of exchange. Like all expressions of love, which are always miraculous in the true sense, the exchange reverses the physical laws. They bring more love both to the giver *and* the receiver.

Page 5. T-1.I.35:1. **Miracles** are expressions of love, but they may not always have observable effects.

Page 6. T-1.I.44:1. The **miracle** is an expression of an inner awareness of Christ and the acceptance of His **Atonement**.

ANSWER 1B. In the first chapter of the Text, there are fifty different descriptions of a **miracle**. Four of these descriptions refer to **miracles** as "expressions of love." A **miracle** always benefits the giver and receiver, who both experience an increase of love. A **miracle** is also an expression of an inner awareness of Christ and transcends physical laws of time and space, although it may not produce observable results. In addition, a **miracle** is an expression of accepting the **Atonement**, which corrects errors and produces healing.

QUESTION 2. How would you compare **miracles** with revelation?

Page 7. T-1.II.1:4-7. **Miracles**, however, are genuinely interpersonal, and result in true closeness to others. Revelation unites you directly with God. **Miracles** unite you directly with your brother. Neither emanates from consciousness, but both are experienced there.

Page 7. T-1.II.2:1-7. Revelation is intensely personal and cannot be meaningfully translated. That is why any attempt to describe it in words is impossible. Revelation induces only experience. **Miracles**, on the other hand, induce action. They are more useful now because of their interpersonal nature. In this phase of learning, working **miracles** is important because freedom from fear cannot be thrust upon you. Revelation is literally unspeakable because it is an experience of unspeakable love.

Page 7. T-1.II.3:1-5. Awe should be reserved for revelation, to which it is perfectly and correctly applicable. It is not appropriate for **miracles** because a state of awe is worshipful, implying that one of a lesser order stands before his Creator. You are a perfect creation, and should experience awe only in the Presence of the Creator of perfection. The **miracle** is therefore a sign of love among equals.

Page 8. T-1.II.5:4-5. Revelation is not reciprocal. It proceeds from God to you, but not from you to God.

ANSWER 2. Revelation is a direct transcendent experience of God and His Love initiated by God in contrast to **miracles**, which induce interpersonal sharing with your brother. Revelation brings about only experience, which is so personal in relation to God that it cannot be fully explained in words. **Miracles** facilitate action, which is more useful for you now because **miracles** help you overcome fear and produce healing in interpersonal relationships. You will respond with awe to revelation because you are in the direct presence of your Creator. It would be inappropriate to experience awe in the sharing that occurs in **miracles** because of your total equality with your brother.

QUESTION 3. What is "the only lack you really need" to correct?

Page 14. T-1.VI.2:1-5.   A sense of separation from God is the only lack you really need correct. This sense of separation would never have arisen if you had not distorted your perception of truth, and had thus perceived yourself as lacking. The idea of order of needs arose because, having made this fundamental error, you had already fragmented yourself into levels with different needs. As you integrate you become one, and your needs become one accordingly. Unified needs lead to unified action, because this produces a lack of conflict.

ANSWER 3. The feeling that you are lacking something can be entirely healed by correcting your false belief that you are separate from God. You had no needs before the separation from your direct awareness of God in Heaven. The separation produced a fragmented concept of yourself that had many different levels of consciousness with many different needs. The healing of your mind is facilitated by the movement from fragmentation to unity, from different needs to unified needs, which lead to unified action, bringing peace to your mind.

QUESTION 4. What is the Holy Spirit's plan called the "**Atonement**" and what will be the end result of this plan?

Page 19. T-2.II.4:2-3. The **Atonement** *principle* was in effect long before the **Atonement** began. The principle was love and the **Atonement** was an *act* of love.
Page 21. T-2.III.2:1. For perfect effectiveness the **Atonement** belongs at the center of the inner altar, where it undoes the separation and restores the wholeness of the mind.
Page 23. T-2.IV.1:5. The **Atonement**, or the final **miracle**, is a remedy and any type of healing is a result.

Page 23. T-2.IV.2:1. A major step in the **Atonement** plan is to undo error at all levels.

ANSWER 4. The **Atonement** is God's plan that the Holy Spirit has established and will carry out. It is a remedy of perfect love. The final result of the **Atonement** will be the undoing of the separation and the healing of the division in your split mind, which will bring it back to the wholeness it had before the separation. The **Atonement** is within your inner altar where it produces the ultimate **miracle** that restores the full awareness of Heaven. It expresses perfect love in action that corrects every error at the level of consciousness in which it occurs.

QUESTION 5A. What is your only responsibility in order to be a **miracle** worker?

Pages 25-26. T-2.V.5:1-3. *The sole responsibility of the miracle worker is to accept the Atonement for himself.* This means you recognize that mind is the only creative level, and that its errors are healed by the **Atonement**. Once you accept this, your mind can only heal.

ANSWER 5A. The only responsibility required of you as a **miracle** worker is to accept the **Atonement** for yourself. Once you accept the **Atonement** for yourself, your own errors are corrected. Then your healed mind becomes a vehicle through which the Holy Spirit can bring healing to other minds.

QUESTION 5B. What is your responsibility in relation to fear?

Page 29. T-2.VI.4:1-6, 8-10. The correction of fear *is* your responsibility. When you ask for release from fear, you are implying that it is not. You should ask, instead, for help in the conditions that have brought the fear about. These conditions always entail a willingness to be separate. At that level you *can* help it. You are much too tolerant of mind wandering, and are passively condoning your mind's miscreations.... The correction is always the same. Before you choose to do anything, ask me if your choice is in accord with mine. If you are sure that it is, there will be no fear.

ANSWER 5B. Controlling and correcting fear is your responsibility. You cannot abdicate your responsibility by asking the Holy Spirit or Jesus to take away your fear for you. Instead, you can ask for divine help in the conditions that brought about your fear and ask the Holy Spirit or Jesus if your choices are in accord with God's Will.

QUESTION 6. How is perception different than knowledge?

Page 40. T-3.III.1:3-10. To know is to be certain. Uncertainty means that you do not know. Knowledge is power because it is certain, and certainty is strength. Perception is temporary. As an attribute of the belief in space and time, it is subject to either fear or love. Misperceptions produce fear and true perceptions foster love, but neither brings certainty because all perception varies. That is why it is not knowledge. True perception is the basis for knowledge, but knowing is the affirmation of truth and beyond all perceptions.
Page 40. T-3.III.2:8-11. Since perceptions change, their dependence on time is obvious. How you perceive at any given time determines what you do, and actions must occur in time. Knowledge is timeless, because certainty is not questionable. You know when you have ceased to ask questions.
Pages 40-41. T-3.III.5:2, 6-13. Certainty is always of God.... Certainty does not require action. When you say you are acting on the basis of knowledge, you are really confusing knowledge with perception. Knowledge provides the strength for creative thinking, but not for right doing. Perception, **miracles** and doing are closely related. Knowledge is the result of revelation and induces only thought. Even in its most spiritualized form perception involves the body. Knowledge comes from the altar within and is timeless because it is certain. To perceive the truth is not the same as to know it.

ANSWER 6. Perceptions are a temporary form of awareness that fluctuates between misperceptions (false perceptions) based on fear and true perceptions fostering love. Knowledge is a stable form of complete awareness coming directly from God, offering total certainty. Perception is part of the experience of time and space and always involves the body. Knowledge transcends time and space and so transcends the body. Replacing false and fearful perceptions with true and loving perceptions is the basis of **miracles** and induces action. Knowledge is the result of direct communication with God that occurs in revelation and induces thought, but is not the basis for action. True perception is a partial awareness of truth. Knowledge is total awareness of truth.

QUESTION 7. What is the authority problem?

Page 48. T-3.VI.8:1-4. The issue of authority is really a question of authorship. When you have an authority problem, it is always because you believe you are the author of yourself and project your delusion onto others. You then perceive the situation as one in which others are literally fighting you for your authorship. This is the fundamental error of all those who believe they have usurped the power of God.

Page 48. T-3.VI.10:3-7. The problem everyone must decide is the fundamental question of authorship. All fear comes ultimately, and sometimes by way of very devious routes, from the denial of Authorship. The offense is never to God, but only to those who deny Him. To deny His Authorship is to deny yourself the reason for your peace, so that you see yourself only in segments. This strange perception *is* the authority problem.

ANSWER 7. The authority problem is the false perception that God is not your Author, and therefore you must be the author of yourself. You project this false and confusing perception onto others, imagining they have the power to determine who you are and how valuable you are. Because you feel you have taken God's power to be your Author, you throw away the peace of God and manifest many types of fear as you falsely imagine you can create yourself. This false belief in self-creation causes confusion, fear, and discontent due to losing the awareness of the peace of God.

QUESTION 8. What are "your greatest strengths now"?

Pages 53-54. T-4.I.4:1-7. Teaching and learning are your greatest strengths now, because they enable you to change your mind and help others to change theirs. Refusing to change your mind will not prove that the separation has not occurred. The dreamer who doubts the reality of his dream while he is still dreaming is not really healing his split mind. You dream of a separated ego and believe in a world that rests upon it. This is very real to you. You cannot undo it by not changing your mind about it. If you are willing to renounce the role of guardian of your thought system and open it to me, I will correct it very gently and lead you back to God.

ANSWER 8. Your greatest strengths now are teaching and learning, which give you the power to change your mind and bring changes to the minds of others. Just because you have doubts about the reality of the dream you are dreaming, your doubts do not change your mind to heal the split in the mind that was the result of the separation. If you want to change your false belief in the ego and in the world the ego shows you, you will have to learn to change your mind and help others change theirs. These changes in perception that bring healing are miracles. Instead of guarding your own thought system based on the ego, you must learn how to open your mind to the divine influence (meaning to the influence of Jesus and/or to the Holy Spirit). Although teaching and learning are your greatest strengths now, applying these strengths to increase your understanding of the Course will ideally lead to another more powerful strength. This is the inner strength that comes from awakening your awareness of Christ within you, which is your true nature in God the Father, the Source of all strength.

QUESTION 9. What is the ego?

Page 58. T-4.II.8:4. The ego is the mind's belief that it is completely on its own.
Page 60. T-4.III.3:2. The ego arose from the separation, and its continued existence depends on your continuing belief in the separation.
Page 61. T-4.III.4:1-8. You who identify with your ego cannot believe God loves you. You do not love what you made, and what you made does not love you. Being made out of the denial of the Father, the ego has no allegiance to its maker. You cannot conceive of the real relationship that exists between God and His creations because of your hatred for the self you made. You project onto the ego the decision to separate, and this conflicts with the love you feel for the ego because you made it. No love in this world is without this ambivalence, and since no ego has experienced love without ambivalence the concept is beyond its understanding. Love will enter immediately into any mind that truly wants it, but it must want it truly. This means that it wants it without ambivalence, and this kind of wanting is wholly without the ego's "drive to get."

ANSWER 9. The ego is simply the false idea of being alone and separate from others and from God. The ego came about because of the separation, and it will persist only as long as you believe in the idea of separation. You have an ambivalent love for the ego because you made it, but you do not truly love it. The ego certainly does not love you or God. As long as you identify with the ego, you cannot believe God loves you, and you cannot have a healthy love for yourself. True love is total giving. However, the ego, which is devoted to getting, cannot understand or appreciate love.

QUESTION 10. What is "the question that *you* must learn to ask in connection with everything"?

A Simple Framework for Understanding the Course

Page 67. T-4.V.6:6-11. Preoccupations with problems set up to be incapable of solution are favorite ego devices for impeding learning progress. In all these diversionary tactics, however, the one question that is never asked by those who pursue them is, "What for?" This is the question that *you* must learn to ask in connection with everything. What is the purpose? Whatever it is, it will direct your efforts automatically. When you make a decision of purpose, then, you have made a decision about your future effort; a decision that will remain in effect unless you change your mind.

ANSWER 10. You must learn to ask, "What is it for?" in relation to everything. You need to have a clear understanding of your purpose in order to direct your efforts. Your recognition of your purpose is a way of setting your goal so that your actions will automatically lead you toward that goal. The decision you make to establish your purpose remains in effect as long as you do not change your mind about that purpose.

QUESTION 11. What is the nature and role of the Holy Spirit, and how is the Holy Spirit related to the **Atonement**?

Page 74. T-5.I.5:1-7. The Holy Spirit is the Christ Mind which is aware of the knowledge that lies beyond perception. He came into being with the separation as a protection, inspiring the **Atonement** principle at the same time. Before that there was no need for healing, for no one was comfortless. The Voice of the Holy Spirit is the Call to **Atonement**, or the restoration of the integrity of the mind. When the **Atonement** is complete and the whole Sonship is healed there will be no Call to return.
Page 74. T-5.I.6:3-6. The Holy Spirit is the Mind of the **Atonement**. He represents a state of mind close enough to One-mindedness that transfer to it is at last possible. Perception is not knowledge, but it can be transferred to knowledge, or cross over into it. It might even be more helpful here to use the literal meaning of transferred or "carried over," since the last step is taken by God.
Page 75. T-5.II.2:1-5. The Holy Spirit is the spirit of joy. He is the Call to return with which God blessed the minds of His separated Sons. This is the vocation of the mind. The mind had no calling until the separation, because before that it had only being, and would not have understood the Call to right thinking. The Holy Spirit is God's Answer to the separation; the means by which the **Atonement** heals until the whole mind returns to creating.

Page 75. T-5.II.3:1-4. The principle of **Atonement** and the separation began at the same time. When the ego was made, God placed in the mind the Call to joy. This Call is so strong that the ego always dissolves at Its sound. That is why you must choose to hear one of two voices within you.

ANSWER 11. God the Father created the Holy Spirit as His Answer to the separation. The Holy Spirit's job is to return the split minds of God's Sons back to One-mindedness, the wholeness of Heaven. The Holy Spirit is the Mind of the **Atonement** that will bring healing by correcting all errors in perception. The Holy Spirit serves as the means of healing perception, but in addition the Holy Spirit is the Christ Mind centered in knowledge that transcends perception. With your necessary cooperation, the Holy Spirit is capable of unifying your perception to such a high degree that it can be transferred to the total knowledge of Heaven. Nevertheless, God your loving Father must take the final step of bringing your split mind back to the completely unified awareness of One-mindedness. The Holy Spirit is the Voice for God and the Call to joy. You must choose to hear within you only one of two voices—the ego's voice or the Holy Spirit's Voice.

QUESTION 12. What is the significance of sharing, and what is the opposite of sharing?

Page 81. T-5.IV.2:1-3, 11. What the ego makes it keeps to itself, and so it is without strength. Its existence is unshared. It does not die; it was merely never born.... The **Atonement** must be understood as a pure act of sharing.
Pages 81-82. T-5.IV.3:1-12. Every loving thought held in any part of the Sonship belongs to every part. It is shared *because* it is loving. Sharing is God's way of creating, and also yours. The ego can keep you in exile from the Kingdom, but in the Kingdom itself it has no power. Ideas of the spirit do not leave the mind that thinks them, nor can they conflict with each other. However, ideas of the ego can conflict because they occur at different levels and also include opposite thoughts at the same level. *It is impossible to share opposing thoughts.* You can share only the thoughts that are of God and that He keeps for you. And of such is the Kingdom of Heaven. The rest remains with you until the Holy Spirit has reinterpreted them in the light of the Kingdom, making them, too, worthy of being shared. When they have been sufficiently purified He lets you give them away. The decision to share them *is* their purification.

A Simple Framework for Understanding the Course

ANSWER 12. Sharing is the way in which love is manifested as healing in the world and also as creating expressions of oneness in Heaven. In contrast to sharing, the ego brings division that separates, producing opposing thoughts that cannot be shared and thus foster conflict. The Holy Spirit can purify your perceptions so they are loving and can be shared. Only loving thoughts can truly be shared, and God preserves your thoughts of love for you in Heaven. Your function in Heaven is to share all of your love, all of your Self, with all the other parts of the Sonship and to receive love from all parts of the Sonship. Heaven itself is a state of love and total sharing in perfect peace, without any of the division or conflict characteristic of the ego.

QUESTION 13A. How are the ego and guilt related?

Page 84. T-5.V.3:1-7. The ego is the part of the mind that believes in division. How could part of God detach itself without believing it is attacking Him? We spoke before of the authority problem as based on the concept of usurping God's power. The ego believes that this is what you did because it believes that it *is* you. If you identify with the ego, you must perceive yourself as guilty. Whenever you respond to your ego you will experience guilt, and you will fear punishment. The ego is quite literally a fearful thought.
Page 84. T-5.V.4:8-13. Guilt is a sure sign that your thinking is unnatural. Unnatural thinking will always be attended with guilt, because it is the belief in sin. The ego does not perceive sin as a lack of love, but as a positive act of assault. This is necessary to the ego's survival because, as soon as you regard sin as a lack, you will automatically attempt to remedy the situation. And you will succeed. The ego regards this as doom, but you must learn to regard it as freedom.

ANSWER 13A. The ego itself is a fearful thought of guilt. This guilt goes all the way back to the separation when you thought you had attacked God and dreamed that you had usurped His power to be your Creator. Responding in any way by identifying with the ego will bring guilt and the fear of punishment associated with guilt. Your ego perceives your mistakes as "sins," attacks on God and others, which foster fear and guilt. But mistakes are actually expressions of a lack of love that can be healed by supplying the love that is lacking.

QUESTION 13B. Will the ego eventually be destroyed?

Pages 87-88. T-5.VI.9:2-6. Every loveless thought must be undone, a word the ego cannot even understand. To the ego, to be undone means to be destroyed. The ego will not be destroyed because it is part of your thought, but because it is uncreative and therefore unsharing, it will be reinterpreted to release you from fear. The part of your mind that you have given to the ego will merely return to the Kingdom, where your whole mind belongs. You can delay the completion of the Kingdom, but you cannot introduce the concept of fear into it.

ANSWER 13B. The ego cannot be destroyed since it is a part of your mind, but it will eventually be *undone*, meaning it will be reinterpreted to release all fear. You will need every part of your mind to bring your split mind back into the wholeness that it has in Heaven. The part of your mind devoted to the ego will be purified of all guilt and fear. This ego part of the mind, which has lacked love and been uncreative and unsharing, will become devoted to love and sharing instead of being focused on illusory separation.

QUESTION 14A. What four false perceptions support the illusion that anger is justified?

Page 91. T-6.in.1:2-7. Anger always involves projection of separation, which must ultimately be accepted as one's own responsibility, rather than being blamed on others. Anger cannot occur unless you believe that you have been attacked, that your attack is justified in return, and that you are in no way responsible for it. Given these three wholly irrational premises, the equally irrational conclusion that a brother is worthy of attack rather than of love must follow. What can be expected from insane premises except an insane conclusion? The way to undo an insane conclusion is to consider the sanity of the premises on which it rests. You cannot *be* attacked, attack *has* no justification, and you *are* responsible for what you believe.

ANSWER 14A. Anger is based on believing the following four false premises: You have been attacked. Your attack in return is justified. You are in no way responsible for your return attack. Your brother is worthy of attack rather than of love. The truth is found in these four opposite beliefs: It is impossible for you in your true nature to be attacked. Attack never has any justification at all. You are responsible for your beliefs, such as false beliefs in the justification of attack. Your brother deserves only love in all circumstances and so do you.

QUESTION 14B. What is the message of the crucifixion?

Page 92. T-6.I.4:1-7. Assault can ultimately be made only on the body. There is little doubt that one body can assault another, and can even destroy it. Yet if destruction itself is impossible, anything that is destructible cannot be real. Its destruction, therefore, does not justify anger. To the extent to which you believe that it does, you are accepting false premises and teaching them to others. The message the crucifixion was intended to teach was that it is not necessary to perceive any form of assault in persecution, because you cannot *be* persecuted. If you respond with anger, you must be equating yourself with the destructible, and are therefore regarding yourself insanely.
Page 94. T-6.I.13:1-2. The message of the crucifixion is perfectly clear:

Teach only love, for that is what you are.

ANSWER 14B. The message of the crucifixion is that the body can be attacked, but you are not a body. Your reality is beyond destruction and so you in your reality cannot be attacked. If you teach that you can be persecuted and attacked, you would be giving the following wrong message: you are an ego that can be persecuted and you are a body that can be assaulted. Instead, the message of the crucifixion is that you are invulnerable because you *are* love. Therefore, you must teach only love. Jesus was able to **forgive** those who crucified him because he knew that the love that he is could not be destroyed by even the most vicious outward assault on the body. Thus Jesus forgave them for what they did *not* do to him in his true nature.

QUESTION 15. The ego functions using the projection of guilt and separation, but what is the alternative to projection?

Pages 96-97. T-6.II.4:1-4. We have learned, however, that there *is* an alternative to projection. Every ability of the ego has a better use, because its abilities are directed by the mind, which has a better Voice. The Holy Spirit extends and the ego projects. As their goals are opposed, so is the result.
Page 97. T-6.II.8:1-3. God created His Sons by extending His Thought, and retaining the extensions of His Thought in His Mind. All His Thoughts are thus perfectly united within themselves and with each other. The Holy Spirit enables you to perceive this wholeness *now*.
Pages 98-99. T-6.II.12:1-8. The difference between the ego's projection and the Holy Spirit's extension is very simple. The ego projects to exclude, and therefore to deceive. The Holy Spirit extends by recognizing Himself in every mind, and thus perceives them as one. Nothing

conflicts in this perception, because what the Holy Spirit perceives is all the same. Wherever He looks He sees Himself, and because He is united He offers the whole Kingdom always. This is the one message God gave to Him and for which He must speak, because that is what He is. The peace of God lies in that message, and so the peace of God lies in you. The great peace of the Kingdom shines in your mind forever, but it must shine outward to make you aware of it.
Page 103. T-6.V.1:7-8. God's extending outward, though not His completeness, is blocked when the Sonship does not communicate with Him as one. So He thought, "My children sleep and must be awakened."

ANSWER 15. In contrast to the ego's use of separation and the projection of guilt, the Holy Spirit uses *extension* to bring healing, wholeness, and peace to the sleeping Sons of God. The purpose of the ego's projection is to produce exclusion and deception. The purpose of the Holy Spirit's extension is to see Himself present within every mind. Thus He perceives them all as joined in perfect oneness, without the separateness the ego projects. Since the Holy Spirit perceives all as one, He offers the whole Kingdom of God to everyone who imagines he is separate. The Holy Spirit Himself is God's Voice for this one message of wholeness that brings peace and healing to the split mind. The Holy Spirit offers you the awareness of the peace of God that is already within you, but you must extend it to others in order to recognize experientially that it is within you.

QUESTION 16. What is the significance of light in relation to your mind and in relation to your brothers and sisters in the Sonship?

Page 117. T-7.III.5:1. God has lit your mind Himself, and keeps your mind lit by His light because His light is what your mind is.
Page 122. T-7.V.10:6-12. Your mind is so powerful a light that you can look into theirs and enlighten them, as I can enlighten yours. I do not want to share my body in communion because this is to share nothing. Would I try to share an illusion with the most holy children of a most holy Father? Yet I do want to share my mind with you because we are of one Mind, and that Mind is ours. See only this Mind everywhere, because only this is everywhere and in everything. It is everything because it encompasses all things within itself.
Pages 122-123. T-7.V.11:1-6. Come therefore unto me, and learn of the truth in you. The mind we share is shared by all our brothers, and as we see them truly they will be healed. Let your mind shine with

mine upon their minds, and by our gratitude to them make them aware of the light in them. This light will shine back upon you and on the whole Sonship, because this is your proper gift to God. He will accept it and give it to the Sonship, because it is acceptable to Him and therefore to His Sons. This is true communion with the Holy Spirit, Who sees the altar of God in everyone, and by bringing it to your appreciation, He calls upon you to love God and His creation.

ANSWER 16. Light is significant to you because God's "light is what your mind is." Light is significant in your relationships because the light God has extended to you can then be extended by you to your brothers and sisters. Your extensions of light can enlighten the minds of others. Jesus can also extend his light to you because he wants to share his mind with you. He wants you to realize there is really only one Christ Mind that everyone shares because it contains within itself everything that exists. True communion is letting the light in your mind shine into the minds of others and having their light return to you. This extension is communion, which brings light and love to the whole Sonship and all of Creation in God.

QUESTION 17. You made the ego, but what does the Course say about letting go of your identification with the ego?

Page 127. T-7.VII.3:2-8. The ego's picture of you is deprived, unloving and vulnerable. You cannot love this. Yet you can very easily escape from this image by leaving it behind. You are not there and that is not you. Do not see this picture in anyone, or you have accepted it *as* you. All illusions about the Sonship are dispelled together as they were made together. Teach no one that he is what you would not want to be.
Page 131. T-7.VIII.6:2. The ego can be completely forgotten at any time, because it is a totally incredible belief, and no one can keep a belief he has judged to be unbelievable.
Page 131. T-7.VIII.7:1-3. The whole purpose of this course is to teach you that the ego is unbelievable and will forever be unbelievable. You who made the ego by believing the unbelievable cannot make this judgment alone. By accepting the **Atonement** for yourself, you are deciding against the belief that you can be alone, thus dispelling the idea of separation and affirming your true identification with the whole Kingdom as literally part of you.

ANSWER 17. When you identify with the ego, you are accepting an unloving illusion and an unbelievable picture of yourself as a separate being. If you can see that this image is unbelievable in everyone you see, you can easily give up this illusion about your identity. If you accept this false image in anyone, you will likewise believe this is what you are. In other words, you will accept this illusion as your reality. You can recognize the unbelievable nature of the ego by accepting the **Atonement**, an act of sharing, which affirms you can never be alone. Learning that you cannot be alone brings the awareness that the idea of separation fostered by the ego is not true. The sharing that occurs in accepting the **Atonement** reminds you that your true identification is with God and with the entire Sonship in His Kingdom.

QUESTION 18. Can you find the divine only by looking within yourself, and what must you do to find your place in God's Kingdom ?

Page 142. T-8.III.4:1-8. When you meet anyone, remember it is a holy encounter. As you see him you will see yourself. As you treat him you will treat yourself. As you think of him you will think of yourself. Never forget this, for in him you will find yourself or lose yourself. Whenever two Sons of God meet, they are given another chance at salvation. Do not leave anyone without giving salvation to him and receiving it yourself. For I am always there with you, in remembrance of *you*.
Page 142. T-8.III.5:7-8, 12. The Holy Spirit teaches you that if you look only at yourself you cannot find yourself, because that is not what you are. Whenever you are with a brother, you are learning what you are because you are teaching what you are.... Give him his place in the Kingdom and you will have yours.
Page 143. T-8.III.6:1. The Kingdom cannot be found alone, and you who are the Kingdom cannot find yourself alone.
Page 143. T-8.III.7:1-4. You can encounter only part of yourself because you are part of God, Who is everything. His power and glory are everywhere, and you cannot be excluded from them. The ego teaches that your strength is in you alone. The Holy Spirit teaches that all strength is in God and *therefore* in you.
Page 146. T-8.IV.8:1-2, 6-7. Freedom is the only gift you can offer to God's Sons, being an acknowledgment of what they are and what He is. Freedom is creation, because it is love.... Your identification is with the Father *and* with the Son. It cannot be with One and not the Other.

ANSWER 18. Certainly you can experience the divine within yourself, but you cannot find your true nature by looking within yourself *alone*. You can find your place in God's Kingdom only by acknowledging

A Simple Framework for Understanding the Course 107

and appreciating your brother's place with you in the Sonship. You can never actually be alone because your true nature is in the Father, the Son, and the Holy Spirit. As you perceive your brother, you will perceive yourself. You are God's Kingdom of freedom, creation, and love, and you will realize this when you see your brother is likewise God's Kingdom of freedom, creation, and love.

QUESTION 19. What is the best way to utilize the body?

Page 151. T-8.VII.2:1-4. Remember that the Holy Spirit interprets the body only as a means of communication. Being the Communication Link between God and His separated Sons, the Holy Spirit interprets everything you have made in the light of what He is. The ego separates through the body. The Holy Spirit reaches through it to others.
Page 151. T-8.VII.3:1-3. If you use the body for attack, it is harmful to you. If you use it only to reach the minds of those who believe they are bodies, and teach them *through* the body that this is not so, you will understand the power of the mind that is in you. If you use the body for this and only for this, you cannot use it for attack.
Page 153. T-8.VII.11:2-3. Help and healing are the normal expressions of a mind that is working through the body, but not *in* it. If the mind believes the body is its goal it will distort its perception of the body, and by blocking its own extension beyond it, will induce illness by fostering separation.

ANSWER 19. The Holy Spirit teaches you that the best way to use the body is as a communication device for healing and for joining with your brother. In contrast to this, the ego uses the body to foster separation and disrupt communication through attack. The Communication Link between God and His sleeping Sons is the Holy Spirit. He encourages minds to communicate with other minds through the body without identifying with the body. This mind to mind extension through the body brings help and healing to others. Using the body for attack instead of the extension of minds will foster separation. Using the body only for communication and extension will bring health to the body as a by-product. Using the body lovelessly will produce sickness as a by-product.

QUESTION 20. What are errors, and what is the best attitude to have about errors of others and about correcting your own errors?

Page 166. T-9.III.2:1-3. To the ego it is kind and right and good to point out errors and "correct" them. This makes perfect sense to the ego, which is unaware of what errors are and what correction is. Errors are of the ego, and correction of errors lies in the relinquishment of the ego.

Page 167. T-9.III.3:1. If you point out the errors of your brother's ego you must be seeing through yours, because the Holy Spirit does not perceive his errors.

Page 167. T-9.III.4:1-2. When you react at all to errors, you are not listening to the Holy Spirit. He has merely disregarded them, and if you attend to them you are not hearing Him.

Page 167. T-9.III.5:1-3. When a brother behaves insanely, you can heal him only by perceiving the sanity in him. If you perceive his errors and accept them, you are accepting yours. If you want to give yours over to the Holy Spirit, you must do this with his.

Page 167. T-9.III.6:4. It is not up to you to change your brother, but merely to accept him as he is.

Pages 167-168. T-9.III.7:1-9. Your brother's errors are not of him, any more than yours are of you. Accept his errors as real, and you have attacked yourself. If you would find your way and keep it, see only truth beside you for you walk together. The Holy Spirit in you **forgives** all things in you and in your brother. His errors are **forgiven** with yours. **Atonement** is no more separate than love. **Atonement** cannot be separate because it comes from love. Any attempt you make to correct a brother means that you believe correction by you is possible, and this can only be the arrogance of the ego. Correction is of God, Who does not know of arrogance.

Page 168. T-9.III.8:1-11. The Holy Spirit **forgives** everything because God created everything. Do not undertake His function, or you will forget yours. Accept only the function of healing in time, because that is what time is for. God gave you the function to create in eternity. You do not need to learn that, but you do need to learn to want it. For that all learning was made. This is the Holy Spirit's use of an ability that you do not need, but that you made. Give it to Him! You do not understand how to use it. He will teach you how to see yourself without condemnation, by learning how to look on everything without it. Condemnation will then not be real to you, and all your errors will be **forgiven**.

ANSWER 20. Errors are mistakes of the ego that can be corrected. Your best attitude toward errors of others is to not react to them at all, but rather leave their correction to the Holy Spirit. If you react to the errors of others as though they are real, you are listening to your own ego and attacking yourself by making your own errors seem real to you. Your brother's errors made by the ego are not real because they are not part of your brother's reality, which has been created by God Himself. You can help the Holy Spirit to heal your brother and yourself by perceiving only the true holiness and divine nature of your brother, which is beyond all the errors of the ego. You cannot correct your brother's errors or even your own errors. The correction of error is the Holy Spirit's function, and you must not try to take over His function by foolishly imagining that correction is your responsibility apart from Him. Nevertheless, correction can happen *through* you although not *by* you. This correction through you is facilitated by simply giving all mistakes to the Holy Spirit and by accepting the **Atonement**, which corrects all errors simply by recognizing they have no reality at all. Errors, sometimes mistakenly called "sins," are merely expressions of a lack of love. The Holy Spirit and the **Atonement** correct errors by providing perfect love that supplies the love that has been lacking.

QUESTION 21. How would you compare the Holy Spirit's **forgiveness** through overlooking errors with the ego's plan of **forgiveness**?

Page 168. T-9.IV.1:1-6. **Atonement** is for all, because it is the way to undo the belief that anything is for you alone. To **forgive** is to overlook. Look, then, beyond error and do not let your perception rest upon it, for you will believe what your perception holds. Accept as true only what your brother is, if you would know yourself. Perceive what he is not and you cannot know what you are, because you see him falsely. Remember always that your Identity is shared, and that Its sharing is Its reality.

Page 169. T-9.IV.4:1, 4-6. The ego, too, has a plan of **forgiveness** because you are asking for one, though not of the right teacher.... The ego's plan is to have you see error clearly first, and then overlook it. Yet how can you overlook what you have made real? By seeing it clearly, you have made it real and *cannot* overlook it.

Page 169. T-9.IV.5:3-6. **Forgiveness** through the Holy Spirit lies simply in looking beyond error from the beginning, and thus keeping it unreal for you. Do not let any belief in its realness enter your mind, or you will also believe that you must undo what you have made in order to be **forgiven**. What has no effect does not exist, and to the Holy Spirit the effects of error are nonexistent. By steadily and consistently cancelling out all its effects, everywhere and in all respects, He teaches that the ego does not exist and proves it.

ANSWER 21. The ego's plan of **forgiveness** is to clearly examine errors and then overlook them, which makes errors seem real so they cannot be overlooked. The Holy Spirit's plan of **forgiveness** is to overlook errors immediately in order to keep them unreal for you. Instead of looking at errors, even just to examine them, the Holy Spirit wants you to look at your brother's reality in Christ because doing so reminds you of your own reality in Christ. Because your Identity in Christ is shared, your perception of your brother will be your perception of yourself. If you identify with your brother's errors and not his reality, you will identify with your own errors and not with your reality. True **forgiveness** always recognizes the difference between your reality and the unreality of errors. Thus you **forgive** *what never happened to you* because the error that is **forgiven** is not real and so does not exist. But if you think the error is real, you will imagine that you have to do something more to correct it than simply handing it over to the Holy Spirit and accepting the **Atonement**, which corrects all errors.

QUESTION 22A. What do bedtime dreams have in common with the dream of this world in apparent banishment from God?

Page 182. T-10.I.2:1-6. You are at home in God, dreaming of exile but perfectly capable of awakening to reality. Is it your decision to do so? You recognize from your own experience that what you see in dreams you think is real while you are asleep. Yet the instant you waken you realize that everything that seemed to happen in the dream did not happen at all. You do not think this strange, even though all the laws of what you awaken to were violated while you slept. Is it not possible that you merely shifted from one dream to another, without really waking?

ANSWER 22A. Dreams seem real while you are sleeping in your bed, but they instantly disappear when you wake up in the morning. This can be compared to how real the dream of this world appears to you now while you are actually sleeping in Heaven. Upon awakening in the morning, you do not think it is strange when your dream self and dream world are replaced by your everyday self and everyday world. Likewise, when you wake up in Heaven, you will think it is perfectly natural to see your earthly self and earthly world disappear, replaced by your true Self in Christ. This comparison is helpful to remember as your motivation for spiritual growth. It is a reminder that your changeless reality in Heaven has been preserved for you by God, Who created you. Your true Self is only awaiting your recognition of what has been hidden but not lost.

QUESTION 22B. Is it helpful for you to sympathize with your brother by agreeing with his belief in his sickness?

Page 185. T-10.III.3:1-5. To believe that a Son of God can be sick is to believe that part of God can suffer. Love cannot suffer, because it cannot attack. The remembrance of love therefore brings invulnerability with it. Do not side with sickness in the presence of a Son of God even if he believes in it, for your acceptance of God in him acknowledges the Love of God he has forgotten. Your recognition of him as part of God reminds him of the truth about himself, which he is denying.

ANSWER 22B. It is not helpful for you to sympathize with your brother in his belief in sickness because your sympathy for him will encourage him to continue to deny the Love of God that is within him. Instead, it is very helpful to see his reality, which is his invulnerability as a holy Son of God. Your recognition of God in him helps him to remember the Love of God that is already within him, but which he is denying in his sickness. Your reality is shared so you can join with him by recognizing the Love of God within both of you, but no good can come from joining with his denial of God's Love that sickness represents.

QUESTION 23A. What does light mean to God and to you?

Page 193. T-11.in.3:1-7. You make by projection, but God creates by extension. The cornerstone of God's creation is you, for His thought system is light. Remember the Rays that are there unseen. The more you approach the center of His thought system, the clearer the light becomes. The closer you come to the foundation of the ego's thought system, the darker and more obscure becomes the way. Yet even the little spark in your mind is enough to lighten it. Bring this light fearlessly with you, and bravely hold it up to the foundation of the ego's thought system.
Page 199. T-11.III.4:6-7. Walk in light and do not see the dark companions, for they are not fit companions for the Son of God, who was created *of* light and *in* light. The Great Light always surrounds you and shines out from you.

ANSWER 23A. God created you by giving Himself to you through extending His Light into you, making you an eternal part of His Light. The Mind of God is light, and He gives His Mind to you by extending light. Thus your mind is light, which you can extend to others just as God has extended His Mind and His Light to you. Thought and light seem to be separate things in your everyday world, but at the spiritual level thought and light are one. As you learn to identify with the spark of light within you, the darkness of the ego will be replaced by increased awareness of your true spiritual nature in God's Light.

QUESTION 23B. What is the relationship between God's Will and your will?

Page 195. T-11.I.7:7. God wills to create, and your will is His.
Page 196. T-11.I.8:3-5. God's Will is that you are His Son. By denying this you deny your own will, and therefore do not know what it is. You must ask what God's Will is in everything, because it is yours.
Page 196. T-11.I.9:1. The projection of the ego makes it appear as if God's Will is outside yourself, and therefore not yours.
Page 196. T-11.I.10:3-4. You are afraid to know God's Will, because you believe it is not yours. This belief is your whole sickness and your whole fear.
Page 196. T-11.I.11:8-9. God's Will is that His Son be One, and united with Him in His Oneness. That is why healing is the beginning of the recognition that your will is His.
Page 199. T-11.III.3:1-5. O my child, if you knew what God wills for you, your joy would be complete! And what He wills has happened, for it was always true. When the light comes and you have said, "God's Will is mine," you will see such beauty that you will know it is not of you. Out of your joy you will create beauty in His Name, for your joy could no more be contained than His. The bleak little world will vanish into nothingness, and your heart will be so filled with joy that it will leap into Heaven, and into the Presence of God.

ANSWER 23B. You are afraid of God's Will because you imagine that your will is different than His, but your spiritual growth depends on recognizing the truth that your will is exactly the same as God's Will. After all, "You *are* the Will of God."[195] If you reject God's Will, it can only mean that you reject yourself. Similarly, your fear of God's Will means you are afraid of yourself. You have manufactured a false self that imagines it wants all sorts of things apart from God, but your true Self wants only to awaken to your eternal oneness with God, which is the same as oneness with God's Will. Sickness affirms your false belief in separateness from God, and healing is the beginning of realizing that God's Will is your will.

QUESTION 24. What are the characteristics of your perceptions of the **real world**, and why do these perceptions lead to awakening in Heaven?

Page 210. T-11.VII.2:1-8. Every loving thought that the Son of God ever had is eternal. The loving thoughts his mind perceives in this world are the world's only reality. They are still perceptions, because he still believes that he is separate. Yet they are eternal because they are loving. And being loving they are like the Father, and therefore cannot die. The **real world** can actually be perceived. All that is necessary is a willingness to perceive nothing else. For if you perceive both good and evil, you are accepting both the false and the true and making no distinction between them.

Page 210. T-11.VII.3:1-9. The ego may see some good, but never only good. That is why its perceptions are so variable. It does not reject goodness entirely, for that you could not accept. But it always adds something that is not real to the real, thus confusing illusion and reality. For perceptions cannot be partly true. If you believe in truth and illusion, you cannot tell which is true. To establish your personal autonomy you tried to create unlike your Father, believing that what you made is capable of being unlike Him. Yet everything true *is* like Him. Perceiving only the **real world** will lead you to the real Heaven, because it will make you capable of understanding it.

Page 211. T-11.VII.4:7-9. To believe that you can perceive the **real world** is to believe that you can know yourself. You can know God because it is His Will to be known. The **real world** is all that the Holy Spirit has saved for you out of what you have made, and to perceive only this is salvation, because it is the recognition that reality is only what is true.

ANSWER 24. Unlike the world of form that contains both unloving false perceptions and loving true perceptions, the **real world** consists of only loving true perceptions. All loving thoughts are eternal, so perceiving the **real world** leads to awakening in Heaven because the content of pure love is so much like God the Father. The **real world** is not reality itself, but gets its name because it is a reflection of reality. Thus the **real world** helps you recognize that reality is only what is true and loving and that love and truth are your reality. If you can perceive the **real world**, you must be seeing without the ego since the ego can see some good, but cannot see only good. Perceiving the **real world** helps you understand Heaven and leads to awakening in Heaven. The Holy Spirit made the **real world** by purifying all the thoughts of the sleeping Sons of God and saving only the loving thoughts called the "blessed residue,"[196] which will go to Heaven with you when you awaken.

QUESTION 25. Is the world outside your mind or inside your mind?

Page 222. T-12.III.7:1-10. If only the loving thoughts of God's Son are the world's reality, the **real world** must be in his mind. His insane thoughts, too, must be in his mind, but an internal conflict of this magnitude he cannot tolerate. A split mind is endangered, and the recognition that it encompasses completely opposed thoughts within itself is intolerable. Therefore the mind projects the split, not the reality. Everything you perceive as the outside world is merely your attempt to maintain your ego identification, for everyone believes that identification is salvation. Yet consider what has happened, for thoughts do have consequences to the thinker. You have become at odds with the world as you perceive it, because you think it is antagonistic to you. This is a necessary consequence of what you have done. You have projected outward what is antagonistic to what is inward, and therefore you would have to perceive it this way. That is why you must realize that your hatred is in your mind and not outside it before you can get rid of it; and why you must get rid of it before you can perceive the world as it really is.

Pages 222-223. T-12.III.9.1, 7-10. The world you perceive is a world of separation.... For it is made out of what you do not want, projected from your mind because you are afraid of it. Yet this world is only in the mind of its maker, along with his real salvation. Do not believe it is outside of yourself, for only by recognizing where it is will you gain control over it. For you do have control over your mind, since the mind is the mechanism of decision.

ANSWER 25. The world you see around you is entirely within your mind. The world is a dream image you have projected so it seems to be outside your mind. Your body is a dream image, which you have mistakenly identified as your separate self in your dream world. There are two worlds in your mind: One is the **real world** of only loving thoughts. The other is your everyday world of both loving and unloving thoughts. But these two worlds in your mind are totally opposed, and only one can be a true reflection of reality. You cannot tolerate seeing both worlds at once in your mind because they contradict each other and you cannot endure this conflict. Therefore, you have projected the part of your mind that does not reflect reality, so you see a world of both loving and unloving thoughts manifested as dream images. Your ego, which is part of your dreaming mind, identifies with your dream images of the world and tells you that you are part of the dream and not the dreamer of the dream. When you realize that the world you see outside is really in your mind, you can use your mind to make decisions that enable you to gain control over your experience of the

A Simple Framework for Understanding the Course 115

world. Instead of denying and projecting your false perceptions onto the outer world, you can recognize and begin to heal the false perceptions within your mind.

QUESTION 26. What enables you to see the **real world** of loving thoughts, and what are the results of having the vision of the **real world**?

Page 228. T-12.VI.4:4-9. Christ's eyes are open, and He will look upon whatever you see with love if you accept His vision as yours. The Holy Spirit keeps the vision of Christ for every Son of God who sleeps. In His sight the Son of God is perfect, and He longs to share His vision with you. He will show you the **real world** because God gave you Heaven. Through Him your Father calls His Son to remember. The awakening of His Son begins with his investment in the **real world**, and by this he will learn to re-invest in himself.

Page 228. T-12.VI.5:1-9. When you have seen this **real world**, as you will surely do, you will remember Us. Yet you must learn the cost of sleeping, and refuse to pay it. Only then will you decide to awaken. And then the **real world** will spring to your sight, for Christ has never slept. He is waiting to be seen, for He has never lost sight of you. He looks quietly on the **real world**, which He would share with you because He knows of the Father's Love for Him. And knowing this, He would give you what is yours. In perfect peace He waits for you at His Father's altar, holding out the Father's Love to you in the quiet light of the Holy Spirit's blessing. For the Holy Spirit will lead everyone home to his Father, where Christ waits as his Self.

Page 229. T-12.VI.6:1-7. Every child of God is one in Christ, for his being is in Christ as Christ's is in God. Christ's Love for you is His Love for His Father, which He knows because He knows His Father's Love for Him. When the Holy Spirit has at last led you to Christ at the altar to His Father, perception fuses into knowledge because perception has become so holy that its transfer to holiness is merely its natural extension. Love transfers to love without any interference, for the two are one. As you perceive more and more common elements in all situations, the transfer of training under the Holy Spirit's guidance increases and becomes generalized. Gradually you learn to apply it to everyone and everything, for its applicability is universal. When this has been accomplished, perception and knowledge have become so similar that they share the unification of the laws of God.

Page 229.T-12.VI.7:1-7. What is one cannot be perceived as separate, and the denial of the separation is the reinstatement of knowledge. At the altar of God, the holy perception of God's Son becomes so

enlightened that light streams into it, and the spirit of God's Son shines in the Mind of the Father and becomes one with it. Very gently does God shine upon Himself, loving the extension of Himself that is His Son. The world has no purpose as it blends into the purpose of God. For the **real world** has slipped quietly into Heaven, where everything eternal in it has always been. There the Redeemer and the redeemed join in perfect love of God and of each other. Heaven is your home, and being in God it must also be in you.
Page 232. T-12.VII.11:7. Through the eyes of Christ, only the **real world** exists and only the **real world** can be seen.

ANSWER 26. **Christ's vision**, which is given to you by Christ and the Holy Spirit, enables you to perceive the **real world** of only loving thoughts that reflect Heaven. But you must accept His vision as yours and not rely on the vision shown to you by your physical eyes.

Perceiving the **real world** helps you identify with your true nature of love and prepares you for awakening. Ultimately, having the vision of the **real world** results in bringing back the memory of God. Seeing the **real world** leads to seeing the **face of Christ**, the image that reminds you of the reality of Christ as your Self. When you see the blazing light of the **face of Christ**, you will perceive only loving thoughts that reflect the knowledge of Heaven. When perception becomes totally loving, it fuses into knowledge because perception and knowledge have become one in love. The Holy Spirit starts by helping you to see love in some situations and later helps you to generalize your learning so you can see love in everything. This produces totally unified perception, which is so close to the unification of awareness in knowledge that the transfer from perception to knowledge becomes possible. Unified perception becomes filled with light and becomes so similar to God's Light that the two lights become one since there is nothing to separate them. Loving thoughts are eternal because they are loving. When all the sleeping Sons of God awaken, the **real world** of only loving thoughts will be taken up into Heaven, the Home of Love. When this final awakening happens, there will no longer be any unloving illusions of separation that cloud the awareness of divine oneness and divine love in Heaven.

QUESTION 27A. Why are you attracted to love and yet afraid of both love and redemption?

Page 235. T-12.VIII.7:10-11. What God did not give you has no power over you, and the attraction of love for love remains irresistible. For it is the function of love to unite all things unto itself, and to hold all things together by extending its wholeness.

Page 242. T-13.III.1:11. Your real terror is of redemption.
Page 242. T-13.III.2:1-9. Under the ego's dark foundation is the memory of God, and it is of this that you are really afraid. For this memory would instantly restore you to your proper place, and it is this place that you have sought to leave. Your fear of attack is nothing compared to your fear of love. You would be willing to look even upon your savage wish to kill God's Son, if you did not believe that it saves you from love. For this wish caused the separation, and you have protected it because you do not want the separation healed. You realize that, by removing the dark cloud that obscures it, your love for your Father would impel you to answer His Call and leap into Heaven. You believe that attack is salvation because it would prevent you from this. For still deeper than the ego's foundation, and much stronger than it will ever be, is your intense and burning love of God, and His for you. This is what you really want to hide.
Page 243. T-13.III.4:3-5. You think you have made a world God would destroy; and by loving Him, which you do, you would throw this world away, which you *would*. Therefore, you have used the world to cover your love, and the deeper you go into the blackness of the ego's foundation, the closer you come to the Love that is hidden there. *And it is this that frightens you.*
Page 243. T-13.III.5:1. You can accept insanity because you made it, but you cannot accept love because you did not.

ANSWER 27A. God gave you love as your reality because Love is His Reality. You are naturally attracted to love because love is attracted to love with an irresistible power. Love unifies all things around love itself by extending its unifying force of oneness. Since you are love and God is Love, you both are naturally attracted to each other. Your union in love has never been interrupted, but your awareness of your union has been interrupted by your illusions that began with the separation and that continue as you hold on to your illusions.

Ironically, you are afraid of both redemption and love. Redemption would expose you directly to God's Love that would replace your illusions with the reality of Heaven. His Love for you is so irresistible that it would awaken your wholehearted love for Him and impel you to leap back into Heaven. But your fear of redemption comes from losing the separation that you made and from unmasking the truth about your separate ego that you falsely claim to be your self. You use a false world and false self that you made to hide your intense and burning love for God and hide God's Love for you. You are afraid of love because you want to hold on to the illusions you have made rather than accept the reality of love that God created in you. Since you are love and can only be love as God created you, your fear of love can only mean that you are afraid of yourself—meaning afraid of your Self—and would rather accept an imaginary self that has no reality.

QUESTION 27B. What happened the first time you requested "special favor" (special love) from God?

Page 244. T-13.III.10:1-6. You who prefer separation to sanity cannot obtain it in your right mind. You were at peace until you asked for special favor. And God did not give it for the request was alien to Him, and you could not ask this of a Father Who truly loved His Son. Therefore you made of Him an unloving father, demanding of Him what only such a father could give. And the peace of God's Son was shattered, for he no longer understood his Father. He feared what he had made, but still more did he fear his real Father, having attacked his own glorious equality with Him.
Page 244. T-13.III.11:1-7. In peace he needed nothing and asked for nothing. In war he demanded everything and found nothing. For how could the gentleness of love respond to his demands, except by departing in peace and returning to the Father? If the Son did not wish to remain in peace, he could not remain at all. For a darkened mind cannot live in the light, and it must seek a place of darkness where it can believe it is where it is not. God did not allow this to happen. Yet you demanded that it happen, and therefore believed that it was so.

ANSWER 27B. Some parts of the Sonship who were in Heaven before the separation asked God for "special favor." They wanted God to give them special love, meaning they wanted more love than God gave every part of the Sonship. God could not agree to unequal love, and so parts of the Sonship joined together to make the separation. They closed off communication with God and fell asleep in Heaven. They dreamed of the illusory world of time and space where the ego, the idea of separation from God, could be believed. God gave His Answer to the instant of separation by creating the Holy Spirit, Who functions as the Communication Link that instantly healed the separation by reestablishing the unity of the whole Sonship with God. However, the dreaming Sons of God still need to wake up from their illusions of separation to restore the peace of mind that they threw away when their desire for special love was denied by God. Because the separation only happened in illusions and did not happen in reality, it did not happen at all. As one of the sleeping parts of the Sonship, you persistently deny your never-ending union with God. You are still insisting that the separation has happened and will continue to do so until you change your mind about the separation and finally wake up in Heaven, where you have been dreaming all along.

QUESTION 28. How are light, vision, love, fear, and Christ related?

Page 249. T-13.V.8:1, 9. Vision depends on light.... Dreams disappear when light has come and you can see.

Pages 249-250. T-13.V.9:1-8. Do not seek vision through your eyes, for you made your way of seeing that you might see in darkness, and in this you are deceived. Beyond this darkness, and yet still within you, is the vision of Christ, Who looks on all in light. Your "vision" comes from fear, as His from love. And He sees for you, as your witness to the **real world**. He is the Holy Spirit's manifestation, looking always on the **real world**, and calling forth its witnesses and drawing them to you. He loves what He sees within you, and He would extend it. And He will not return unto the Father until He has extended your perception even unto Him. And there perception is no more, for He has returned you to the Father with Him.

Page 250. T-13.V.10:1-6. You have but two emotions, and one you made and one was given you. Each is a way of seeing, and different worlds arise from their different sights. See through the vision that is given you, for through **Christ's vision** He beholds Himself. And seeing what He is, He knows His Father. Beyond your darkest dreams He sees God's guiltless Son within you, shining in perfect radiance that is undimmed by your dreams. And this *you* will see as you look with Him, for His vision is His gift of love to you, given Him of the Father for you.

Page 250. T-13.V.11:1-7. The Holy Spirit is the light in which Christ stands revealed. And all who would behold Him can see Him, for they have asked for light. Nor will they see Him alone, for He is no more alone than they are. Because they saw the Son, they have risen in Him to the Father. And all this will they understand, because they looked within and saw beyond the darkness the Christ in them, and recognized Him. In the sanity of His vision they looked upon themselves with love, seeing themselves as the Holy Spirit sees them. And with this vision of the truth in them came all the beauty of the world to shine upon them.

Page 252. T-13.VI.8:4, 8. God's guiltless Son is only light.... The holy light that shines forth from God's Son is the witness that his light is of his Father.

Page 252. T-13.VI.10:1-4. Child of Light, you know not that the light is in you. Yet you will find it through its witnesses, for having given light to them they will return it. Each one you see in light brings your light closer to your awareness. Love always leads to love.

ANSWER 28. Christ is light and love, and He gives His vision through the medium of light and love. Unlike vision with your physical eyes that perceive a transitory world of fear and darkness, **Christ's vision** shows you the **real world** of only light and love. To receive **Christ's vision** requires that you receive His light that enables you to perceive the **face of Christ** in the **real world**. There are only two emotions: fear and love. You made the illusion of fear. God created love as the extension of His Reality. **Christ's vision** enables you to choose love instead of fear. Your physical eyes were made to see both images of fear and darkness and images of love and light, just as the physical world that you see has both false perceptions of fear as well as true perceptions of love. When you accept **Christ's vision** from the Holy Spirit, you see the **real world** of only light and love without darkness and fear. The Holy Spirit Himself is the light that reveals Christ to you, and His light connects every part of Christ with God the Father. **Christ's vision** through the Holy Spirit shows you Christ and His holiness as your Self, leading to your awakening in Heaven.

QUESTION 29A. How would you compare partial awareness with the awareness of wholeness?

Page 258. T-13.VIII.2:1-5. The very real difference between perception and knowledge becomes quite apparent if you consider this: There is nothing partial about knowledge. Every aspect is whole, and therefore no aspect is separate. You are an aspect of knowledge, being in the Mind of God, Who knows you. All knowledge must be yours, for in you is all knowledge. Perception, at its loftiest, is never complete.
Page 258. T-13.VIII.3:1. Perfect perception, then, has many elements in common with knowledge, making transfer to it possible.
Page 259. T-13.VIII.5:1-3. This is the **miracle** of creation; *that it is one forever.* Every **miracle** you offer to the Son of God is but the true perception of one aspect of the whole. Though every aspect *is* the whole, you cannot know this until you see that every aspect is the same, perceived in the same light and therefore one.
Page 259. T-13.VIII.6:3-7. There is one **miracle**, as there is one reality. And every **miracle** you do contains them all, as every aspect of reality you see blends quietly into the one Reality of God. The only **miracle** that ever was is God's most holy Son, created in the one Reality that is his Father. **Christ's vision** is His gift to you. His Being is His Father's gift to Him.

Page 259. T-13.VIII.7:4-6. Knowledge is far beyond your individual concern. You who are part of it and all of it need only realize that it is of the Father, not of you. Your role in the redemption leads you to it by re-establishing its oneness in your mind.
Pages 259-260. T-13.VIII.8:1. When you have seen your brothers as yourself you will be released to knowledge, having learned to free yourself through Him Who knows of freedom.

ANSWER 29A. Perception is partial awareness, which means that it is very different from knowledge that is total awareness of wholeness that exists in Heaven. There are parts in the knowledge of Heaven, but the parts are not limited. Each unique part or aspect in Heaven contains the whole, meaning each part has the total awareness of knowledge and no part is separate from any other part. You are a part of Christ and yet are simultaneously the whole of Christ. This is a paradox that seems contradictory and unbelievable in your everyday perception, but in the knowledge of Heaven it is how perfect equality in the Sonship is maintained. It is how God can have only one Son as the Christ, and how every part of that one Christ is equally loved by God. Similarly, there is only one **miracle** and one **holy instant**. Every **miracle** you perform in the **holy instant** in everyday life is in fact an expression of the one **miracle** and the one **holy instant**. This is also a paradox that cannot be explained with the partial awareness of perception.

QUESTION 29B. If you love everyone except one person whom you see as guilty, what will the result be?

Page 262. T-13.IX.7:1-6. Guilt makes you blind, for while you see one spot of guilt within you, you will not see the light. And by projecting it the world seems dark, and shrouded in your guilt. You throw a dark veil over it, and cannot see it because you cannot look within. You are afraid of what you would see there, but it is not there. *The thing you fear is gone.* If you would look within you would see only the **Atonement**, shining in quiet and in peace upon the altar to your Father.
Page 265. T-13.X.11:1-7. You cannot enter into real relationships with any of God's Sons unless you love them all and equally. Love is not special. If you single out part of the Sonship for your love, you are imposing guilt on all your relationships and making them unreal. You can love only as God loves. Seek not to love unlike Him, for there is no love apart from His. Until you recognize that this is true, you will have no idea what love is like. No one who condemns a brother can see himself as guiltless and in the peace of God.

ANSWER 29B. Excluding anyone from your love by perceiving guilt will prevent you from understanding or experiencing the true nature of love. Your love must be a reflection of God's Love. You cannot have real relationships until you love everyone equally as God does because true love has no specialness in it. You cannot look upon some parts of the Sonship as more worthy of love than other parts without fostering specialness and guilt within your own mind, which will darken your awareness of God's Love within you.

QUESTION 30. What is the importance of your power of decision?

Page 275. T-14.III.4:2-6. The ego is the choice for guilt; the Holy Spirit the choice for guiltlessness. The power of decision is all that is yours. What you can decide between is fixed, because there are no alternatives except truth and illusion. And there is no overlap between them, because they are opposites which cannot be reconciled and cannot both be true. You are guilty or guiltless, bound or free, unhappy or happy.

Page 276. T-14.III.9:1, 5. Whenever you choose to make decisions for yourself you are thinking destructively, and the decision will be wrong.... Every decision is made for the whole Sonship, directed in and out, and influencing a constellation larger than anything you ever dreamed of.

Page 276. T-14.III.11:1-2. It will never happen that you must make decisions for yourself. You are not bereft of help, and Help that knows the answer.

Page 277. T-14.III.12:1-6. Would you deny the truth of God's decision, and place your pitiful appraisal of yourself in place of His calm and unswerving value of His Son? Nothing can shake God's conviction of the perfect purity of everything that He created, for it *is* wholly pure. Do not decide against it, for being of Him it must be true. Peace abides in every mind that quietly accepts the plan God set for its **Atonement**, relinquishing its own. You know not of salvation, for you do not understand it. Make no decisions about what it is or where it lies, but ask the Holy Spirit everything, and leave all decisions to His gentle counsel.

Page 277. T-14.III.13:4-6. The Holy Spirit knows that all salvation is escape from guilt. He is the strong protector of the innocence that sets you free. And it is His decision to undo everything that would obscure your innocence from your unclouded mind.

Page 277. T-14.III.14:1-3, 7. Let Him, therefore, be the only Guide that you would follow to salvation. He knows the way, and leads you gladly on it. With Him you will not fail to learn that what God wills for you *is* your will.... Forget Him not and He will make every decision for you, for your salvation and the peace of God in you.

ANSWER 30. Your mind has the power of decision to direct your path, but you do not have the power to choose your alternatives. You are limited to only two unchanging alternatives: You can choose either the ego or the Holy Spirit. Choosing the ego is a choice for guilt, illusion, and unhappiness. Choosing the Holy Spirit is a choice for holiness, truth, and happiness. If you make your decisions by and for yourself alone, you will be choosing the ego, which will convince you that you are alone. Instead, you can ask for help from the Holy Spirit and let Him make your decisions for you. His decisions for you will affirm God's decision that you are His holy Son and will lead you to the peace of God and to awakening in Heaven. Your decisions affect the entire Sonship in ways you cannot possibly understand. One of your most important decisions is to accept the **Atonement**, which is the Holy Spirit's plan that will undo all your errors and will lead to your awakening in Heaven.

QUESTION 31A. Who is called to enter the circle of **Atonement**?

Pages 283-284. T-14.V.8:3-7. Within its holy circle is everyone whom God created as His Son. Joy is its unifying attribute, with no one left outside to suffer guilt alone. The power of God draws everyone to its safe embrace of love and union. Stand quietly within this circle, and attract all tortured minds to join with you in the safety of its peace and holiness. Abide with me within it, as a teacher of **Atonement**, not of guilt.
Page 284. T-14.V.11:1-3, 5. Each one you see you place within the holy circle of **Atonement** or leave outside, judging him fit for crucifixion or for redemption. If you bring him into the circle of purity, you will rest there with him. If you leave him without, you join him there.... Refuse to accept anyone as without the blessing of **Atonement**, and bring him into it by blessing him.

ANSWER 31A. You are called to enter the circle of **Atonement** and so is every Son of God. When you accept the **Atonement**, you accept your own holiness in this circle of purity where Jesus stands beside you. As you stand within the circle of **Atonement**, your role is to be a teacher of guiltlessness, who attracts others who stand outside believing in their guilt. If you see any brother outside as guilty, you will join him outside the circle. As a teacher of God, your function is to see your brother's holiness and welcome him to join you within the circle of **Atonement** where you can give him your embrace of love. As you give the blessing of the **Atonement**, you simultaneously receive the blessing of **Atonement**, which is an experience of sharing and union in the perfect Love of God.

QUESTION 31B. What does the Holy Spirit ask of you?

Page 288. T-14.VII.6:1, 6-11. The Holy Spirit asks of you but this; bring to Him every secret you have locked away from Him.... He sees for you, and unless you look with Him He cannot see. The vision of Christ is not for Him alone, but for Him with you. Bring, therefore, all your dark and secret thoughts to Him, and look upon them with Him. He holds the light, and you the darkness. They cannot coexist when both of You together look on them. His judgment must prevail, and He will give it to you as you join your perception to His.

ANSWER 31B. The Holy Spirit asks you to give Him every bit of pain and every unloving secret thought you have hidden in darkness. He will bring you the light of **Christ's vision** to shine away every dark secret you bring to Him. You cannot release your darkness by yourself alone, but you can join with the Holy Spirit so you can both look with **Christ's vision**. When you join your perception with the Holy Spirit's, your dark secret illusions will dissolve in the light of truth. What you do not bring to the light will remain hidden because the Holy Spirit cannot heal what you want to keep for yourself.

QUESTION 32A. Holiness is yours, but what can you do with your mind to help others with your holiness?

Page 292. T-14.IX.5:1-7. In this world you can become a spotless mirror, in which the Holiness of your Creator shines forth from you to all around you. You can reflect Heaven here. Yet no reflections of the images of other gods must dim the mirror that would hold God's reflection in it. Earth can reflect Heaven or hell; God or the ego. You need but leave the mirror clean and clear of all the images of hidden darkness you have drawn upon it. God will shine upon it of Himself. Only the clear reflection of Himself can be perceived upon it.

Page 292. T-14.IX.7:1, 4. Could you but realize for a single instant the power of healing that the reflection of God, shining in you, can bring to all the world, you could not wait to make the mirror of your mind clean to receive the image of the holiness that heals the world.... All bring their different problems to its healing light, and all their problems find but healing there.

Page 292. T-14.IX.8:1, 3-4. The response of holiness to any form of error is always the same.... Its one response is healing, without regard for what is brought to it. Those who have learned to offer only healing, because of the reflection of holiness in them, are ready at last for Heaven.

ANSWER 32A. The best way to let your holiness help others is to clean your own mind so it becomes a pure reflection of the Holiness coming from God. Then holiness will shine through you to the world. Through cleaning your mind, you become a vehicle for healing others and healing yourself. Cleaning your mind means letting go of images of fear, unforgiveness, and separation and replacing them with images of love, **forgiveness**, and sharing that symbolize Heaven. When the mirror of your mind reflects only God's Holiness, you become a vehicle for healing that solves all errors and problems.

QUESTION 32B. What are the two categories of thought you need to adopt as your way of perceiving your brother and yourself?

Page 294. T-14.X.7:1. The only judgment involved is the Holy Spirit's one division into two categories; one of love, and the other the call for love.
Page 295. T-14.X.11:4-6. Every interpretation you would lay upon a brother is senseless. Let the Holy Spirit show him to you, and teach you both his love and his call for love. Neither his mind nor yours holds more than these two orders of thought.
Pages 295-296. T-14.X.12:1-9. The **miracle** is the recognition that this is true. Where there is love, your brother must give it to you because of what it is. But where there is a call for love, you must give it because of what you are. Earlier I said this course will teach you how to remember what you are, restoring to you your Identity. We have already learned that this Identity is shared. The **miracle** becomes the means of sharing It. By supplying your Identity wherever It is not recognized, you will recognize It. And God Himself, Who wills to be with His Son forever, will bless each recognition of His Son with all the Love He holds for him. Nor will the power of all His Love be absent from any **miracle** you offer to His Son.

ANSWER 32B. The Holy Spirit teaches you that there are only two categories for correctly evaluating your brother's behavior and your own behavior. One category is the expression of love and the other is the call for love. If your brother is expressing love, he will give it to you because love is sharing and union. If your brother is expressing anything besides love, he is calling for love in the mistaken belief that he is lacking love. The best response you can have to such a brother is to supply the love that he is calling for. The love that comes to him through you reminds him of the love that is already within him, and this brings healing. In fact, this is an expression of a **miracle** in which there is an exchange of love between the giver and receiver, who both gain love without loss to either one. Your Identity is love, and you share your Identity with your brother. As you recognize love in your brother and give him love, you are acknowledging his Identity and reminding yourself of your own Identity. The power of the **miracle** comes from recognizing and sharing your Identity of love with your brother, and your recognition is blessed by God Himself.

QUESTION 33. What are the features of the **holy instant**?

Page 304. T-15.I.13:4-8. The Holy Spirit gives their blessed instant to you through your giving it. As you give it, He offers it to you. Be not unwilling to give what you would receive of Him, for you join with Him in giving. In the crystal cleanness of the release you give is your instantaneous escape from guilt. You must be holy if you offer holiness.
Pages 310-311. T-15.IV.6:5-8. The **holy instant** is a time in which you receive and give perfect communication. This means, however, that it is a time in which your mind is open, both to receive and give. It is the recognition that all minds are in communication. It therefore seeks to change nothing, but merely to accept everything.
Page 311. T-15.IV.8:6. For the **holy instant** is given and received with equal willingness, being the acceptance of the single Will that governs all thought.
Page 311. T-15.IV.9:1-2. The necessary condition for the **holy instant** does not require that you have no thoughts that are not pure. But it does require that you have none that you would keep.
Page 312. T-15.V.1:1-4. The **holy instant** is the Holy Spirit's most useful learning device for teaching you love's meaning. For its purpose is to suspend judgment entirely. Judgment always rests on the past, for past experience is the basis on which you judge. Judgment becomes impossible without the past, for without it you do not understand anything.
Page 314. T-15.V.10:1-2, 8-10. All your relationships are blessed in the **holy instant**, because the blessing is not limited. In the **holy instant** the Sonship gains as one, and united in your blessing it becomes one to you.... Yet in the **holy instant** you unite directly with God, and all your brothers join in Christ. Those who are joined in Christ are in

no way separate. For Christ is the Self the Sonship shares, as God shares His Self with Christ.

Page 314. T-15.V.11:4-6. In the **holy instant** there is no conflict of needs, for there is only one. For the **holy instant** reaches to eternity, and to the Mind of God. And it is only there love has meaning, and only there can it be understood.

Page 315. T-15.VI.5:5. The **holy instant** thus becomes a lesson in how to hold all of your brothers in your mind, experiencing not loss but completion.

ANSWER 33. When the **holy instant** is experienced, the mind is open to both giving and receiving in perfect communication with the entire Sonship. The **holy instant** is the Holy Spirit's gift, given to you as you give it to your brother. It is an experience of sharing in the present moment without reference to the past or future. In the **holy instant**, all judgment is suspended since the past, which is the basis of judgment, is set aside. That does not mean the mind must be perfectly clear in order to experience the **holy instant**. Some fleeting false perceptions may pass through your mind, yet it is still possible to experience the **holy instant** as long as you can let go of these false perceptions by not clinging to them. The **holy instant** of sharing offers holiness with no hint of guilt. The **holy instant** is a communion in which you experience your completion. It is a recognition of union with God the Father, the Holy Spirit, and the Sonship joined in Christ. Christ is the one Self that every part of the Sonship shares equally, while each part is also the whole of the one Christ. The **holy instant** provides your best means of truly understanding the limitless nature of love because it extends to eternity and to the Mind of God, the Home of Love.

QUESTION 34A. What is the link between the special relationship and guilt?

Page 317. T-15.VII.1:7. For every relationship on which the ego embarks *is* special.

Page 317. T-15.VII.2:1-7. The ego establishes relationships only to get something. And it would keep the giver bound to itself through guilt. It is impossible for the ego to enter into any relationship without anger, for the ego believes that anger makes friends. This is not its statement, but it *is* its purpose. For the ego really believes that it can get and keep *by making guilty*. This is its one attraction; an attraction so weak that it would have no hold at all, except that no one recognizes it. For the ego always seems to attract through love, and has no attraction at all to anyone who perceives that it attracts through guilt.

Page 317. T-15.VII.4:1, 6. We said before that the ego attempts to maintain and increase guilt, but in such a way that you do not recognize what it would do to you.... And thus it embarks on an endless, unrewarding chain of special relationships, forged out of anger and dedicated to but one insane belief; that the more anger you invest outside yourself, the safer you become.

Page 319. T-15.VII.10:3-4. All anger is nothing more than an attempt to make someone feel guilty, and this attempt is the only basis the ego accepts for special relationships. Guilt is the only need the ego has, and as long as you identify with it, guilt will remain attractive to you.

ANSWER 34A. The special relationship is a relationship in which both partners are focused on getting special love. Each partner's ego wants to get specialness from the other, so the special relationship is based on taking rather than giving. The ego fosters the special relationship by offering an illusion of love to attract you, while hiding the truth that such a relationship based on getting must foster guilt and not love. The ego always seeks specialness to gain from the loss of others. Thus specialness is a form of attack, which the ego will tell you is a "sin," rather than a "mistake." Because seeking specialness always involves an attack, it fosters guilt. In special hate relationships, this attack that produces guilt is overt. This direct attack is a way of gaining specialness by deflating another's ego to inflate your own ego. In the more common special love relationships, the attack is always disguised as an expression of love, which is merely an illusion of love. This indirect attack involves taking your partner's specialness so he loses his specialness and you gain from his loss. This mentality of taking to acquire specialness causes guilt and is the exact result the ego is seeking as its purpose. The ego will always hide this goal since you would reject it if you could clearly see that it is based on the attraction of guilt rather than the attraction of love. When special love relationships fail, the love is revealed as an illusion and both partners are angry. As all anger, this anger is an attempt to make another person feel guilty. This projection of guilt is a way of denying one's original attacking goal of acquiring specialness at the expense of one's partner.

QUESTION 34B. Do you need to understand **miracles** in order to perform them?

Page 332. T-16.II.2:4-8. A better and far more helpful way to think of **miracles** is this: You do not understand them, either in part or in whole. Yet they have been done through you. Therefore your understanding cannot be necessary. Yet it is still impossible to accomplish what you do not understand. And so there must be Something in you that *does* understand.

Page 333. T-16.II.4:1-5. You have done **miracles**, but it is quite apparent that you have not done them alone. You have succeeded whenever you have reached another mind and joined with it. When two minds join as one and share one idea equally, the first link in the awareness of the Sonship as One has been made. When you have made this joining as the Holy Spirit bids you, and have offered it to Him to use as He sees fit, His natural perception of your gift enables Him to understand it, and you to use His understanding on your behalf. It is impossible to convince you of the reality of what has clearly been accomplished through your willingness while you believe that you must understand it or else it is not real.

ANSWER 34B. **Miracles** do not require your understanding in order to perform them. In fact, the spiritual nature of **miracles** is so radically different than your everyday experience in the world that you do not understand them. However, it is very helpful to know that you can perform **miracles** as expressions of love by letting them happen *through* you. Thus there must be "Something" acting through you, and this Something must understand what **miracles** are. This Something is, of course, the Holy Spirit. The **miracle** happens whenever your mind joins with your brother's mind and you both share one idea equally. This is the beginning of reestablishing your awareness of oneness with the whole Sonship. It is natural for the Holy Spirit to facilitate **miracles** since He is the eternal link that connects all parts of the Sonship with each other and with God. Your connection during a **miracle** with one of your brothers is uplifting for you and your brother, but it is also for the benefit of the whole Sonship. Consequently, you must offer your **miracles** to the Holy Spirit to use as He sees fit in ways you cannot possibly imagine.

QUESTION 35A. What is the nature of love in the special love relationship?

Page 341. T-16.V.3:1, 4, 6-8. The special love relationship is the ego's most boasted gift, and one which has the most appeal to those unwilling to relinquish guilt.... No one considers it bizarre to love and hate together, and even those who believe that hate is sin merely feel guilty, but do not correct it.... For this world *is* the opposite of Heaven, being made to be its opposite, and everything here takes a direction exactly opposite of what is true. In Heaven, where the meaning of love is known, love is the same as union. Here, where the illusion of love is accepted in love's place, love is perceived as separation and exclusion. Page 341.T-16.V.4:1-2. It is in the special relationship, born of the hidden wish for special love from God, that the ego's hatred triumphs. For the special relationship is the renunciation of the Love of God, and the attempt to secure for the self the specialness that He denied.

ANSWER 35A. Love in a special relationship is not love it all. Rather, it is merely an illusion of love. Love in a special relationship is really special love, which pretends to offer union, while, in fact, it only fosters separateness based on specialness. In Heaven love is union, and God's Love is shared as a state of union with God and with all your brothers and sisters, sharing equally in the one Christ. Because the special relationship embraces the acquisition of specialness instead of love, it is a rejection of God's Love based on union.

QUESTION 35B. What is traded in the bargain of a special love relationship?

Page 342. T-16.V.7:1-7. Most curious of all is the concept of the self which the ego fosters in the special relationship. This "self" seeks the relationship to make itself complete. Yet when it finds the special relationship in which it thinks it can accomplish this it gives itself away, and tries to "trade" itself for the self of another. This is not union, for there is no increase and no extension. Each partner tries to sacrifice the self he does not want for one he thinks he would prefer. And he feels guilty for the "sin" of taking, and of giving nothing of value in return. How much value can he place upon a self that he would give away to get a "better" one?
Page 342. T-16.V.8:1-3. The "better" self the ego seeks is always one that is more special. And whoever seems to possess a special self is "loved" for what can be taken from him. Where both partners see this special self in each other, the ego sees "a union made in Heaven."

ANSWER 35B. In the special relationship, each partner attempts to trade his unworthy "self" for the more worthy "self" of the other and thereby acquire the other person's specialness for himself. Thus each partner in a special relationship wants to take something better from his partner and give something less valuable in return. This is a selfish bargain that has nothing to do with love. After all, this relationship is about taking without giving and results in guilt, not the union of true love. Each partner is seeking specialness and not love, so the special relationship fosters selfishness and merely the illusion of love. However, eventually the selfishness of the special relationship will rudely shatter the illusion of love. When this happens, each partner will blame the other for breaking the bargain. Thus illusory love will change into overt hate. When partners in a special relationship break up, they often fail to take responsibility for manufacturing the illusion of love based on taking rather than giving.

QUESTION 36A. What will **forgiveness** show you in the **real world**?

Page 352. T-17.II.1:1-2, 6-9. Can you imagine how beautiful those you **forgive** will look to you? In no fantasy have you ever seen anything so lovely.... For you will see the Son of God. You will behold the beauty the Holy Spirit loves to look upon, and which He thanks the Father for. He was created to see this for you, until you learned to see it for yourself. And all His teaching leads to seeing it and giving thanks with Him.
Pages 352-353. T-17.II.2:1-3. This loveliness is not a fantasy. It is the **real world**, bright and clean and new, with everything sparkling under the open sun. Nothing is hidden here, for everything has been **forgiven** and there are no fantasies to hide the truth.
Page 354. T-17.II.6:1-3. All this beauty will rise to bless your sight as you look upon the world with forgiving eyes. For **forgiveness** literally transforms vision, and lets you see the **real world** reaching quietly and gently across chaos, removing all illusions that had twisted your perception and fixed it on the past. The smallest leaf becomes a thing of wonder, and a blade of grass a sign of God's perfection.
Page 354. T-17.II.7:1-2. From the **forgiven** world the Son of God is lifted easily into his home. And there he knows that he has always rested there in peace.
Page 354. T-17.II.8:5. Go out in gladness to meet with your Redeemer, and walk with Him in trust out of this world, and into the **real world** of beauty and **forgiveness**.

ANSWER 36A. Practicing **forgiveness** will show you the beauty and holiness of the **real world**, which is the world of all loving thoughts that is a reflection of Heaven. With your physical vision replaced by **Christ's vision** of the **real world**, you will use your **forgiving** perception to see the beauty and true divine holiness of the Son of God as you look upon your brothers and sisters in Christ. Through the eyes of **forgiveness**, you will even look with wonder on the loveliness you will see in the smallest ordinary objects of the world of form, which will appear to you as symbols of God's perfection.

QUESTION 36B. What happens when two people join in a **holy relationship**?

Page 362. T-17.V.1:1. The **holy relationship** is the expression of the **holy instant** in living in this world.
Page 362. T-17.V.2:1. The **holy relationship**, a major step toward the perception of the **real world**, is learned. It is the old, unholy relationship, transformed and seen anew.
Page 362. T-17.V.3:1-2, 9. This invitation is accepted immediately, and the Holy Spirit wastes no time in introducing the practical results of asking Him to enter. At once His goal replaces yours.... For once the unholy relationship has accepted the goal of holiness, it can never again be what it was.
Page 363. T-17.V.5:2, 5. Only a radical shift in purpose could induce a complete change of mind about what the whole relationship is for.... A relationship, undertaken by two individuals for their unholy purposes, suddenly has holiness for its goal.
Page 363. T-17.V.6:1-2, 8. This is the time for *faith*. You let this goal be set for you.... And your relationship has sanity as its purpose.
Page 364. T-17.V.11:1-2. You undertook, together, to invite the Holy Spirit into your relationship. He could not have entered otherwise.
Page 365. T-17.V.14:1-3, 7-9. You and your brother stand together in the holy presence of truth itself. Here is the goal, together with you. Think you not the goal itself will gladly arrange the means for its accomplishment?... You *are* joined in purpose, but remain still separate and divided on the means. Yet the goal is fixed, firm and unalterable, and the means will surely fall in place because the goal is sure. And you will share the gladness of the Sonship that it is so.

ANSWER 36B. When two people join in a **holy relationship**, a **holy instant** occurs and the Holy Spirit enters the relationship. The partners join for a common purpose with common interests, but the Holy Spirit replaces the partners' goals with His goal of holiness. An unholy special relationship based on a trade of specialness can be transformed into a **holy relationship** by the Holy Spirit entering that relationship and replacing the old goal of specialness with the new goal of holiness. The Holy Spirit is allowed to come into the relationship only because of the invitation of both partners. Faith is needed by both partners to maintain the Holy Spirit's new goal of holiness. The partners may be uncertain about the means of pursuing and achieving their common purpose of holiness. However, persistently holding on to the goal of holiness will allow the Holy Spirit to quite naturally provide the means for accomplishing that goal of holiness.

A Simple Framework for Understanding the Course 133

QUESTION 37. When you are uncertain about a situation, what do you need to consider and clarify in order be led by the Holy Spirit?

Page 366. T-17.VI.2:1-9. In any situation in which you are uncertain, the first thing to consider, very simply, is "What do I want to come of this? What is it *for*?" The clarification of the goal belongs at the beginning, for it is this which will determine the outcome. In the ego's procedure this is reversed. The situation becomes the determiner of the outcome, which can be anything. The reason for this disorganized approach is evident. The ego does not know what it wants to come of the situation. It is aware of what it does not want, but only that. It has no positive goal at all.

Page 366. T-17.VI.3:1, 7. Without a clear-cut, positive goal, set at the outset, the situation just seems to happen, and makes no sense until it has already happened.... The absence of a criterion for outcome, set in advance, makes understanding doubtful and evaluation impossible.

Page 366. T-17.VI.4:1-6. The value of deciding in advance what you want to happen is simply that you will perceive the situation as a means to *make* it happen. You will therefore make every effort to overlook what interferes with the accomplishment of your objective, and concentrate on everything that helps you meet it. It is quite noticeable that this approach has brought you closer to the Holy Spirit's sorting out of truth and falsity. The true becomes what can be used to meet the goal. The false becomes the useless from this point of view. The situation now has meaning, but only because the goal has made it meaningful.

Page 366. T-17.VI.5:1-2, 9. The goal of truth has further practical advantages. If the situation is used for truth and sanity, its outcome must be peace.... The Holy Spirit knows that the situation is as the goal determines it, and is experienced according to the goal.

Page 367. T-17.VI.6:1-7. The goal of truth requires faith. Faith is implicit in the acceptance of the Holy Spirit's purpose, and this faith is all-inclusive. Where the goal of truth is set, there faith must be. The Holy Spirit sees the situation as a whole. The goal establishes the fact that everyone involved in it will play his part in its accomplishment. This is inevitable. No one will fail in anything.

ANSWER 37. When you are involved in any situation, you need to clearly identify the goal by asking yourself, "What outcome do I want?" Knowing the positive result that you want in the beginning will actually determine the outcome. The ego will let the situation evolve all by itself without any positive goal in mind, and thus anything might happen. The value of setting the goal is that it will enable you to perceive the situation as a means of achieving the goal. Therefore, you will disregard everything in the situation that interferes with reaching the goal. You will focus all your attention and efforts toward the aspects of the situation that will help you accomplish the goal. The Course recommends making truth the goal of every situation because that is the Holy Spirit's purpose. With the goal of truth, you will be helped by the Holy Spirit to disregard whatever is false in any situation and accept what is true in any situation. Everything you experience in a situation and the situation itself will be is determined by the goal of truth you set for it in the beginning. By setting and maintaining the goal of truth, you will be placing your faith in the Holy Spirit. Investing your faith in the Holy Spirit's purpose of truth means that every person involved in the situation will play his part in manifesting the goal of truth. The Holy Spirit will inspire everyone to bring about the inevitable outcome of truth. Truth always brings the recognition of holiness, resulting in peace of mind.

QUESTION 38. What is required of you to manifest the **miracle** of the **holy instant**?

Pages 380-381. T-18.IV.2:1-3, 8-9. Trust not your good intentions. They are not enough. But trust implicitly your willingness, whatever else may enter.... The **miracle** of the **holy instant** lies in your willingness to let it be what it is. And in your willingness for this lies also your acceptance of yourself as you were meant to be.
Page 381. T-18.IV.3:3, 5-7. Your difficulty with the **holy instant** arises from your fixed conviction that you are not worthy of it.... God did not create His dwelling place unworthy of Him. And if you believe He cannot enter where He wills to be, you must be interfering with His Will. You do not need the strength of willingness to come from you, but only from His Will.
Page 381. T-18.IV.4:1-2, 7. The **holy instant** does not come from your little willingness alone. It is always the result of your small willingness combined with the unlimited power of God's Will.... Your willingness is needed only to make it possible to teach you what they are.
Page 382. T-18.IV.6:4-8. And it is only fear that you will add, if you prepare yourself for love. The preparation for the **holy instant** belongs to Him Who gives it. Release yourself to Him Whose function is release. Do not assume His function for Him. Give Him but what He asks, that you may learn how little is your part, and how great is His.
Page 383. T-18.V.2:1-6. Never approach the **holy instant** after you have tried to remove all fear and hatred from your mind. That is *its* function. Never attempt to overlook your guilt before you ask the Holy

Spirit's help. That is *His* function. Your part is only to offer Him a little willingness to let Him remove all fear and hatred, and to be **forgiven**. On your little faith, joined with His understanding, He will build your part in the **Atonement** and make sure that you fulfill it easily.

Page 384. T-18.V.6:1. When you feel the holiness of your relationship is threatened by anything, stop instantly and offer the Holy Spirit your willingness, in spite of fear, to let Him exchange this instant for the holy one that you would rather have.

ANSWER 38. **Holy instant**s come to everyone. But their impact and frequency depend on how you respond to them. You can open the door to the benefits of the **holy instant** if you are willing to do so. The **holy instant** requires your willingness to let it be the **miracle** that it is. Your willingness to accept the **miracle** of the **holy instant** is a foreshadowing of your eventual acceptance of yourself as the **miracle** of God that you truly are. In order to give your willingness to the **holy instant**, you must give up your false belief that you are not worthy of it, which is directly related to your false belief that you are not worthy of God. When you give your willingness to the **holy instant**, you are merely relying on God's Will for you to be aware of His presence. Bear in mind that you do not have to give a great amount of willingness. You are only asked for a "little willingness" as your small part to go along with the much greater part of willingness supplied by God's Will for you. You do not have to remove your fear, hate, and guilt before you open yourself to the **holy instant** or before you call upon the Holy Spirit. After all, the **holy instant** and the Holy Spirit have been given to you as your means of releasing you from your inner blocks if you only give your little willingness to be healed. Remember that at any time you can ask the Holy Spirit to replace an instant of blockage with a **holy instant** that you deserve as a holy Son of God.

QUESTION 39A. What is it like to go beyond the limitations imposed by the body?

Page 397. T-18.VI.11:1-11. Everyone has experienced what he would call a sense of being transported beyond himself. This feeling of liberation far exceeds the dream of freedom sometimes hoped for in special relationships. It is a sense of actual escape from limitations. If you will consider what this "transportation" really entails, you will realize that it is a sudden unawareness of the body, and a joining of yourself and something else in which your mind enlarges to encompass it. It becomes part of you, as you unite with it. And both become whole, as neither is perceived as separate. What really happens is that you have given up the illusion of a limited awareness, and lost your fear of union. The love that instantly replaces it extends to what has freed you, and unites with it. And while this lasts you are not uncertain of your Identity, and would not limit It. You have escaped from fear to peace, asking no questions of reality, but merely accepting it. You have accepted this instead of the body, and have let yourself be one with something beyond it, simply by not letting your mind be limited by it.

Page 387. T-18.VI.12:1-5. This can occur regardless of the physical distance that seems to be between you and what you join; of your respective positions in space; and of your differences in size and seeming quality. Time is not relevant; it can occur with something past, present or anticipated. The "something" can be anything and anywhere; a sound, a sight, a thought, a memory, and even a general idea without specific reference. Yet in every case, you join it without reservation because you love it, and would be with it. And so you rush to meet it, letting your limits melt away, suspending all the "laws" your body obeys and gently setting them aside.

Pages 387-388. T-18.VI.13:1-6. There is no violence at all in this escape. The body is not attacked, but simply properly perceived. It does not limit you, merely because you would not have it so. You are not really "lifted out" of it; it cannot contain you. You go where you would be, gaining, not losing, a sense of Self. In these instants of release from physical restrictions, you experience much of what happens in the **holy instant**; the lifting of the barriers of time and space, the sudden experience of peace and joy, and, above all, the lack of awareness of the body, and of the questioning whether or not all this is possible.

ANSWER 39A. The feeling of going beyond the body happens to everyone. You experience a decrease or a complete absence of body awareness and in addition experience being united with something or someone beyond the limitations of your small self. You let go of the illusion of separation and directly experience that love is union. In this state, you have let go of fear and accepted that your true identity is love. In your experience of love as union, you can unite with anything and transcend the ordinarily accepted "laws" of time and space that govern the body and limit you. This transportation is just an increase in your awareness of your true Self. Also, this transportation is a clear example of the **holy instant** in which there is a release from time and space, an experience of joy and peace, a release of body awareness, and a reassessment of your true identity.

QUESTION 39B. What is the Course really recommending when it says "you need do nothing"?

Page 390. T-18.VII.7:1-9. To do anything involves the body. And if you recognize you need do nothing, you have withdrawn the body's value from your mind. Here is the quick and open door through which you slip past centuries of effort, and escape from time. This is the way in which sin loses all attraction *right now*. For here is time denied, and past and future gone. Who needs do nothing has no need for time. To do nothing is to rest, and make a place within you where the activity of the body ceases to demand attention. Into this place the Holy Spirit comes, and there abides. He will remain when you forget, and the body's activities return to occupy your conscious mind.
Page 390. T-18.VII.8:1-5. Yet there will always be this place of rest to which you can return. And you will be more aware of this quiet center of the storm than all its raging activity. This quiet center, in which you do nothing, will remain with you, giving you rest in the midst of every busy doing on which you are sent. For from this center will you be directed how to use the body sinlessly. It is this center, from which the body is absent, that will keep it so in your awareness of it.

ANSWER 39B. The Course quotation "you need do nothing" is often misinterpreted to mean that you do not have to do any **meditation**. The exact opposite is true. The Manual encourages teachers of God to set aside two daily periods for **"quiet times"** to direct the mind to God as was learned in the Workbook lessons. In relation to Workbook **meditation** practices, the words "do nothing" refer to doing nothing with your body. Keeping the body still helps release the awareness of time and opens the quiet mind to experiencing the **holy instant**. The Course encourages a wide variety of **meditation** practices as long as they do not reinforce the false belief in sinfulness and unworthiness. By letting the body do nothing in **meditation**, you can find a place of rest within since the body does not divert your attention. During every **quiet time** of **meditation**, you can return to the place of rest where you do nothing. In this quiet center within, you can find peace from the busy activities of the world. This inner rest provides spiritual nourishment, which afterwards will help you navigate through the world without investing in the belief in sin.

QUESTION 40. What is the body's relationship to the ego, to love, to your Self, and to God?

Page 390. T-18.VIII.1:1-2. It is only the awareness of the body that makes love seem limited. For the body *is* a limit on love.
Page 390. T-18.VIII.2:5-6. The body is a tiny fence around a little part of a glorious and complete idea. It draws a circle, infinitely small,

around a very little segment of Heaven, splintered from the whole, proclaiming that within it is your kingdom, where God can enter not.
Page 391. T-18.VIII.3:1-6. Within this kingdom the ego rules, and cruelly. And to defend this little speck of dust it bids you fight against the universe. This fragment of your mind is such a tiny part of it that, could you but appreciate the whole, you would see instantly that it is like the smallest sunbeam to the sun, or like the faintest ripple on the surface of the ocean. In its amazing arrogance, this tiny sunbeam has decided it is the sun; this almost imperceptible ripple hails itself as the ocean. Think how alone and frightened is this little thought, this infinitesimal illusion, holding itself apart against the universe. The sun becomes the sunbeam's "enemy" that would devour it, and the ocean terrifies the little ripple and wants to swallow it.
Page 391. T-18.VIII.6:1-6. Like to the sun and ocean your Self continues, unmindful that this tiny part regards itself as you. It is not missing; it could not exist if it were separate, nor would the Whole be whole without it. It is not a separate kingdom, ruled by an idea of separation from the rest. Nor does a fence surround it, preventing it from joining with the rest, and keeping it apart from its Creator. This little aspect is no different from the whole, being continuous with it and at one with it. It leads no separate life, because its life *is* the oneness in which its being was created.
Page 391. T-18.VIII.7:1. Do not accept this little, fenced-off aspect as yourself. The sun and ocean are as nothing beside what you are.
Page 392. T-18.VIII.8:1-2. Love knows no bodies, and reaches to everything created like itself. Its total lack of limit *is* its meaning.
Pages 392-393. T-18.VIII.11:1-2, 6. The **holy instant** is your invitation to love to enter into your bleak and joyless kingdom, and to transform it into a garden of peace and welcome. Love's answer is inevitable.... And your shining Self will lift the tiny aspect that you tried to hide from Heaven straight to Heaven.

ANSWER 40. The body is intended to be a limitation. It limits your awareness of love, your awareness of your Self, and your awareness of God. The ego relies on the body to prove to you that you are limited and separate. The ego tells you that you are the body, a concrete form that appears to be undeniably real in a concrete world. Through this false identification with the body, the ego substitutes the Reality of Heaven, your true Home, with the apparent reality of this world of form, the home of the body. "The ego is the part of the mind that believes your existence is defined by separation."[197] Although the ego fosters the belief in the body as your reality, it is only a tiny part of the mind that believes it is separate from your Whole Mind that exists forever in Heaven. This tiny part of your mind dominated by the ego cannot be separate from the Whole, yet it can and does provide the illusion of separation. This tiny part of your mind that is sleeping and dreaming of illusions in Heaven has the ability to cause you to lose your awareness of the knowledge of God, given to you in your creation. It is only this tiny part that needs to be transformed in order to bring you salvation. When this happens, your awareness of being in Heaven will be entirely restored. To prepare yourself for awakening, you must learn to let go of your identification with the limitations presented by the ego and the body. This means you must learn to shift your identification toward the limitlessness of love, the limitlessness of your Self, and the limitlessness of God. The way for you to open your mind to the belief in limitlessness is to give your little willingness to welcoming the **holy instant** that will reveal the divine aspects of your true nature beyond limitations.

QUESTION 41. What is the truth about sin and its effects?

Page 402. T-19.II.1:1-2, 6. It is essential that error be not confused with sin, and it is this distinction that makes salvation possible. For error can be corrected, and the wrong made right.... Sin calls for punishment as error for correction, and the belief that punishment *is* correction is clearly insane.
Page 402. T-19.II.2:1-7. Sin is not an error, for sin entails an arrogance which the idea of error lacks. To sin would be to violate reality, and to succeed. Sin is the proclamation that attack is real and guilt is justified. It assumes the Son of God is guilty, and has thus succeeded in losing his innocence and making himself what God created not. Thus is creation seen as not eternal, and the Will of God open to opposition and defeat. Sin is the grand illusion underlying all the ego's grandiosity. For by it God Himself is changed, and rendered incomplete.
Page 402. T-19.II.3:1-4. The Son of God can be mistaken; he can deceive himself; he can even turn the power of his mind against himself. But he *cannot* sin. There is nothing he can do that would really change his reality in any way, nor make him really guilty. That is what sin would do, for such is its purpose.

ANSWER 41. The idea of sin is that your reality, your true nature created by God, can be violated. If you believe that your reality can be violated or changed in any way, then the ramifications of that belief are that you will invite a whole series of other false beliefs. These additional false beliefs are the beliefs that God made a mistake when He created you, that you have offended God, that you should feel guilty, and that you are now separate from God, which is the foundation of your belief in the ego.

The Course maintains that you are now thinking insanely if you believe in sin. An insane person does not know who he is, and you cannot know who you are as long as you believe you are capable of sin. God knows you are made of His Love and deserve only love. Sin tells you that you are guilty and therefore deserve punishment. You are investing in arrogance and even insanity whenever you disagree with what God knows about who you are and what you deserve. By giving up the arrogance of the ego and the belief in sin, you can accept that all your mistakes have done nothing to change your reality and that all your mistakes are correctable. Since all errors are correctable, there is absolutely no justification for sin, guilt, or punishment.

All correction starts with the basic understanding of what needs to be corrected and what does not need to be corrected. Your illusions are what always need to be corrected, and sin is the grand illusion that supports the illusion of the ego itself. What never needs to be corrected is your God-given true nature of love that only needs your acceptance just as it is. That's why your salvation is merely awakening to what has always been true. All mistakes are expressions of a lack of love. All mistakes are corrected by supplying the love that was previously lacking. By supplying the love, you realize that love is your true nature and that your inner love had only been hidden from your awareness and not lost.

QUESTION 42. What role does love play and what role does your brother play in lifting the veil that separates you from your Home in Heaven?

Pages 420-421. T-19.IV.D.5:1-9. Every obstacle that peace must flow across is surmounted in just the same way; the fear that raised it yields to the love beyond, and so the fear is gone. And so it is with this. The desire to get rid of peace and drive the Holy Spirit from you fades in the presence of the quiet recognition that you love Him. The exaltation of the body is given up in favor of the spirit, which you love as you could never love the body. And the appeal of death is lost forever as love's attraction stirs and calls to you. From beyond each of the obstacles to love, Love Itself has called. And each has been surmounted by the power of the attraction of what lies beyond. Your wanting fear seemed to be holding them in place. Yet when you heard the Voice of Love beyond them, you answered and they disappeared.

Page 422. T-19.IV.D.11:4-7. Before complete **forgiveness** you still stand unforgiving. You are afraid of God *because* you fear your brother.

Those you do not **forgive** you fear. And no one reaches love with fear beside him.
Page 422. T-19.IV.D.12:7. Brother, you need **forgiveness** of your brother, for you will share in madness or in Heaven together.
Page 423. T-19.IV.D.14:1-4. Behold your Friend, the Christ Who stands beside you. How holy and how beautiful He is! You thought He sinned because you cast the veil of sin upon Him to hide His loveliness. Yet still He holds **forgiveness** out to you, to share His Holiness.
Page 423. T-19.IV.D.15:8-10. Redemption has been given you to give your brother, and thus receive it. Whom you **forgive** is free, and what you give you share. **Forgive** the sins your brother thinks he has committed, and all the guilt you think you see in him.

ANSWER 42. God calls you to awaken and accept your place in Heaven. But since God is Love, it is equally true that His Love calls you to awaken. Also, you love God, Who created you out of Love. You are irresistibly drawn by the attraction of love, which overcomes every obstacle on your path to awakening. Fear is replaced by love. Your resistance to peace is replaced by love. The misguided glorification of the body is replaced by love. The foolish appeal of death is replaced by love. Love Itself will awaken you with the realization that you are love because you remain just as God created you.

You will fear your brother if you do not **forgive** him, and your fear of your brother contributes to your fear of God. You must learn to **forgive** your brother in order to let go of your fear of him and your fear of God. Your brother whom you have **forgiven** becomes your savior who joins with you in your awakening.

How you perceive your brother will determine how you perceive yourself. You will mistakenly believe you are guilty as long as you believe your brother is guilty. Your **forgiveness** reveals to you that your brother is holy as part of the one Christ and reminds you that you are just as holy and just as much a part of the one Christ as he is.

QUESTION 43A. What will the Holy Spirit do for you when you accept His plan as your one function?

Pages 433-434 T-20.IV.8:4-12. Once you accept His plan as the one function that you would fulfill, there will be nothing else the Holy Spirit will not arrange for you without your effort. He will go before you making straight your path, and leaving in your way no stones to trip on, and no obstacles to bar your way. Nothing you need will be denied you. Not one seeming difficulty but will melt away before you reach it. You need take thought for nothing, careless of everything except the only purpose that you would fulfill. As that was given you, so will its fulfillment be. God's guarantee will hold against all obstacles, for it rests on certainty and not contingency. It rests on *you*. And what can be more certain than a Son of God?

ANSWER 43A. God has a plan for your life. By accepting His plan as your most important function, you give the Holy Spirit permission to arrange everything about your life to facilitate the accomplishment of your part in God's plan. God promises you that you will fulfill your purpose and has assigned the Holy Spirit to give you every possible assistance. The Holy Spirit cannot fail to perform this function.

QUESTION 43B. What is the vision that carries "the memory of what you are"?

Page 447. T-21.I.8:1-6. Beyond the body, beyond the sun and stars, past everything you see and yet somehow familiar, is an arc of golden light that stretches as you look into a great and shining circle. And all the circle fills with light before your eyes. The edges of the circle disappear, and what is in it is no longer contained at all. The light expands and covers everything, extending to infinity forever shining and with no break or limit anywhere. Within it everything is joined in perfect continuity. Nor is it possible to imagine that anything could be outside, for there is nowhere that this light is not.
Page 447. T-21.I.9:1-4. This is the vision of the Son of God, whom you know well. Here is the sight of him who knows his Father. Here is the memory of what you are; a part of this, with all of it within, and joined to all as surely as all is joined in you. Accept the vision that can show you this, and not the body.

ANSWER 43B. The "vision of the Son of God" holds the "memory of what you are." The memory of your true nature recalls your Identity in Heaven where you are fully aware of being both part of the one Christ and paradoxically the whole Christ. This vision of the Son of God is also called the "**face of Christ**." There are lower levels of seeing the shining **face of Christ** that can even be perceived as you look at the divine presence in your brother. But when you see the **face of Christ** in the vision of the Son of God, you will be seeing the unmistakable blazing light at the deepest level of the **real world**. It is only an image of Christ, but it reflects the reality of Christ that you are. It is a vision of a vast circle of light that expands infinitely, encompassing everything that exists. This vision is the "doorway" to Heaven. When you see this vast expanding circle of blazing light, it will remind you of your intense

A Simple Framework for Understanding the Course 143

love for God. With your true nature of love revealed, you will leap into God's Arms as He takes the final step of lifting your mind back to the Mind of Christ in Heaven. This is your final awakening that must come to every Son of God because this is God's Will for you.

QUESTION 44. What's important to know about the power and the effects of your decision making?

Page 448. T-21.II.2:1-7. This is the only thing that you need do for vision, happiness, release from pain and the complete escape from sin, all to be given you. Say only this, but mean it with no reservations, for here the power of salvation lies:

> *I am responsible for what I see.*
> *I choose the feelings I experience, and I decide upon*
>   *the goal I would achieve.*
> *And everything that seems to happen to me I ask for,*
>   *and receive as I have asked.*

Deceive yourself no longer that you are helpless in the face of what is done to you. Acknowledge but that you have been mistaken, and all effects of your mistakes will disappear.

Page 448. T-21.II.3:1-8. It is impossible the Son of God be merely driven by events outside of him. It is impossible that happenings that come to him were not his choice. His power of decision is the determiner of every situation in which he seems to find himself by chance or accident. No accident nor chance is possible within the universe as God created it, outside of which is nothing. Suffer, and you decided sin was your goal. Be happy, and you gave the power of decision to Him Who must decide for God for you. This is the little gift you offer to the Holy Spirit, and even this He gives to you to give yourself. For by this gift is given you the power to release your savior, that he may give salvation unto you.

Page 450. T-21.II.11:1-5. It is as needful that you recognize you made the world you see, as that you recognize that you did not create yourself. *They are the same mistake.* Nothing created not by your Creator has any influence over you. And if you think what you have made can tell you what you see and feel, and place your faith in its ability to do so, you are denying your Creator and believing that you made yourself. For if you think the world you made has power to make you what it wills, you are confusing Son and Father; effect and Source.

ANSWER 44. The most important thing to know about the power of your decision making is that all your experiences are the result of your own decisions. You are experiencing exactly what you have asked for in every situation. Understanding that you are always responsible for your own experiences frees you from imagining that you are a helpless victim of something outside of your own control. If you feel you are a victim in any situation, you can let go of this mistaken belief and free yourself from the effects of believing you are a victim.

Since your decision making is so powerful in the effects it brings to you, you must be very careful about what goal you decide you want to achieve. If you choose the ego to be your guide for decision making, you will choose goals that will reinforce the belief in separation and that will produce suffering. Your wisest choice, which will bring you happiness, is to let the Holy Spirit be your guide. You can safely let the Holy Spirit decide for you because He will choose the goal of holiness and will "decide for God for you." By giving the Holy Spirit the power to choose holiness for you, you will in turn see holiness in your brother. Seeing holiness in your brother frees him to believe in his own holiness, and he will become your savior, reminding you of your holiness.

God the Father is the First Cause. You, as His Son, are the effect. Because you are the effect of God, you cannot create yourself. The mistake of believing you created yourself is the exact same mistake as believing you did not make the world. These two mistakes can be corrected by deciding to believe that God created you and by looking at the logical ramifications of this belief. If God created you, He must have created you like Himself as an expression of perfect holiness and perfect love. Since God is Spirit without a body, He must have created you only as a spiritual being and not as a body. Logically, a world of bodies and a world filled with expressions of hate, suffering, and war could not possibly have been made by God. Because the God of Love could not have made this world of discontent, it must be an illusory world manufactured by those who have identified with their bodies. If you believe the world of form can make decisions for you, you must believe God did not create you. When you disown God as your Father, you end up believing you have created yourself. The ego, your false identity, which you have made as a means of denying God, mistakenly believes that you can create yourself, making yourself into whatever you want to be. Also, your ego can mistakenly believe your fabricated illusions have power over you and have taken away your free will. Nevertheless, your reality remains forever in God. Only what God created in you is real and has any influence over you. What God did not create in you does not exist and therefore cannot influence you, except in the imaginings of your ego. Thus you have never lost your innate holiness, love, and perfection given to you by God, even when your ego imagines that the world has taken away your power of decision and has made you into a victim. In truth, you cannot be a victim of anything outside of your own power of decision making.

QUESTION 45. What does **forgiveness** really **forgive**, and who walks with you on your path of **forgiveness**?

Page 505. T-24.III.1:1-8. **Forgiveness** is the end of specialness. Only illusions can be **forgiven**, and then they disappear. **Forgiveness** is release from all illusions, and that is why it is impossible but partly to **forgive**. No one who clings to one illusion can see himself as sinless, for he holds one error to himself as lovely still. And so he calls it "unforgivable," and makes it sin. How can he then give his **forgiveness** wholly, when he would not receive it for himself? For it is sure he would receive it wholly the instant that he gave it so. And thus his secret guilt would disappear, **forgiven** by himself.

Page 509. T-24.V.3:1-7. Where could your peace arise *but* from **forgiveness**? The Christ in you looks only on the truth, and sees no condemnation that could need **forgiveness**. He is at peace *because* He sees no sin. Identify with Him, and what has He that you have not? He is your eyes, your ears, your hands, your feet. How gentle are the sights He sees, the sounds He hears. How beautiful His hand that holds His brother's, and how lovingly He walks beside him, showing him what can be seen and heard, and where he will see nothing and there is no sound to hear.

Page 510. T-24.V.7:1-2, 4-10. Yet is He quiet, for He knows that love is in you now, and safely held in you by that same hand that holds your brother's in your own. Christ's hand holds all His brothers in Himself.... He reaches through them, holding out His hand, that everyone may bless all living things, and see their holiness. And He rejoices that these sights are yours, to look upon with Him and share His joy. His perfect lack of specialness He offers you, that you may save all living things from death, receiving from each one the gift of life that your **forgiveness** offers to your Self. The sight of Christ is all there is to see. The song of Christ is all there is to hear. The hand of Christ is all there is to hold. There is no journey but to walk with Him.

ANSWER 45. **Forgiveness** always **forgives** only illusions. **Forgiveness** is accomplished by looking past illusions and by looking for what is real. If you think that what you are forgiving is real, you will not be able to **forgive** wholeheartedly without resentment. By realizing that everything you **forgive** is unreal, you understand there is no reason to withhold your **forgiveness**. True **forgiveness** merely recognizes that illusions are unreal and offer nothingness, and so you lose nothing by giving them up. **Forgiveness** sees value only in what is real and affirms the value it sees.

God brings His Love and Holiness into all of reality, and **forgiveness** is the perception of the reality of this love and holiness. Your brother is real, although his body and the mistakes of his ego are illusions. You can **forgive** only your brother's mistakes and your own mistakes—meaning you **forgive** your brother's illusions about himself and your own illusions about your brother. If you see with your ego, you will have condemning judgments in which you will see guilt in yourself and in your brother. Your **forgiveness** is merely a letting go of your own false judgments, which are all illusions. Since illusions are nothing and not real, they did not happen in reality and so did not happen at all. Thus **forgiveness** merely **forgives** *what never happened*.

When you look at your brother with the forgiving eyes of Christ, you will see that there is nothing there in his reality that needs to be **forgiven**. Thus you can **forgive** wholeheartedly without resentment and can have peace of mind. As you learn to **forgive**, you will understand that Christ walks with you on your path. As you increasingly open yourself to **Christ's vision**, you will increasingly see the reality of the beauty, love, and holiness of your brother. You will gladly take your brother's hand. He will just as gladly take your hand as you each recognize the divine love within. You will become saviors for each other in your process of awakening, and you will both take the hand of Christ. At first, when using **Christ's vision** to perceive the holiness of your brother, you will see some of the light shining through the **face of Christ**. When the time is right, you will experience a higher level of consciousness and will see the deepest level of the **face of Christ**, which involves seeing the vision of a blazing light. Perceiving this final vision of the Son of God awakens the memory of God, and then your Father Himself will take the final step of lifting you back to Heaven.

QUESTION 46A. What's the importance of having two different makers of the world?

Page 524. T-25.III.4:1-3. There is another Maker of the world, the simultaneous Corrector of the mad belief that anything could be established and maintained without some link that kept it still within the laws of God; not as the law itself upholds the universe as God created it, but in some form adapted to the need the Son of God

believes he has. Corrected error is the error's end. And thus has God protected still His Son, even in error.
Page 524. T-25.III.5:1-4. There is another purpose in the world that error made, because it has another Maker Who can reconcile its goal with His Creator's purpose. In His perception of the world, nothing is seen but justifies **forgiveness** and the sight of perfect sinlessness. Nothing arises but is met with instant and complete **forgiveness**. Nothing remains an instant, to obscure the sinlessness that shines unchanged, beyond the pitiful attempts of specialness to put it out of mind, where it must be, and light the body up instead of it.
Page 524. T-25.III.6:1-4. Everyone here has entered darkness, yet no one has entered it alone. Nor need he stay more than an instant. For he has come with Heaven's Help within him, ready to lead him out of darkness into light at any time. The time he chooses can be any time, for help is there, awaiting but his choice.

ANSWER 46A. It is not enough to recognize that God did not create the world and that you and all the other sleeping Sons of God made the illusory world of form. You must also understand that there is another Maker of the world Who is the Holy Spirit. God had to protect His Sons from their illusions of separation by assigning the Holy Spirit the task of bringing reflections of God's laws into the world of form. The Holy Spirit is the Maker of the **real world**, the **face of Christ**, and the **Atonement** to facilitate His role as the Corrector of the illusory belief in separation. The sleeping Sons of God made the world for the purpose of expressing specialness. God responded immediately by creating the Holy Spirit, Who became the Maker of the world that brought in God's purpose of **forgiveness**. Because there are two makers of the world, you have two choices: You can choose the ego's expressions of darkness made to proclaim specialness, or you can choose the Holy Spirit's help, including His expressions of the light that reflect Heaven.

QUESTION 46B. What is the importance of your special function?

Page 530. T-25.VI.4:1-3. Such is the Holy Spirit's kind perception of specialness; His use of what you made, to heal instead of harm. To each He gives a special function in salvation he alone can fill; a part for only him. Nor is the plan complete until he finds his special function, and fulfills the part assigned to him, to make himself complete within a world where incompletion rules.
Page 530. T-25.VI.5:1-11. Here, where the laws of God do not prevail in perfect form, can he yet do *one* perfect thing and make *one* perfect

choice. And by this act of special faithfulness to one perceived as other than himself, he learns the gift was given to himself, and so they must be one. **Forgiveness** is the only function meaningful in time. It is the means the Holy Spirit uses to translate specialness from sin into salvation. **Forgiveness** is for all. But when it rests on all it is complete, and every function of this world completed with it. Then is time no more. Yet while in time, there is still much to do. And each must do what is allotted him, for on his part does all the plan depend. He *has* a special part in time for so he chose, and choosing it, he made it for himself. His wish was not denied but changed in form, to let it serve his brother and himself, and thus become a means to save instead of lose.

Page 530. T-25.VI.7:1-10. The Holy Spirit needs your special function, that His may be fulfilled. Think not you lack a special value here. You wanted it, and it is given you. All that you made can serve salvation easily and well. The Son of God can make no choice the Holy Spirit cannot employ on his behalf, and not against himself. Only in darkness does your specialness appear to be attack. In light, you see it as your special function in the plan to save the Son of God from all attack, and let him understand that he is safe, as he has always been, and will remain in time and in eternity alike. This is the function given you for your brother. Take it gently, then, from your brother's hand, and let salvation be perfectly fulfilled in you. Do this *one* thing, that everything be given you.

ANSWER 46B. Participating in the separation, you made specialness as a means of separating yourself from your brother. Since you have asked for specialness, the Holy Spirit gives you one particular type of specialness. Unlike the ego, the Holy Spirit uses the idea of specialness positively by giving you a *special function*. Your special function is the role assigned to you alone. No one else can fulfill your special function in God's plan of salvation designed to awaken all of God's children. Because God's plan of salvation is based on the practical application of **forgiveness**, your special function is always a specific expression of **forgiveness** that is assigned to you. Your **forgiveness** that you give to specific brothers and sisters is essential for you to complete your part in God's plan and is absolutely necessary for the overall completion of God's plan. Your special function of **forgiveness** is always a blessing to your brother that acknowledges his holiness and reminds you of your holiness. This acknowledgment is necessary for your brother and you so you both can awaken to your eternal holiness in Heaven.

QUESTION 47. What can you do to let go of time—meaning let go of the past and future in order to accept the eternal now?

Page 551. T-26.V.6:1-10. **Forgiveness** is the great release from time. It is the key to learning that the past is over. Madness speaks no more. There *is* no other teacher and no other way. For what has been undone no longer is. And who can stand upon a distant shore, and dream himself across an ocean, to a place and time that have long since gone by? How real a hindrance can this dream be to where he really is? For this is fact, and does not change whatever dreams he has. Yet can he still imagine he is elsewhere, and in another time. In the extreme, he can delude himself that this is true, and pass from mere imagining into belief and into madness, quite convinced that where he would prefer to be, he *is*.

Page 551. T-26.V.9:1-5. Forget the time of terror that has been so long ago corrected and undone. Can sin withstand the Will of God? Can it be up to you to see the past and put it in the present? You can *not* go back. And everything that points the way in the direction of the past but sets you on a mission whose accomplishment can only be unreal.

Page 552. T-26.V.13:1-4. Each day, and every minute in each day, and every instant that each minute holds, you but relive the single instant when the time of terror took the place of love. And so you die each day to live again, until you cross the gap between the past and present, which is not a gap at all. Such is each life; a seeming interval from birth to death and on to life again, a repetition of an instant gone by long ago that cannot be relived. And all of time is but the mad belief that what is over is still here and now.

Page 552. T-26.V.14:1-5. **Forgive** the past and let it go, for it *is* gone. You stand no longer on the ground that lies between the worlds. You have gone on, and reached the world that lies at Heaven's gate. There is no hindrance to the Will of God, nor any need that you repeat again a journey that was over long ago. Look gently on your brother, and behold the world in which perception of your hate has been transformed into a world of love.

ANSWER 47. Before you can let go of the idea of time, you must first recognize that time is entirely an illusion. According to the Course, the "tiny tick of time" called the "separation" was healed immediately by God when He responded by creating the Holy Spirit as His Answer. Perfect peace continued undisturbed in Heaven where you remain even now while dreaming of separation. The instant of separation is now gone, yet this one instant appears to you as the illusion of the passage of time.

Forgiveness is your best means of letting go of the illusion of time. **Forgiveness** always releases illusions and then replaces them with the recognition of reality. Currently you are dreaming in Heaven where the formlessness of spirit in the eternal now is the only reality. Yet the part of your sleeping mind that is dominated by the ego has dreamed up a world of space and time and is lost in the illusions of sin. **Forgiveness** overlooks every illusion in your dream world that is not a reflection of Heaven. **Forgiveness** looks for reflections of God's Love and the divine presence within the overall illusion of space and time.

Since God instantly corrected the original error of the separation when He created the Holy Spirit, why is it important to realize that the separation was a mistake? Perhaps you have heard the common saying: "Those who do not learn from history are doomed to repeat it." Although the original mistake of the separation was healed long ago, with the passage of time you are amazingly repeating that same error. You are reliving the first instant of separation so each successive instant has been merely an expression of holding on to the past. You are reliving what the Course calls the "time of terror." Thus you are unknowingly experiencing a *post-traumatic stress disorder* (PTSD), which is defined as an anxiety disorder that is an ongoing result of a traumatic event, in this case the trauma of the separation.

But is there any karmic debt that must be paid for the mistake of the original separation? No, since God has already corrected this mistake. God knows you deserve only love. Cause and effect exist because God is the Cause and you are His Effect. However, God does not believe in karma or any karmic retribution. When you experience what you call "karma," you are merely receiving the results of your past behavior that you assign to yourself based on what you consciously or subconsciously feel you deserve. If you feel you have done good deeds, you will reward yourself. If you feel you have done bad deeds, you will punish yourself. This self-imposed accounting system fosters a guilty self-image. To remove this guilty self-image requires only a change in thinking that will allow you to accept yourself as the innocent Son of God that you already are. True **forgiveness** enables you to substitute the ego's false and unloving perception of you with the Holy Spirit's true and loving perception of your true nature. This change in thinking, called a **miracle**, releases your illusions about yourself, including the illusion that your past determines your present condition.

Forgiveness reminds you that there is no need to relive the original trauma of the separation, which is gone forever and can never return, except in your deluded imaginings. **Forgiveness** teaches you to let go of your fear of this past trauma and replace it with the eternal now.

Forgiveness overlooks the world of fear you have manufactured because of your fear of the separation. Instead of illusions, **forgiveness** reveals to you the world of loving perceptions that is the **real world**, which leads to awakening in Heaven. **Forgiveness** enables you to let go of your only block to awakening in Heaven. This persistent block is your current ego condition of perpetuating your misguided belief in a nonexistent separation between you and God and between you and your brothers and sisters.

QUESTION 48. Why can't you **forgive** your brother while still believing he is guilty?

Pages 568-569. T-27.II.2:1-10. The unhealed cannot pardon. For they are the witnesses that pardon is unfair. They would retain the consequences of the guilt they overlook. Yet no one can **forgive** a sin that he believes is real. And what has consequences must be real, because what it has done is there to see. **Forgiveness** is not pity, which but seeks to pardon what it thinks to be the truth. Good cannot *be* returned for evil, for **forgiveness** does not first establish sin and then **forgive** it. Who can say and mean, "My brother, you have injured me, and yet, because I am the better of the two, I pardon you my hurt." His pardon and your hurt cannot exist together. One denies the other and must make it false.
Page 569. T-27.II.3:1-3, 9-11. To witness sin and yet **forgive** it is a paradox that reason cannot see. For it maintains what has been done to you deserves no pardon. And by giving it, you grant your brother mercy but retain the proof he is not really innocent.... **Forgiveness** cannot be for one and not the other. Who **forgives** is healed. And in his healing lies the proof that he has truly pardoned, and retains no trace of condemnation that he still would hold against himself or any living thing.
Page 569. T-27.II.4:1-7. **Forgiveness** is not real unless it brings a healing to your brother and yourself. You must attest his sins have no effect on you to demonstrate they are not real. How else could he be guiltless? And how could his innocence be justified unless his sins have no effect to warrant guilt? Sins are beyond **forgiveness** just because they would entail effects that cannot be undone and overlooked entirely. In their undoing lies the proof that they are merely errors. Let yourself be healed that you may be forgiving, offering salvation to your brother and yourself. False **forgiveness** sees sin as real and cannot overlook reality.

ANSWER 48. If you believe your brother is actually guilty, you cannot overlook your belief that guilt is real. If you attempt to overlook your brother's guilt, you will feel you are hiding the truth about him by this kind of **forgiveness** that you will believe is self-deception. Fortunately, true **forgiveness** can overlook guilt because of the simple truth that your brother is just as holy now as when God created him. There is nothing your brother can do to lose that God-given holiness.

True **forgiveness** sees sins as merely illusions. Illusions are easy to overlook because they are not real. False **forgiveness** says that your brother has really hurt you, but you are better than him so you pity him and pardon him for his harmfulness. True **forgiveness** says that your actions have produced no effect on your reality since you in your true nature cannot be harmed by illusions. By demonstrating that your brother's mistakes have not harmed you in any way, you prove to him that his actions have had no effect that would warrant the belief in guilt. True **forgiveness** recognizes the truth of holiness in your brother and reminds you of your own holiness. True **forgiveness** unites you with your brother as your equal. When your **forgiveness** brings him healing, you in turn receive the healing that you have given. You offer your brother salvation from self-condemnation. Then he becomes your mirror in which you see your own salvation from self-condemnation reflected back to you. Thus you become saviors for each other.

QUESTION 49A. What is the "central figure" playing the role of the "hero"?

Page 585. T-27.VIII.1:1. The body is the central figure in the dreaming of the world.
Page 586. T-27.VIII.3:1-5. The body's serial adventures, from the time of birth to dying are the theme of every dream the world has ever had. The "hero" of this dream will never change, nor will its purpose. Though the dream itself takes many forms, and seems to show a great variety of places and events wherein its "hero" finds itself, the dream has but one purpose, taught in many ways. This single lesson does it try to teach again, and still again, and yet once more; that it is cause and not effect. And you are its effect, and cannot be its cause.
Page 586. T-27.VIII.4:1-5. Thus are you not the dreamer, but the dream. And so you wander idly in and out of places and events that it contrives. That this is all the body does is true, for it is but a figure in a dream. But who reacts to figures in a dream unless he sees them as if they were real? The instant that he sees them as they are they have no more effects on him, because he understands he gave them their effects by causing them and making them seem real.

ANSWER 49A. The following sentence brings clarity to Chapter 27: "The body is the central figure in the dreaming of the world." This quote comes from the section titled "The Hero of the Dream," and it is saying that the hero of your dream of separation is the body. Just think of all the time and energy you spend in taking care of the body. This emphasis on the body is the ego's means of keeping you locked into the false belief that separation is your reality. The body is only an illusion, but it is a very convincing actor in the drama of your dream. The body gives you the false impression that you are the effect of the dream and you are not the cause. Yet you are in fact the dreamer who has caused the dream and the body within it. Awakening, when it finally comes, will be a release from the illusion of the body and an acceptance of the formlessness of your true spiritual nature in the one Self—in the one Christ.

QUESTION 49B. How is the "complete picture of the Son of God" described in Chapter 28 different from the "vision of the Son of God" and the "**face of Christ**" described in other chapters?

Pages 599-600. T-28.IV.8:1-6. The Holy Spirit's function is to take the broken picture of the Son of God and put the pieces into place again. This holy picture, healed entirely, does He hold out to every separate piece that thinks it is a picture in itself. To each He offers his Identity, which the whole picture represents, instead of just a little, broken bit that he insisted was himself. And when he sees this picture he will recognize himself. If you share not your brother's evil dream, this is the picture that the **miracle** will place within the little gap, left clean of all the seeds of sickness and of sin. And here the Father will receive His Son, because His Son was gracious to himself.
Page 600. T-28.IV.9:1-7. I thank You, Father, knowing You will come to close each little gap that lies between the broken pieces of Your holy Son. Your Holiness, complete and perfect, lies in every one of them. And they are joined because what is in one is in them all. How holy is the smallest grain of sand, when it is recognized as being part of the completed picture of God's Son! The forms the broken pieces seem to take mean nothing. For the whole is in each one. And every aspect of the Son of God is just the same as every other part.

ANSWER 49B. Chapter 28 describes the "broken picture of the Son of God" to represent all the sleeping parts of the Sonship. The broken pieces of the Son of God are all the seekers who have identified with the ego and their bodies and who seem to live in the world of space and time. The function of the Holy Spirit is to show the "whole picture" of the Son of God to each seeker, who thought he was only a broken and separate part. When the seeker sees the "completed picture of the God's Son," his mind is healed, and he recognizes himself as the holy Son of God. This happens because this completed picture shows the seeker the image of his true Identity as the one Christ. This picture of his Identity is only an image, but seeing this reflection is the place where the Father receives His Son. This place is the "holy meeting place" where God takes the final step of awakening His Son from his dreams of separation.

The broken pieces of the Son of God seem to be the forms of each seeker's physical body in a limited world of separate forms. But all the various forms are merely illusions of separation and so mean nothing. The truth is revealed by seeing the whole picture of the Son of God. This revealed truth is that every seeker is an aspect of the Son of God and simultaneously each aspect is paradoxically the whole. Since each aspect is a part of the one Son of God and the whole of the one Son of God, every aspect is perfectly equal to every other aspect.

The "completed picture of God's Son" is exactly the same as what other sections of the Course call the "vision of the Son of God" and also call the "**face of Christ**." When **Christ's vision** given by the Holy Spirit reveals the deepest level of seeing the **face of Christ**, you will see a perfect image of your Self. This image of the Son of God, which is seen in a blazing light, will bring back the memory of God. As you awaken in Heaven, you will accept your paradoxical nature— the truth that you are a part of Christ and also the whole Christ.

QUESTION 50. In addition to Jesus, called your "elder brother" in the Course, who is your savior and why is this savior so important?

Page 611. T-29.III.3:2-12. You cannot wake yourself. Yet you can let yourself be wakened. You can overlook your brother's dreams. So perfectly can you **forgive** him his illusions he becomes your savior from your dreams. And as you see him shining in the space of light where God abides within the darkness, you will see that God Himself is where his body is. Before this light the body disappears, as heavy shadows must give way to light. The darkness cannot choose that it remain. The coming of the light means it is gone. In glory will you see your brother then, and understand what really fills the gap so long perceived as keeping you apart. There, in its place, God's witness has set forth the gentle way of kindness to God's Son. Whom you **forgive** is given power to **forgive** you your illusions. By your gift of freedom is it given unto you.

Pages 611-612. T-29.III.4:1-4. Make way for love, which you did not create, but which you can extend. On earth this means **forgive** your brother, that the darkness may be lifted from your mind. When light has come to him through your **forgiveness**, he will not forget his savior, leaving him unsaved. For it was in your face he saw the light that he would keep beside him, as he walks through darkness to the everlasting light.
Page 612. T-29.III.5:1-7. How holy are you, that the Son of God can be your savior in the midst of dreams of desolation and disaster. See how eagerly he comes, and steps aside from heavy shadows that have hidden him, and shines on you in gratitude and love. He is himself, but not himself alone. And as his Father lost not part of him in your creation, so the light in him is brighter still because you gave your light to him, to save him from the dark. And now the light in you must be as bright as shines in him. This is the spark that shines within the dream; that you can help him waken, and be sure his waking eyes will rest on you. And in his glad salvation you are saved.

ANSWER 50. The Course calls Jesus your "elder brother," and he is your savior as you open yourself to him. Yet any one of your brothers has the potential to be your savior. You and your brothers are asleep in Heaven and dreaming of this world. You can continue to dream together, or you can wake up together. You do not have the power to awaken yourself. You do have the power to heal your brother's mind, which helps him to awaken. In turn, your brother blesses you for your **forgiveness** and becomes your savior by empowering you to **forgive** yourself. By helping your brother to heal his mind, you can heal your own mind, leading to your awakening. Your primary means of healing others and likewise healing yourself is **forgiveness**, which heals the perception of separation. When you **forgive** your brother, you join with him and overcome the sense of separation manufactured by dreams of space and time. You are your brother's savior and your brother is your savior because **forgiveness** is mutually beneficial.

As you **forgive** your brother's dreams, your own dreams give way to your perception of the divine presence. The body is the gap that seems to separate you from your brother. The solid illusion that your brother's body presents to normal consciousness becomes transparent as the light of God shines through because of your **forgiveness**. When you **forgive** your brother, you see the light in him, and he also sees the light within you. You even give your light and love to him, and he gives his light and love to you. Light and love are actually exchanged in this **miracle** of **forgiveness**, reminding you both that you have never lost the light of Heaven, even while you seem to be immersed in your dark dreams. God created light and love, and you can extend both on earth through **forgiveness**. This is your way to claim the light and love that is your true nature and your brother's true nature.

QUESTION 51. What is an idol, and how do idols affect you and your relationships with others?

Page 619. T-29.VIII.1:6-8. An idol is an image of your brother that you would value more than what he is. Idols are made that he may be replaced, no matter what their form. And it is this that never is perceived and recognized.

Page 619. T-29.VIII.2:1-2, 4. Let not their form deceive you. Idols are but substitutes for your reality.... They have the power to supply your lacks, and add the value that you do not have.

Page 620. T-29.VIII.3:1-2, 5. An idol is a false impression, or a false belief; some form of anti-Christ, that constitutes a gap between the Christ and what you see. An idol is a wish, made tangible and given form, and thus perceived as real and seen outside the mind.... All forms of anti-Christ oppose the Christ.

Page 620. T-29.VIII.4:1. This world of idols *is* a veil across the **face of Christ**, because its purpose is to separate your brother from yourself.

Page 620. T-29.VIII.5:1-3. What is an idol? Nothing! It must be believed before it seems to come to life, and given power that it may be feared.

Page 621. T-29.VIII.8:4-9, 11-13. The world believes in idols. No one comes unless he worshipped them, and still attempts to seek for one that yet might offer him a gift reality does not contain. Each worshipper of idols harbors hope his special deities will give him more than other men possess. It must be more. It does not really matter more of what; more beauty, more intelligence, more wealth, or even more affliction and more pain. But more of something is an idol for.... Be not deceived by forms the "something" takes. An idol is a means for getting more. And it is this that is against God's Will.

Page 621. T-29.VIII.9:5-11. For more than Heaven can you never have. If Heaven is within, why would you seek for idols that would make of Heaven less, to give you more than God bestowed upon your brother and on you, as one with Him? God gave you all there is. And to be sure you could not lose it, did He also give the same to every living thing as well. And thus is every living thing a part of you, as of Himself. No idol can establish you as more than God. But you will never be content with being less.

ANSWER 51. An idol is something that you accept and value as being worth more than reality. An idol is a substitute for God or Heaven or any other aspect of the divine presence. An idol is always a belief in something that does not exist, but which seems more desirable than reality. Therefore, idols must be unreal, but they remain appealing as long as you invest in illusions. You would not believe in your illusions if you could not see them as being valuable. Idols serve the purpose of sustaining your belief in your world of illusions.

For example, as long as you value idols, you will see only an image of your brother, such as his body. Also, you will not truly value your brother or see his reality in God. Thus idols allow you to persistently separate yourself from your brother and support the belief in your ego. Idols are always false beliefs. Because idols are false, holding on to them means that you do not want the truth. Idols represent the wish for what can never be true, and so idols are the currency of self-deception. If you decide you want to see the **face of Christ** and wake up in Heaven, you will have to let go of the idols that blind you to the divine presence underlying all of life.

Holding on to idols demonstrates a desire to have specialness. The wish to be better than your brother is the foundation of specialness, and therefore specialness always seeks more of something. Idols offer more of something—more of anything unreal—in order to fulfill the manufactured need for specialness. If you want to let go of idols, you will have to release your striving for specialness and accept your true equality with your brother.

QUESTION 52A. When you join your brother in the one purpose of **forgiveness**, whose hand do you hold and whose face will you see?

Page 636. T-30.V.7:1-8. When brothers join in purpose in the world of fear, they stand already at the edge of the **real world**. Perhaps they still look back, and think they see an idol that they want. Yet has their path been surely set away from idols toward reality. For when they joined their hands it was Christ's hand they took, and they will look on Him Whose hand they hold. The **face of Christ** is looked upon before the Father is remembered. For He must be unremembered till His Son has reached beyond **forgiveness** to the Love of God. Yet is the Love of Christ accepted first. And then will come the knowledge They are One.

ANSWER 52A. When you take your brother's hand by joining in the purpose of **forgiveness**, you are likewise taking the hand of Christ. As you look upon your brother's face, you can see the divine light shining through him to reveal the **face of Christ**. There are different levels of seeing the **face of Christ**, just as the sun can be seen while being partially obscured by clouds. When you look at your brother, you may be seeing the **face of Christ** only dimly at the lower levels of the **real world** of loving thoughts. Eventually you will be able to see the **face of Christ** as a blazing light expanding infinitely at the deepest level of the **real world**. This final vision must be seen before you can completely remember your Father and His infinite Love for you. Only then will you let go of all your fear of God and recognize your place in the Sonship and awaken in Heaven.

QUESTION 52B. Why is anger never justified and **forgiveness** always justified?

Page 638. T-30.VI.1:1-9. Anger is *never* justified. Attack has *no* foundation. It is here escape from fear begins, and will be made complete. Here is the **real world** given in exchange for dreams of terror. For it is on this **forgiveness** rests, and is but natural. You are not asked to offer pardon where attack is due, and would be justified. For that would mean that you **forgive** a sin by overlooking what is really there. This is not pardon. For it would assume that, by responding in a way which is not justified, your pardon will become the answer to attack that has been made. And thus is pardon inappropriate, by being granted where it is not due.

Page 638. T-30.VI.2:1-5. Pardon is *always* justified. It has a sure foundation. You do not **forgive** the unforgivable, nor overlook a real attack that calls for punishment. Salvation does not lie in being asked to make unnatural responses which are inappropriate to what is real. Instead, it merely asks that you respond appropriately to what is not real by not perceiving what has not occurred.

Page 638. T-30.VI.3:1-8. This understanding is the only change that lets the **real world** rise to take the place of dreams of terror. Fear cannot arise unless attack is justified, and if it had a real foundation pardon would have none. The **real world** is achieved when you perceive the basis of **forgiveness** is quite real and fully justified. While you regard it as a gift unwarranted, it must uphold the guilt you would "**forgive**." Unjustified **forgiveness** is attack. And this is all the world can ever give. It pardons "sinners" sometimes, but remains aware that they have sinned. And so they do not merit the **forgiveness** that it gives.

Pages 638-639. T-30.VI.4:1. This is the false **forgiveness** which the world employs to keep the sense of sin alive.

Page 639. T-30.VI.5:1-4. **Forgiveness** recognized as merited will heal. It gives the **miracle** its strength to overlook illusions. This is how you learn that you must be **forgiven** too. There can be no appearance that can not be overlooked.

ANSWER 52B. If you feel you have been attacked and harmed, you will believe your anger in return is justified. To believe anger is justified, you must also believe the combination of the ego and the body is your identity because egos and bodies can be attacked and harmed. But what if you are not an ego and not a body? What if you are actually invulnerable because your true Identity exists in Heaven? What if you can actually never be a victim because even in this world of dreams, you are responsible for everything that you experience? All your experiences come to you only at your own invitation. The Course maintains you are indeed invulnerable and you can never be a victim. Thus your anger is never justified. Your anger is merely a projection of guilt upon your brother and a failure to perceive the true holiness that is in all your brothers and sisters and, of course, in you as well.

Forgiveness is always justified because you pardon only illusions that never existed in the first place. Thus **forgiveness** is merely the giving up of the judgments of separation in your mind to recognize you were never separate from your brother. If it is true that anger is never justified, then it makes sense that pardon is always deserved. **Forgiveness** recognizes that your brother never deserves your anger and your brother always deserves your love. The mistakes your brother makes at the form level are expressions of a lack of love. If you see your brother's mistake and supply him with the love that was lacking, you will be offering him healing that he needs. The healing you offer him will help him to correct his mistakes and will likewise heal your own mind along with his. The light and love you give are given back to you, and **forgiveness** allows this exchange, called a **"miracle,"** to happen. The nightmares of this dreaming world are always grievances against others and against the world itself. **Miracles** of **forgiveness** replace grievances in your brother and also replace self-condemning grievances in your own mind. **Forgiveness** is always justified because healing is always justified.

QUESTION 53A. What self-concept masks do you wear?

Page 656. T-31.V.2:1-9. A concept of the self is made by you. It bears no likeness to yourself at all. It is an idol, made to take the place of your reality as Son of God. The concept of the self the world would teach is not the thing that it appears to be. For it is made to serve two purposes, but one of which the mind can recognize. The first presents the face of innocence, the aspect acted on. It is this face that smiles and charms and even seems to love. It searches for companions and it looks, at times with pity, on the suffering, and sometimes offers solace. It believes that it is good within an evil world.

Page 656. T-31.V.3:1-4. This aspect can grow angry, for the world is wicked and unable to provide the love and shelter innocence deserves. And so this face is often wet with tears at the injustices the world accords to those who would be generous and good. This aspect never makes the first attack. But every day a hundred little things make small assaults upon its innocence, provoking it to irritation, and at last to open insult and abuse.

Page 656. T-31.V.4:1-4. The face of innocence the concept of the self so proudly wears can tolerate attack in self-defense, for is it not a well-known fact the world deals harshly with defenseless innocence? No one who makes a picture of himself omits this face, for he has need of it. The other side he does not want to see. Yet it is here the learning of the world has set its sights, for it is here the world's "reality" is set, to see to it the idol lasts.

Pages 656-657. T-31.V.5:1-4. Beneath the face of innocence there is a lesson that the concept of the self was made to teach. It is a lesson in a terrible displacement, and a fear so devastating that the face that smiles above it must forever look away, lest it perceive the treachery it hides. The lesson teaches this: "I am the thing you made of me, and as you look on me, you stand condemned because of what I am." On this conception of the self the world smiles with approval, for it guarantees the pathways of the world are safely kept, and those who walk on them will not escape.

ANSWER 53A. Your concept of yourself is not you, but just the idea you hold of what you are. It bears no resemblance to you at all. Your concept of yourself has an outer aspect and a hidden inner aspect. The *face of innocence* is the outer aspect of your concept of yourself. It is the image you project to the world. The face of innocence is the outer mask that you want to present to others as who you are. The face of innocence says, "I am a good person in an evil world and would not hurt anyone. Then again, if someone attacked me first, I would, of course, reluctantly have to attack back merely to protect myself from being unfairly treated. I am innocent because my anger is justified. After all, I am being forced to act in self-defense."

Below the face of innocence is a hidden mask that has two aspects you do not want others to see. It is the mask of devastating fear, hate, condemnation, and self-condemnation. The two aspects of this hidden mask are the broken *victim* and the heartless *victimizer*. In both aspects, raw emotions rage against the world and against yourself. The conscious mind of the face of innocence does not dare to look upon this hidden mask that lurks in the subconscious mind. As you entertain the possibility of believing this hidden mask is really in your mind, the face of innocence will naturally want to dismiss the idea that the hidden mask could be part of your concept of yourself. Fortunately, the hidden mask of raw emotions is just as unreal as the face of innocence. Both the face of innocence and the mask of the victim and victimizer are only false beliefs you have made into a false concept of yourself.

QUESTION 53B. What is the benefit of admitting that your concept of yourself is mistaken?

Page 659. T-31.V.14:1-3. The concept of the self has always been the great preoccupation of the world. And everyone believes that he must find the answer to the riddle of himself. Salvation can be seen as nothing more than the escape from concepts.
Page 660. T-31.V.17:1-9. The world can teach no images of you unless you want to learn them. There will come a time when images have all gone by, and you will see you know not what you are. It is to this unsealed and open mind that truth returns, unhindered and unbound. Where concepts of the self have been laid by is truth revealed exactly as it is. When every concept has been raised to doubt and question, and been recognized as made on no assumptions that would stand the light, then is the truth left free to enter in its sanctuary, clean and free of guilt. There is no statement that the world is more afraid to hear than this:

> *I do not know the thing I am, and therefore do not know what I am doing, where I am, or how to look upon the world or on myself.*

Yet in this learning is salvation born. And What you are will tell you of Itself.

ANSWER 53B. Although you can let your concept of yourself persist as long as you want, there is a benefit from admitting you are mistaken about your inner and outer self-images. The benefit comes from taking off the masks, allowing you to truly admit you really do not know who or what you are. Instead of relying on the images you manufacture, you can open your mind to the experience of your true Self. Indeed, your true Self will find ways to speak to you of the reality within you that your concepts have hidden. Concepts—whether good or bad—have inherent limitations. True freedom transcends concepts that block your reality. An open mind will make room for the Truth to present Itself.

QUESTION 54. What choice does Christ ask you to make, and what temptations need to be avoided?

Page 666. T-31.VIII.1:1-6. Temptation has one lesson it would teach, in all its forms, wherever it occurs. It would persuade the holy Son of God he is a body, born in what must die, unable to escape its frailty, and bound by what it orders him to feel. Would you be this, if Christ appeared to you in all His glory, asking you but this:

> *Choose once again if you would take your place among the saviors of the world, or would remain in hell, and hold your brothers there.*

For He *has* come, and He *is* asking this.

Page 666. T-31.VIII.2:1-4. How do you make the choice? How easily is this explained! You always choose between your weakness and the strength of Christ in you. And what you choose is what you think is real.

Pages 666-667. T-31.VIII.3:2-7. In every difficulty, all distress, and each perplexity Christ calls to you and gently says, "My brother, choose again." He would not leave you comfortless, alone in dreams of hell, but would release your mind from everything that hides His face from you. His Holiness is yours because He is the only power that is real in you. His strength is yours because He is the Self that God created as His only Son.

Page 667. T-31.VIII.4:1-2. The images you make cannot prevail against what God Himself would have you be. Be never fearful of temptation, then, but see it as it is; another chance to choose again, and let Christ's strength prevail in every circumstance and every place you raised an image of yourself before.

Page 667. T-31.VIII.5:1-5. Learn, then, the happy habit of response to all temptation to perceive yourself as weak and miserable with these words:

> *I am as God created me. His Son can suffer nothing. And I am His Son.*

Thus is Christ's strength invited to prevail, replacing all your weakness with the strength that comes from God and that can never fail.

Page 667. T-31.VIII.6:1, 4-5. You *are* as God created you, and so is every living thing you look upon, regardless of the images you see.... A **miracle** has come to heal God's Son, and close the door upon his dreams of weakness, opening the way to his salvation and release. Choose once again what you would have him be, remembering that *every* choice you make establishes your own identity as you will see it and believe it is.

Page 668. T-31.VIII.9:4-7. Hear me, my brothers, hear and join with me. God has ordained I cannot call in vain, and in His certainty I rest content. For you *will* hear, and you *will* choose again. And in this choice is everyone made free.

ANSWER 54. According to the Course, Christ is asking you to choose between being a savior for others and saving yourself as well or remaining lost in the illusion that says you are a body and not the holy Son of God. You always make your choice based on what you think is real. If you think Christ is what is real in you, you will choose to follow Christ and to rely on His strength. Your reliance on His strength is the acceptance of your own strength since Christ in you is your true Self. If you mistakenly think the images you have made of yourself are your reality, you will choose your weakness rather than the strength of Christ. The truth is that Christ is the only source of power within you because He is the Self that is your true nature and every seeker's true nature.

The major temptation you need to avoid is investing in the idea that you are a body and not the holy Son of God. If you give in to the false belief that you are a body, you will believe in your weakness as your reality. Each time you give in to this convincing illusion of being a body, you have a new opportunity to choose again for the Christ in you that will strengthen you. Jesus is your elder brother, who has perfectly identified with Christ and wants you to also identify with Christ. Jesus wants you to join with him in choosing to free your brothers and to free yourself in the process.

QUESTION 55. Who is a teacher of God, and what are his stages of learning trust?

Page 3. M-1.1:1-2. A teacher of God is anyone who chooses to be one. His qualifications consist solely in this; somehow, somewhere he has made a deliberate choice in which he did not see his interests as apart from someone else's.

Page 10. M-4.I.A.3:1-8. First, they must go through what might be called "a period of undoing." This need not be painful, but it usually is so experienced. It seems as if things are being taken away, and it is rarely understood initially that their lack of value is merely being recognized. How can lack of value be perceived unless the perceiver is in a position where he must see things in a different light? He is not yet at a point at which he can make the shift entirely internally. And so the plan will sometimes call for changes in what seem to be external circumstances. These changes are always helpful. When the teacher of God has learned that much, he goes on to the second stage.

Page 10. M-4.I.A.4:1-7. Next, the teacher of God must go through "a period of sorting out." This is always somewhat difficult because, having learned that the changes in his life are always helpful, he must now decide all things on the basis of whether they increase the helpfulness or hamper it. He will find that many, if not most of the things he valued before will merely hinder his ability to transfer what he has learned to new situations as they arise. Because he has valued what is really valueless, he will not generalize the lesson for fear of loss and sacrifice. It takes great learning to understand that all things, events, encounters and circumstances are helpful. It is only to the extent to which they are helpful that any degree of reality should be accorded them in this world of illusion. The word "value" can apply to nothing else.

Page 10. M-4.I.A.5:1-2, 5-8. The third stage through which the teacher of God must go can be called "a period of relinquishment." If this is interpreted as giving up the desirable, it will engender enormous conflict....Therefore, the period of overlap is apt to be one in which the teacher of God feels called upon to sacrifice his own best interests on behalf of truth. He has not realized as yet how wholly impossible such a demand would be. He can learn this only as he actually does give up the valueless. Through this, he learns that where he anticipated grief, he finds a happy lightheartedness instead; where he thought something was asked of him, he finds a gift bestowed on him.

Pages 10-11. M-4.I.A.6:1-4, 9. Now comes "a period of settling down." This is a **quiet time**, in which the teacher of God rests a while in reasonable peace. Now he consolidates his learning. Now he begins to see the transfer value of what he has learned.... The teacher of God needs this period of respite.

Page 11. M-4.I.A.7:1-2, 8. The next stage is indeed "a period of unsettling." Now must the teacher of God understand that he did not really know what was valuable and what was valueless.... He must learn to lay all judgment aside, and ask only what he really wants in every circumstance.

Page 11. M-4.I.A.8:1-10. And finally, there is "a period of achievement." It is here that learning is consolidated. Now what was seen as merely shadows before become solid gains, to be counted on in all "emergencies" as well as tranquil times. Indeed, the tranquility is their result; the outcome of honest learning, consistency of thought and full transfer. This is the stage of real peace, for here is Heaven's state fully reflected. From here, the way to Heaven is open and easy. In fact, it is here. Who would "go" anywhere, if peace of mind is already complete? And who would seek to change tranquility for something more desirable? What could be more desirable than this?

ANSWER 55. A teacher of God is anyone who chooses to be one. His choice implies he has studied the spiritual principles of the Course and demonstrates his understanding by making a deliberate choice to join with another in a **holy relationship**. This choice always involves joining with another in a common purpose with common interests, not separate interests. Trust is the most important characteristic of a teacher of God. The stages of learning trust are listed below:

1. A Period of Undoing — This is a time of change in which the teacher of God may experience the pain of giving up things that seem worthwhile, but are not really valuable. There is a recognition that changes are always helpful.

2. A Period of Sorting Out — The teacher of God makes difficult choices based on whether they increase helpfulness or hinder it.

3. A Period of Relinquishment — This stages starts with the teacher of God feeling conflicted about giving up things that make him mistakenly think he is making a sacrifice. Later in this stage, he finds out his apparent sacrifices were actually blessings in disguise.

4. A Period of Settling Down — This is a relatively peaceful time of respite in which the teacher of God consolidates his learning. He increases his ability to generalize his learning to new situations and relationships.

5. A Period of Unsettling — This is a period of reassessment in which he finds out he did not really know what was valuable and valueless. He must ask for only what is truly valuable and learn to give up all judgment.

6. A Period of Achievement — In this stage, there is peace of mind because learning has been consolidated. Here the teacher of God maintains consistency of thought and has learned to generalize his learning to all situations and all relationships. His mind has become a reflection of Heaven, and so he has successfully prepared his mind for the final step of awakening in his Home in the Arms of God.

QUESTION 56A. How is the **face of Christ** completely revealed?

Page 16. M-4.X.2:1-13. How do the open-minded **forgive**? They have let go all things that would prevent **forgiveness**. They have in truth abandoned the world, and let it be restored to them in newness and in joy so glorious they could never have conceived of such a change. Nothing is now as it was formerly. Nothing but sparkles now which seemed so dull and lifeless before. And above all are all things welcoming, for threat is gone. No clouds remain to hide the **face of Christ**. Now is the goal achieved. **Forgiveness** is the final goal of the curriculum. It paves the way for what goes far beyond all learning. The curriculum makes no effort to exceed its legitimate goal. **Forgiveness** is its single aim, at which all learning ultimately converges. It is indeed enough.

ANSWER 56A. The deepest level of seeing the **face of Christ** with all of its blazing light can only be seen after all that covers it has been removed. Every covering of the **face of Christ** is merely an illusion based on a false perception. **Forgiveness** is the only aim of the Course because it removes every obstructing illusion, every false perception. **Forgiveness** dissolves all man-made images, and the last image that remains is the spotless **face of Christ**. Although the **face of Christ** is an image, it is an all-encompassing image made by the Holy Spirit as His answer to all the images of specialness and separation made by man. Since the **face of Christ** is an image, it is in the world of form, yet it is the one form that leads to formlessness because it perfectly reflects Heaven. Thus seeing it awakens the memory of God, just before He lifts you back to your heavenly Home.

QUESTION 56B. How does a teacher of God improve his ability to make decisions?

Page 26. M-9.1:1-2, 8-9. Changes are required in the *minds* of God's teachers. This may or may not involve changes in the external situation.... Relationships in particular must be properly perceived, and all dark cornerstones of unforgiveness removed. Otherwise the old thought system still has a basis for return.
Page 26. M-9.2:1-4. As the teacher of God advances in his training, he learns one lesson with increasing thoroughness. He does not make his own decisions; he asks his Teacher for His answer, and it is this he follows as his guide for action. This becomes easier and easier, as the teacher of God learns to give up his own judgment. The giving up of judgment, the obvious prerequisite for hearing God's Voice, is usually a fairly slow process, not because it is difficult, but because it is apt to be perceived as personally insulting.

ANSWER 56B.   The teacher of God improves his ability to make decisions by giving up judgment. This setting aside of reliance on his own judgment increases his ability to listen to the Voice for God, the Holy Spirit. The teacher of God always turns to the Holy Spirit and asks Him to decide for God for him and trusts in His answer to every question. Then he follows the Holy Spirit's guidance in all his actions.

QUESTION 57. What does the teacher of God need to know about judgment?

Page 27. M-10.2:1-9. It is necessary for the teacher of God to realize, not that he should not judge, but that he cannot. In giving up judgment, he is merely giving up what he did not have. He gives up an illusion; or better, he has an illusion of giving up. He has actually merely become more honest. Recognizing that judgment was always impossible for him, he no longer attempts it. This is no sacrifice. On the contrary, he puts himself in a position where judgment *through* him rather than *by* him can occur. And this judgment is neither "good" nor "bad." It is the only judgment there is, and it is only one: "God's Son is guiltless, and sin does not exist."

Page 27. M-10.3:1-7. The aim of our curriculum, unlike the goal of the world's learning, is the recognition that judgment in the usual sense is impossible. This is not an opinion but a fact. In order to judge anything rightly, one would have to be fully aware of an inconceivably wide range of things; past, present and to come. One would have to recognize in advance all the effects of his judgments on everyone and everything involved in them in any way. And one would have to be certain there is no distortion in his perception, so that his judgment would be wholly fair to everyone on whom it rests now and in the future. Who is in a position to do this? Who except in grandiose fantasies would claim this for himself?

Page 28. M-10.4:1-10. Remember how many times you thought you knew all the "facts" you needed for judgment, and how wrong you were! Is there anyone who has not had this experience? Would you know how many times you merely thought you were right, without ever realizing you were wrong? Why would you choose such an arbitrary basis for decision making? Wisdom is not judgment; it is the relinquishment of judgment. Make then but one more judgment. It is this: There is Someone with you Whose judgment is perfect. He does know all the facts; past, present and to come. He does know all the effects of His judgment on everyone and everything involved in any way. And He is wholly fair to everyone, for there is no distortion in His perception.

Page 28. M-10.5:1, 7-13. Therefore lay judgment down, not with regret but with a sigh of gratitude.... His sense of care is gone, for he has none. He has given it away, along with judgment. He gave himself to Him Whose judgment he has chosen now to trust, instead of his own. Now he makes no mistakes. His Guide is sure. And where he came to judge, he comes to bless. Where now he laughs, he used to come to weep.

Page 28. M-10.6:1-2, 6-10. It is not difficult to relinquish judgment. But it is difficult indeed to try to keep it.... All of the loneliness and sense of loss; of passing time and growing hopelessness; of sickening despair and fear of death; all these have come of it. And now he knows that these things need not be. Not one is true. For he has given up their cause, and they, which never were but the effects of his mistaken choice, have fallen from him. Teacher of God, this step will bring you peace. Can it be difficult to want but this?

ANSWER 57. The teacher of God knows he must learn to give up judgment because he realizes why judgments by him cannot be relied upon for accuracy. He remembers the many times in the past when his judgments were totally wrong. He knows that judgments based on his own personal viewpoint, coming from his ego perspective, are merely illusions. When he gives up making his own judgments, he is honestly seeing the illusory nature of his own limited ego. By giving up the illusion of judgment, he accepts that no human being can have the all-encompassing awareness that would be required to always make judgments that are correct and fair to everyone. The teacher of God knows that accurate judgment is impossible for him and only the Holy Spirit is qualified to make totally accurate judgments. Therefore, the teacher of God lets judgment happen *through* him by listening to the guidance of the Holy Spirit and acting on His judgment. The judgment that happens through the Holy Spirit is that false beliefs in sin and guilt have never changed the perfect holiness of the Son of God.

QUESTION 58A. How do teachers of God spend their time?

Page 40. M-16.3:4-8. At the outset, we can safely say that time devoted to starting the day right does indeed save time. How much time should be so spent? This must depend on the teacher of God himself. He cannot claim that title until he has gone through the workbook, since we are learning within the framework of our course. After completion of the more structured practice periods, which the workbook contains, individual need becomes the chief consideration. Pages 40-41. M-16.4:1-9. This course is always practical. It may be that the teacher of God is not in a situation that fosters quiet thought as he awakes. If this is so, let him but remember that he chooses to spend time with God as soon as possible, and let him do so. Duration is not the major concern. One can easily sit still an hour with closed eyes and accomplish nothing. One can as easily give God only an instant, and in that instant join with Him completely. Perhaps the one generalization that can be made is this; as soon as possible after waking take your **quiet time**, continuing a minute or two after you begin to find it difficult. You may find that the difficulty will diminish and drop away. If not, that is the time to stop.

Page 41. M-16.5:1-8. The same procedures should be followed at night. Perhaps your **quiet time** should be fairly early in the evening, if it is not feasible for you to take it just before going to sleep. It is not wise to lie down for it. It is better to sit up, in whatever position you prefer. Having gone through the workbook, you must have come to some conclusions in this respect. If possible, however, just before going to sleep is a desirable time to devote to God. It sets your mind into a pattern of rest, and orients you away from fear. If it is expedient to spend this time earlier, at least be sure that you do not forget a brief period,—not more than a moment will do,—in which you close your eyes and think of God.

ANSWER 58A. Becoming a teacher of God requires taking the time to first complete the one year of structured daily Workbook lessons as a foundation for future less structured daily practice. The Manual recommends that the teacher of God set aside **quiet time**s every morning and evening to connect with God. The term "**quiet times**" is another term for **meditation** practices that usually focus on a thought of God. As was learned in Workbook lessons, the teacher of God sits erect for **meditation** practices and does not lie down, which can induce drowsiness.

QUESTION 58B. What must the teacher of God do to be able to allow healing to happen through him?

Page 48. M-18.4:1-9. In order to heal, it thus becomes essential for the teacher of God to let all his own mistakes be corrected. If he senses even the faintest hint of irritation in himself as he responds to anyone, let him instantly realize that he has made an interpretation that is not true. Then let him turn within to his eternal Guide, and let Him judge what the response should be. So is he healed, and in his healing is his pupil healed with him. The sole responsibility of God's teacher is to accept the **Atonement** for himself. **Atonement** means correction, or the undoing of errors. When this has been accomplished, the teacher of God becomes a **miracle** worker by definition. His sins have been **forgiven** him, and he no longer condemns himself. How can he then condemn anyone? And who is there whom his **forgiveness** can fail to heal?

ANSWER 58B. Before the teacher of God can allow healing to happen through him, he must first focus on healing his own mind. When he experiences the least bit of irritation, he must realize that he has made an incorrect interpretation originating from his ego. Then he must turn to the Holy Spirit for guidance and allow His judgment to replace the false judgment he had previously made. In order to be a healer, meaning a **miracle** worker, the teacher of God has the one necessary responsibility of accepting the **Atonement** for himself. This enables his mind to be healed. When the mind of the teacher of God is healed, the mind of his pupil is automatically healed at the same time. By accepting the **Atonement**, the teacher of God is allowing his own mistakes to be **forgiven**, and he releases inner self-condemnation. The **forgiveness** he receives and loss of self-condemnation are passed along to his pupil through the action of the Holy Spirit, Who unites all the minds of the sleeping Sons of God.

QUESTION 59A. What does the teacher of God need to learn to make progress and to heal others?

Page 55. M-22.1:1-12. Healing and **Atonement** are not related; they are identical. There is no order of difficulty in **miracles** because there are no degrees of **Atonement**. It is the one complete concept possible in this world, because it is the source of a wholly unified perception. Partial **Atonement** is a meaningless idea, just as special areas of hell in Heaven are inconceivable. Accept **Atonement** and you are healed. **Atonement** is the Word of God. Accept His Word and what remains to make sickness possible? Accept His Word and every miracle has been accomplished. To **forgive** is to heal. The teacher of God has taken accepting the **Atonement** for himself as his only function. What is there, then, he cannot heal? What **miracle** can be withheld from him?
Page 55. M-22.2:1, 5. The progress of the teacher of God may be slow or rapid, depending on whether he recognizes the **Atonement's** inclusiveness, or for a time excludes some problem areas from it.... Anywhere along the way, the necessary realization of inclusiveness may reach him.
Page 55. M-22.3:1. That **forgiveness** is healing needs to be understood, if the teacher of God is to make progress.
Pages 55-56. M-22.4:1-9. Certainly sickness does not appear to be a decision. Nor would anyone actually believe he wants to be sick. Perhaps he can accept the idea in theory, but it is rarely if ever consistently applied to all specific forms of sickness, both in the individual's perception of himself and of all others as well. Nor is it at this level that the teacher of God calls forth the **miracle** of healing. He overlooks the

A Simple Framework for Understanding the Course

mind *and* body, seeing only the **face of Christ** shining in front of him, correcting all mistakes and healing all perception. Healing is the result of the recognition, by God's teacher, of who it is that is in need of healing. This recognition has no special reference. It is true of all things that God created. In it are all illusions healed.

Page 56. M-22.6:1-2. The offer of **Atonement** is universal. It is equally applicable to all individuals in all circumstances.

ANSWER 59A. The **Atonement** and healing are identical. When you accept the **Atonement**, God's plan of perfect love, you heal your own mind. In receiving the blessing of healing yourself, you become a **miracle** worker, who allows others to be healed along with you. This is your only function as a teacher of God. At first the teacher of God will bring healing to a few others and accept the **Atonement** only in some situations. As the teacher of God makes progress, he applies the acceptance of **Atonement** for himself to more and more situations. Finally he will generalize his learning to apply the acceptance of the **Atonement** for himself to every single problem at all times. Also, to make progress, the teacher of God needs to learn that **forgiveness** is healing. The teacher of God knows that every sick person has made a decision to be sick, while not being consciously aware of that decision. However, analyzing the ego that made the choice for sickness is not the job of the healer. To heal others the teacher of God must know for certain who is in need of healing. The ego is not this "who" because the ego is nothing but an illusion that doesn't have any reality. The "who" that needs healing is the sleeping Son of God. In order to facilitate healing through the Holy Spirit, the teacher of God overlooks what is not the Son of God and looks for the Son of God. This process of overlooking and looking is **forgiveness**. The body and the part of the mind ruled by the ego are overlooked. Looking for the Son of God is accomplished by seeing only the **face of Christ**, which is identical to accepting the **Atonement**. Welcoming the **face of Christ** and inviting the **Atonement** are exactly the same because they both bring the same result of correcting all errors and healing all perception.

QUESTION 59B. Why is it helpful to call on the name of Jesus Christ as a part of healing?

Page 58. M-23.2:1-8. We have repeatedly said that one who has perfectly accepted the **Atonement** for himself can heal the world. Indeed, he has already done so. Temptation may recur to others, but never to this One. He has become the risen Son of God. He has overcome death because he has accepted life. He has recognized himself as God created him, and in so doing he has recognized all living things as part of him. There is now no limit on his power, because it is the power of God. So has his name become the Name of God, for he no longer sees himself as separate from Him.

Page 58. M-23.3:1-11. What does this mean for you? It means that in remembering Jesus you are remembering God. The whole relationship of the Son to the Father lies in him. His part in the Sonship is also yours, and his completed learning guarantees your own success. Is he still available for help? What did he say about this? Remember his promises, and ask yourself honestly whether it is likely that he will fail to keep them. Can God fail His Son? And can one who is one with God be unlike Him? Who transcends the body has transcended limitation. Would the greatest teacher be unavailable to those who follow him?

Page 58. M-23.4:1-7. The name of Jesus Christ as such is but a symbol. But it stands for love that is not of this world. It is a symbol that is safely used as a replacement for the many names of all the gods to which you pray. It becomes the shining symbol for the Word of God, so close to what it stands for that the little space between the two is lost, the moment that the name is called to mind. Remembering the name of Jesus Christ is to give thanks for all the gifts that God has given you. And gratitude to God becomes the way in which He is remembered, for love cannot be far behind a grateful heart and thankful mind. God enters easily, for these are the true conditions for your homecoming.

Page 59. M-23.5:1-11. Jesus has led the way. Why would you not be grateful to him? He has asked for love, but only that he might give it to you. You do not love yourself. But in his eyes your loveliness is so complete and flawless that he sees in it an image of his Father. You become the symbol of his Father here on earth. To you he looks for hope, because in you he sees no limit and no stain to mar your beautiful perfection. In his eyes Christ's vision shines in perfect constancy. He has remained with you. Would you not learn the lesson of salvation through his learning? Why would you choose to start again, when he has made the journey for you?

ANSWER 59B. The Manual explains that Jesus has a special place in healing because he is the risen Son of God and the One who has perfectly accepted the **Atonement** and healed the world. The name of Jesus "has become the Name of God" because he knows he is in no way separate from God. He has the unlimited power of God because he recognized his Identity as God created him and his oneness with all living things that are part of him. Every time you remember the name of Jesus Christ, you are remembering the Name of God. Workbook

Lessons 183 and 184 recommend repeating the Name of God as a form of meditation. Since the name of Jesus Christ "has become the Name of God," the Manual is indirectly saying that as an option you can use the name of Jesus Christ in your meditation practice to stand for the Name of God.

Jesus has accepted his rightful role as the awakened Son of God, and in so doing he has ensured that you will also accept your rightful place in the Sonship as the awakened Son of God. Jesus is always available to you if you call upon him for help and healing. Calling on the name of Jesus, who has perfectly accepted the **Atonement**, opens you to likewise accept the **Atonement** to correct your errors and your perception. Any name is only a symbol, but since the name of Jesus has become the Name of God, it calls upon the perfect love that is the **Atonement**. The name of Jesus symbolizes the Love of God. His name as a symbol reflects the reality so closely that calling his name brings the divine love it represents. Invoking the name of Jesus brings forth the memory of God's many gifts to you and inspires your gratitude, which leads to remembering God Himself and awakening in His Arms.

QUESTION 60. Where is the Course curriculum leading you?

Page 68. M-28.1:1-5, 10. Very simply, the resurrection is the overcoming or surmounting of death. It is a reawakening or a rebirth; a change of mind about the meaning of the world. It is the acceptance of the Holy Spirit's interpretation of the world's purpose; the acceptance of the **Atonement** for oneself. It is the end of dreams of misery, and the glad awareness of the Holy Spirit's final dream. It is the recognition of the gifts of God.... It is the single desire of the Son for the Father.

Page 68. M-28.2:4-6. Love is no longer feared, but gladly welcomed. Idols have disappeared, and the remembrance of God shines unimpeded across the world. Christ's face is seen in every living thing, and nothing is held in darkness, apart from the light of **forgiveness**.

Page 68. M-28.3:1-13. Here the curriculum ends. From here on, no directions are needed. Vision is wholly corrected and all mistakes undone. Attack is meaningless and peace has come. The goal of the curriculum has been achieved. Thoughts turn to Heaven and away from hell. All longings are satisfied, for what remains unanswered or incomplete? The last illusion spreads across the world, forgiving all things and replacing all attack. The whole reversal is accomplished. Nothing is left to contradict the Word of God. There is no opposition to the truth. And now the truth can come at last. How quickly will it come as it is asked to enter and envelop such a world!

Page 69. M-28.5:1-9. Now there are no distinctions. Differences have disappeared and Love looks on Itself. What further sight is needed? What remains that vision could accomplish? We have seen the **face of Christ**, His sinlessness, His Love behind all forms, beyond all purposes. Holy are we because His Holiness has set us free indeed! And we accept His Holiness as ours; as it is. As God created us so will we be forever and forever, and we wish for nothing but His Will to be our own. Illusions of another will are lost, for unity of purpose has been found.

Page 69. M-28.6:1-9. These things await us all, but we are not prepared as yet to welcome them with joy. As long as any mind remains possessed of evil dreams, the thought of hell is real. God's teachers have the goal of wakening the minds of those asleep, and seeing there the vision of Christ's face to take the place of what they dream. The thought of murder is replaced with blessing. Judgment is laid by, and given Him Whose function judgment is. And in His Final Judgment is restored the truth about the holy Son of God. He is redeemed, for he has heard God's Word and understood its meaning. He is free because he let God's Voice proclaim the truth. And all he sought before to crucify are resurrected with him, by his side, as he prepares with them to meet his God.

ANSWER 60. The curriculum of the Course is leading you to one goal, one universal destination, described in many different ways. When you reach this final destination, your mind will be changed so there will be a reawakening or rebirth, which overcomes death. This will be a release of all dark illusions and the acceptance of the Holy Spirit's final dream. The one last illusion the Holy Spirit will show you is the **face of Christ** that will bring back the memory of God. This will be the same as fully accepting the **Atonement** in which all errors will be corrected. This will fulfill the desire of the Son for the Father. **Forgiveness** will finally complete its task of releasing you from all your idols so you can accept the holiness, light, and love that are your true nature. You will accept the Will of God as your own will. Your transformation will not be entirely new because you will simply be returning to the acceptance of yourself as God created you. In the **face of Christ**, you will see your true Self, and your sleep and past nightmares will be gone forever. The practice of giving up your judgment and accepting the judgment of the Holy Spirit will prepare you for God's Final Judgment. This judgment reaffirms that you are God's holy Son and that you have never been separate from His eternal Love. This is the final resurrection. In this last stage of your redemption, God takes the final step of welcoming you to the eternal joy of Heaven. You will laugh at the great irony that all your wanderings have brought you back to the Home that you have never left, except in your illusions of separation.

AN OPTION FOR STUDY GROUP LEADERS

~ o ~

Many people study the Course by themselves. However, the Course encourages the student and teacher relationship as the ideal way to learn the Course. The most common way to find a teacher is to attend a local Course study group. There is no standardized format for how to run a study group. Typically, every leader has his or her own personal style of running a Course study group.

I have attended many different study groups with different leaders. Recently I attended a new study group in which I knew no one. One member wondered if there was a positive purpose behind us leaving Heaven to come to this world or if leaving Heaven was a mistake. Participants offered a variety of opinions. One woman turned to the leader and asked her directly, "Is the Course saying that coming to this world was a mistake? If it was a mistake, I want to know that because that's not what I understand from reading the Course."

I waited for the leader to respond, since the group respected her as an authority on the Course. Nevertheless, she said nothing. Finally I spoke up for the first time and explained that the Course maintains that the separation was a mistake in which we foolishly closed off our awareness of the eternal bliss of Heaven and experienced "the time of terror." After the meeting, I showed the woman who had asked the question a Course quotation supporting the idea that the separation was a mistake. She responded firmly but kindly, "Well, everybody interprets the Course differently." Obviously she was unconvinced by my explanation, since I was a newcomer whom she did not know. I did not tell her I write Course books. I said to her, "I feel inwardly agitated that I cannot seem to explain this idea to you. But my being agitated means I am not focusing on loving you. Since the whole purpose of the Course is to teach me how to become more loving, I want you to know that I can see you are a loving person, and that's all that's important." She smiled appreciatively, and we hugged.

In my opinion, if you are a leader of a study group, you have two responsibilities: One responsibility is to coordinate the meeting in a way that encourages loving communication. The other responsibility is to serve a teaching function. If group members say something that is slightly inaccurate, you do not need to rush in with an immediate correction. On the other hand, if a member says something that is obviously not a true perception of the Course, you have a leadership obligation to provide clarity so that member and the other members can gain a better understanding of the Course. In the study group I just described, the leader accepted her responsibility to facilitate loving communication, but she did not accept her teaching responsibility to give clarity to the group. Now I am recommending an optional study guide that would help leaders fulfill their teaching function.

As a high school student, I learned that unlike the students, each teacher had a special textbook with the answers to all the questions. Similar to a special teacher's textbook with answers included, the prior section titled "Sixty Answers to Sixty Questions" can be used as an optional curriculum guide if you are a teacher of God who leads study groups. This guide gives you an optional way of helping study group members to better understand the Course.

If you are a study group leader, you can use this study guide in the following way: You encourage every student to bring a copy of the Course to each meeting (ideally the second edition that has the page numbers used in this guide). You choose a question from this guide to present to the study group. However, instead of reading the question aloud right away, you ask members to turn to the page number of the Course that is listed right below the question. Then you have members read the particular paragraph or paragraphs listed in the guide right next to each page number.

After all the relevant paragraphs are read, you ask the members for comments. Following the members' comments, you read the question you have chosen from the guide. You let members of your study group come up with answers they would like to share before you read the answer written in this guide and before you give your own answer to the question. Letting your members speak first will encourage their participation. Before offering your comments, you inwardly ask the Holy Spirit to guide your thoughts and words so you can be truly helpful. Since "giving and receiving are the same," you will learn as much from group members as they will learn from you. Of course, you and everyone else will learn from the Holy Spirit, God's Teacher.

> When pupil and teacher come together, a teaching-learning situation begins. For the teacher is not really the one who does the teaching. God's Teacher speaks to any two who join together for learning purposes. The relationship is holy because of that purpose, and God has promised to send His Spirit into any holy relationship. In the teaching-learning situation, each one learns that giving and receiving are the same.[198]

CLOSING SUMMARY

~ o ~

All the answers provided in the prior section are correct, but not the last word on any topic. If you asked ten experienced Course students these same questions, their answers would most likely offer ten different interpretations. Yet the basic ideas would be similar and harmonize. Thus it is not necessary for you to recall every idea presented in this book. But it would be helpful to remember that forgiveness, Christ's vision, the holy instant, the holy relationship, miracles, meditation, and the Atonement are the seven tools of the Holy Spirit. This understanding will be your framework for studying the entire Course Text and doing all 365 daily Workbook lessons.

In this book, these seven tools were first identified as separate keys, and then their interrelationships were explained. These various interrelationships are important because they illustrate how all seven tools of the Holy Spirit work together. The Holy Spirit helps you to perform miracles by correcting perception, which involves replacing false perceptions with true perceptions. Now your mind is divided between false perceptions guided by the ego and true perceptions guided by the Holy Spirit. But the Holy Spirit uses the seven keys to Heaven to heal the division in the mind and eventually bring about "total perception."[199] This unified perception of all true perceptions reveals the deepest level of the real world. Seeing the blazing light of the face of Christ in the real world, you are transformed by the memory of God returning. The return of this memory of God completes the unification of the mind. Thus the seven keys of the Holy Spirit have served their ultimate purpose of opening the door to Heaven.

Forgiveness, Christ's vision, the holy instant, the holy relationship, miracles, meditation, and the Atonement are all important concepts to remember as a framework for understanding and applying the Course. Yet of these seven keys, the master key is true forgiveness. Practicing the "overlooking" aspect of the process of forgiveness helps you see illusions as illusions and totally disregard them. Equally helpful is the "looking" aspect of forgiveness that allows you to look for and see the divine presence of holiness in everyone you meet and in yourself as well. Through releasing illusions and perceiving the reality of the divine presence, forgiveness heals the perception of separation leading to the unification of the mind, which is necessary for awakening in Heaven.

2. T-7.VI.4:6, p. 124
3. T-8.III.1:3, p. 141
4. W-191.6:1, p. 363
5. T-22.III.2:1, pp. 474-475
6. T-24.in.2:1, p. 499
7. T-9.IV.8:3, p. 170
8. T-12.V.7:1-7, p. 226
9. T-12.V.8:3-7, p. 227
10. W.ep.3:3, p. 487
11. T-5.III.9:3-4, p. 80
12. T-30.V.7:5, p. 637
13. T-5.I.5:1-7, 6:1-6, p. 74
14. T-8.VI.4:1-4, 5:1, pp. 148-149
15. T-4.V.5:1-8, 6:1, p. 66
16. T-4.V.6:6-11, p. 67
17. W-93.5:1-9, 6:1-7, pp. 161-162
18. T-8.I.2:1-3, p. 138
19. T-4.VI.1:1-7, p. 67
20. W-66.7:2-5, p. 111
21. T-4.VI.4:1-4, p. 68
22. T-4.VI.3:3-8, p. 68
23. T-4.VI.5:1-8, p. 68
24. W-133.6:1-2, p. 245
25. W-133.7:3-5, p. 246
26. W-133.8:1-4, p. 246
27. W-133.11:2-3, p. 246
28. W-133.13:1-4, p. 347
29. W-133.14:3, p. 347
30. T-20.IV.8:4, 6-8, pp. 433-434
31. T-6.IV.3:2-4, 4:1-3, p. 101
32. C-2.5:1, p. 81
33. T-13.IV.5:1-2, p. 246
34. T-15.V.10:8-10, p. 314
35. T-21.IV.3:4-5, pp. 454-455
36. M-16.4:7, 5:1-5, p. 41
37. Geoffrey D. Falk, *Stripping the Gurus*, Chapter XXIII, "Up the Asana" (Amrit Desai), posted on strippingthegurus.com
38. T-4.IV.5:1-3, p. 68
39. T-14.IV.9:3-8, p. 281
40. W-67.4:3-4, p. 113
41. W-157.9:1-4, p. 297
42. T-19.IV.D.2:3, p. 420
43. T-in.1:7, p. 1
44. W-342.1:7, p. 474
45. T-31.VII.12:6, p. 665
46. W-256.1:9, p. 422
47. W-159.8:1, p. 301
48. T-25.VI.3:1, p. 529
49. W-108.1:3-5, 2:1-3, 3:1-3, p.195

50. W-108.1:3-5, 2:1-3, 3:1-3, p.195
51. T-15.I.15:4-11, p. 304
52. T-17.III.8:2, p. 357
53. T-18.IX.13:3-4, p. 394
54. T-22.II.12:1, 7-8, p. 474
55. T-19.IV.B.8:3, p. 414
56. T-30.V.7:2-8, pp. 636-637
57. T-22.VI.4:1-8, p. 481
58. C-in.1:1-3, p. 77
59. T-1.I.25:1-2, 26:1-3, 27:1-2, pp. 4-5
60. T-4.VI.8:2-3, p. 69
61. Kenneth Wapnick, *Absence From Felicity*, Copyright 1991 by the Foundation for *A Course In Miracles*, R.R. Box 71, Roscoe, N.Y. 12776-9506, p. 287
62. T-15.IV.6:5-8, pp. 310-311
63. T-17.II.5:1, p. 353
64. T-14.VIII.2:10-16, 3:1, pp. 289-290
65. C-3.4:1-12, p. 83
66. C-3.8:1-6, p. 84
67. T-3.IV.7:4, p. 43
68. T-1.VI.2:1-5, 3:1-6, p. 14
69. T-11.IV.6:1-7, 7:1-5, pp. 202-202
70. C-3.4:1, p. 83
71. T-3.III.4:1-6, p. 40
72. C-3.4:3, p. 83
73. T-21.I.8:1-6, 9:1-6, p. 447
74. W-15.2:2, p. 25
75. T-8.III.1:3, p. 141
76. T-7.VI.4:6, p. 124
77. W-167.12:1-7, p. 320
78. W-167.12:5, p. 320
79. C-4.6:9-10, 7:1-7, 8:1-3, p. 86
80. T-14.VII.7:5-8, p. 289
81. T-17.II.1:1-9, p. 352
82. W-46.1:1-5, 21-5, p. 73
83. T-18.IX.10:1-7, 11:1-7, 12:1-6, pp. 395-396
84. T-4.VII.5:4, p. 70
85. T-4.VII.5:1-8, p. 70
86. T-15.VI.4:1-7, p. 315
87. W-192.3:1, p. 365
88. W-192.1:1-2, p. 365
89. W-192.2:1-7, p. 365
90. W-192.4:1-3, p. 365
91. W-192.5:5-7, p. 365
92. T-19.III.5:1, p. 404
93. T-25.VI.4:1-3, 5:1-11, p. 530
94. C-3.7:5-8, 8:1-6, p. 84
95. T-30.V.1:6, p. 635
96. M-29.5:7, p. 71
97. T-9.IV.1:1-6, p. 168

98. T-9.IV.4:1-6, p. 169
99. T-9.III.7:2, p. 167
100. T-9.III.7:7, pp. 167-168
101. T-9.IV.5:3, p. 169
102. T-9.IV.2:1-7, p. 168
103. W-78.7:2-4, p. 140
104. W-134.15:1-3, p. 250
105. W-161.8:1, p. 305
106. W-161.10:1-4, 11:1-5, pp. 305-306
107. W-161.5:2, p. 304
108. W-78. 5:3-6, 7:1, pp. 139-40
109. W-121.11:1-4, 12:1-3, 13:1-3, pp. 215-216
110. W-161.10:2, p. 305
111. W-161.4:1, p. 304
112. W-161.9:1-4, p. 305
113. W-161.11:7-8, p. 306
114. W-161.12:1-6, p. 306
115. W-126.6:1-6, 7:1-6, pp. 227-228
116. W-108.2:1-3, 3:1-3, 4:1-2, p. 195
117. W-15.1:1-7, p. 25
118. W-30.2:1, p. 47
119. T-18.IX.5:1-4, p. 394
120. W-30.2:1-5, p. 25
121. T-31.VII.12:6, p. 665
122. T-3.V.9:1, p. 46
123. T-13.VIII.5:5-6, p. 259
124. W-158.7:1-5, p. 299
125. W-158.8:3-4, 9:1-6, 10:1-5, p. 299
126. T-1.I.21:1-2, p. 4
127. W-159.4:1-6, p. 300
128. W-pII.13.3:1-4, p. 580
129. T-9.IV.6:1-3, p. 169
130. T-25.IX.8:1, p. 540
131. T-13.VIII.6:3-7, p. 259
132. W-91.1:4-7, p. 156
133. T-31.VII.13:1-7, p. 665
134. T-17.III.8:2, p. 357
135. T-13.VIII.5:4, p. 259
136. T-22.II.12:1-8, p. 474
137. W-in.4:1-2, 5:1-3, p. 1
138. T-22.in.4:2-3, p. 467
139. T-17.VII.8:11-13, 9:1-6, p. 369
140. T-22.in.4:6, p. 468
141. T-19.IV.1:5, p. 406
142. T-18.V.3:1-9, p. 383
143. T-18.V.5:1-2, 5-6, pp. 383-384
144. T-3.V.6:1-5, p. 45
145. T-1.VII.4:1, p. 16
146. W-41. 6:1-6, 7:1-4, pp. 63-64
147. W-44.7:1-5, 9:1, 10:1-3, p. 70
148. W-41.9:2-3, p. 64

149. W-44.8:1-3, p. 70
150. W-pII.in.3:1-4, 4:6, p. 398
151. W-pII.in.1:1-3, p. 398
152. W-108.2:2, p. 195
153. T-11.IV.4:5, p. 201
154. T-11.IV.5:5, p. 201
155. T-1.VII.4:2, p. 16
156. T-5.III.9:3, p. 80
157. T-2.VII.3:5-9, p. 32
158. T-2.III.3:1-7, pp. 21-22
159. C-in.1:1-6, p. 77
160. T-14.I.1:7, p. 270
161. M-18.4:1-10, p. 48
162. T-2.VI.7:8, p. 30
163. T-1.III.3:1-4, 4:1-4, p. 9
164. M-23.4:1-2, p. 58
165. M-23.2:8, p. 58
166. T-14.V.2:1, p. 282
167. T-14.V.9:3-5, p. 284
168. T-14.V.11:1-6. p. 284
169. W-79.2:1-2, p. 141
170. T-18.I.5:2-6, 6:1-9, pp. 372-373
171. T-11.VII.2:1-8, p. 15
172. W-pII.8.1:1-4, 2:1-6, p. 443
173. T-17.II.5:5, 6:1-3, p. 353
174. T-14.V.3:5, p. 282
175. T-18.IX.9:1-7, p. 395
176. T-16.V.3:7, p. 341
177. T-12.VI.6:1-4, 7, p. 229
178. T-12.VIII.7:9-11, 8:1-9, p. 235
179. M-4.X.2:7-13, p. 16
180. Song of Prayer S-2.III.7:2-8
181. T-19.IV.D.2:1-3, p. 420
182. T-1.VII.5:1-11, p. 16
183. T-1.VII.5:11, p. 16
184. T-1.VII.5:8, p. 16
185. W-342.pII.1:1-8, p. 474
186. W-67.pI, p. 113
187. W-67.pI.5:2, p. 114
188. W-67.pI.4:3-4, p. 113
189. W-108.2:1, p. 195
190. W-108.3:3, p. 195
191. Luke 11:34
192. T-25.VI.3:2-5, p. 529
193. T-31.VII.8:3-7, 9:1-2, p. 664
194. T-20.VIII.2:10, 3:1-6, 4:1-4, p. 443
195. T-7.VII.10:1, p. 129
196. T-5.V.2:2, p. 83
197. T-4.VII.1:5, p. 69
198. M-2.5:1-5. p. 6
199. T-12.VIII.8:3, p. 235

CPSIA information can be obtained
at www.ICGtesting.com
Printed in the USA
FSOW04n1300260716
22940FS